I0709633

STINKHORN

STINKHORN

How Nature's Most Foul-Smelling Mushroom
Can Change the Way We Listen

Siôn Parkinson

Sternberg Press

To Hannah, and our family.

CONTENTS

*Nel mezzo del cammin di nostra vita
mi ritrovai per una selva oscura,
ché la diritta via era smarrita.*

Dante, *Divinna Comedia*, Canto 1,
lines 1–3

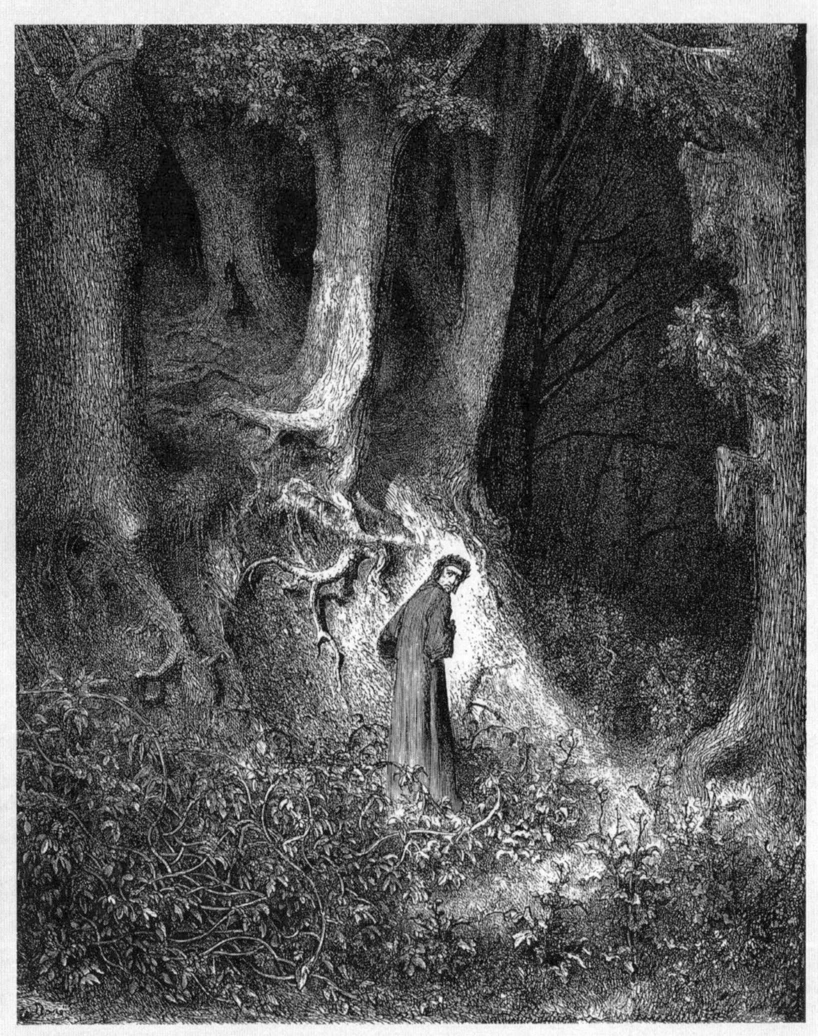

Midway upon the journey of our life / I found myself within a forest dark, /
For the straightforward pathway had been lost.

Inf. I, lines 1–3

0. Introduction

Smells off

0.1   The forest floor is covered in leaf litter, creeping vines, grasping bramble tendrils, tree suckers, water sprouts … From this entanglement a figure emerges, hunched as if they themselves have sprung up out of the earth overnight under a gibbous moon, the stiff folds of their robe echoing the gnarled texture of the trunks that flank them. Though they have their back to us, their face, illuminated as if caught in the beam of a flashlight, is turned round to reveal an anxious expression, unsure whether to proceed or not. While their body is oriented towards the top right of the frame and the shadowy maw of the forest, their head is drawn to something else happening, or having just happened, in the opposite direction, an event we can still see impressed upon their face: fright, an emotion prolonged forever by the resounding of something sensed beyond the bounds of the scene itself.

0.11   What is the sound that precedes the image? What noise has the figure in the picture just heard that has spooked them so, causing their neck to twist so that their eyes become fixed upon us over their shoulder? The snap of a twig? The sudden rush of wind in the trees? The grunt of some crepuscular animal disturbed in its den? The honk of a hunting horn drifting in from the ecotone? From this or these misshapen notes, might they have hallucinated a voice crying out from the dark: *Hey, you! Stop! Wait!* Rather, has the sound come from within their own head? The voice of guilt, perhaps, or the prick of conscience.

0.111   In attending to an image like this, the critical mind makes a noise enough to startle its subject. If this is true, it is us, the interlopers in this woodland scene, who are the source of the discomposing sound.

0.12   An image is "listenable," argues David Toop.[1] Its sound is *implied*, in the classical Latin sense of the word meaning "enfolded" or "entangled," within the various cues that exist both within the time and space of the image, and at a distance from it. In theatrical language, we might say that we can detect certain "noises off."

0.13   Like noises, smells too have a tail to them. If images can sound, this book risks the proposition that sound, in smelling, transforms the conditions of all listening, musical or otherwise. Using the figure of the stinkhorn fungus and a multisensory analysis of its powerful odor and sonic association with flies, I will explore the ways in which certain types of "bad" smells *inform*, not merely influence, how we make sense of sound. What these two modes of interpretation—listening and smelling—hope to reveal is not only the source of these types of sounds drifting in from offstage or offscreen, but the qualities of their "offness."

A deviant path

0.2   There's a point deep within many a passion project where one finds oneself, like the awakening figure in Gustave Doré's illustration for Dante's *Divine Comedy*, suddenly lost in the forest of one's own subject without the faintest clue how to navigate yourself, or your reader, out of it. I, like Dante's wayfinder, started this project precisely midway through the journey of life ("midway," that is, according to an estimation by the Office for National Statistics of the average life expectancy of a male born in Scotland towards the end of the 1970s). If Dante, aided by the ancient poet Virgil, is the reader's guide as they travel with him through the entangled forest into the depths of Hell, then I am the guide to the reader of this book as we travel together towards our reeking subject and Stink itself. By the end, I hope to show the potentiality of a malodorous medium—a mushroom, for example—as a listening device.

0.21   There are many other reasons to liken this book to a journey through a forest. Foremost because it is the forest where I've spent much of my time over the last five years in search of the source of a single scent and the noises that invariably accompany it. I present them together here, sound and smell, in the figure of the phallic stinkhorn fungus and the humming that precedes it.

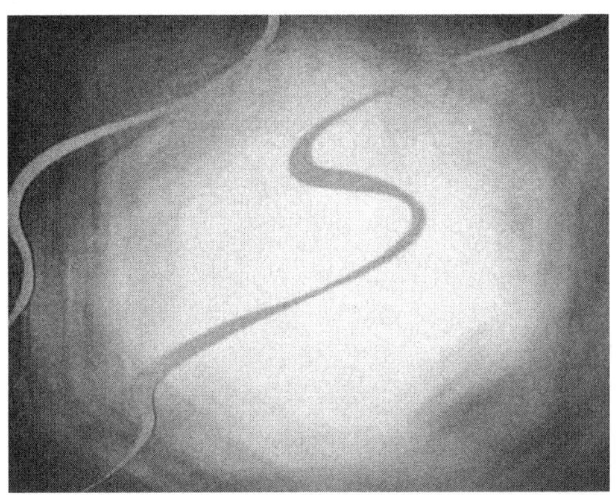

0.22   Stinkhorns hold a special place in the history of how plant enthusiasts and botanical artists have described the natural world. As I discuss in chapter two, the history of printed mycological literature starts with a short sixteen-page pamphlet from 1564 on the dune stinkhorn titled *The Description of the Phallus* by Adriaen de Jonghe, better known by his Latinized name Hadrianus Junius. Within the pages of this book, I have inserted a careful and complete reproduction of Junius's monograph, translated in its entirety for the first time by Caroline Spearing. This should be of interest to not only mycologists and amateur mushroomers, but to anyone with an interest in past perceptions of fungi. More than out of generosity, the reason I've chosen to share Junius's description with you here is to show how, for nearly five hundred years, stinkhorns have eluded true, that is, total representation in art and writing. Whether this can be put down to a lack of language to describe smells (as I discuss in chapter one), or because of the sheer potency of their stench, when it comes to stinkhorns it seems artists and authors are forced to drift about their edges rather than approach them directly.

0.221   A meandering route is sometimes necessary when trying to advance towards a subject using its nonvisual characteristics as the primary clues to its whereabouts. As a matter of course, we must lose the straight path (Dante: "*la diritta via*") so a more deviant one can be found. I have not set out to be deliberately discursive or abstruse. Neither am I claiming to be striking out into this particular forest alone, or to have bent the bracken first. Writing this now, I'm reminded of Ivor Cutler's song "The Path," spoken aloud by Cutler in his typically equable and endearing west coast Scottish monotone:

> Many feet make one path.
> I like to walk on a foot path.
> I walk over the grass and turn to see if I have made a path.
> Two feet once only is not enough.
> I return to the foot path to feel one of the bunch.
> I add my feet.
> I look back.
> What a path we made![2]

0.222   I hope to add my own two feet to "the bunch" who have gone before, including Junius, but also those whose arguments for listening beyond the auditory have given me confidence to stray farther from the path they have only started to define. I'm thinking chiefly about John Cage who, like me, frequently trampled through the forest in search of mushrooms and music. But in this book, silence is no longer the quarry. Stink is.

0.23   Others who have led the way in this area include Seth Kim-Cohen whose book *In the Blink of an Ear* argues for a "non-cochlear sonic art."[3] Kim-Cohen is compelling in his advocacy for a theorization of sound that should, at last, be afforded the same conceptual dimension the visual arts (or "gallery arts," as he usefully defines it) have enjoyed for over a hundred years since Duchamp, an aesthetic advantage he sets up in contrast to the persistent, essentialist understanding of "sound as sound" proclaimed by Cage and Pierre Schaeffer sometime around the 1950s.

0.231   David Toop, too, cuts a wide swathe in his book *Sinister Resonance,* a study of the latencies of silent mediums—such as painting and literature—as auditory devices. Both Toop's and

Kim-Cohen's ambitious texts, published within a year of each other —2010 and 2009 respectively—implore us to consider sound beyond the ear to the brain. Mine throws the nose into this heady mix.

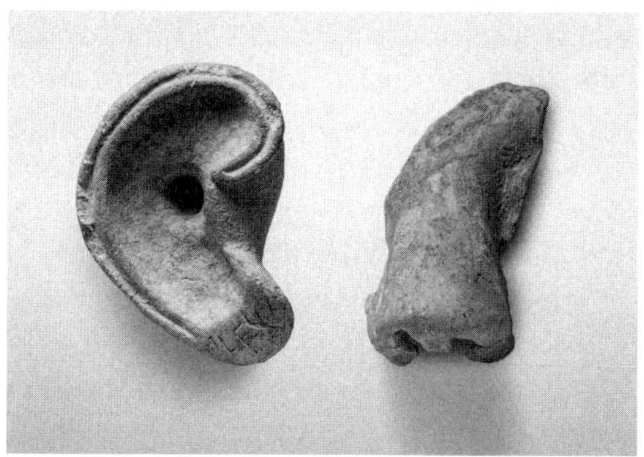

0.24   My ambition is not to bypass, but to broaden the still emerging path of sound studies, an area of artistic and academic interest which, despite a couple of notable exceptions just described, has predominantly focused on the constricted idea of sound as a fixed thing, wedded to the ear and hearing if not alone, then above all other sense modalities. As such, my claim for the olfactory as a counter-example to the aural does not mean to contradict Toop, Kim-Cohen, or other demands for conceptual or silent mediums to matter to the conditions of listening—an experience Toop generously describes as the "subtle perceptual entwinement of our senses" (though I note he inexplicably excludes smelling from this sensory knot).[4] Rather, it only bolsters their demands further by insisting that smelling should also be included as part of the clamorous discussions about what can and cannot constitute a listening experience.

0.25   This book, therefore, begins with the idea that the tendency for empirical or phenomenological approaches to sound as sound has largely ignored the potentialities of other sensory and conceptual modes of listening—smelling in particular. If the former practices can be described as overwhelmingly "ear led," then this book proposes to expand our conception of listening to consider sound via an alternative nose-led approach.

Nose-led

0.3   To follow your nose means to trust your instincts, to privilege that which cannot be seen. As such, to lead with one's nose means to expect to occasionally bump into seemingly immovable or deeply rooted ideas; obstacles which one must step over or go around in order to keep pressing onwards. It means presuming to sometimes end up mired in thick, claggy footnotes that will want to slow you down or reroute your attention. It also means having to slosh through puddles of language and meaning before being forced to select which terminology will provide the surest footing. But it's my belief that it is exactly this stumbling, bumping, tripping, and sloshing (verbs which themselves connote a type of muted soundscape) that will lead us someplace unexpected and sonically rich.

0.31   "Nose-led," of course, signifies the act of sniffing. I must admit here, however, that lacking the sophisticated snout of a professional perfumer or the chemical vocabulary of a material scientist—or, for that matter, the discriminating knowledge of a mycologist or the formal training of a musician or composer—my methods have necessarily taken on a kind of dilettantism in the sense of being drawn towards something intuitively rather than knowingly. An image comes to mind of a cartoon character floating, body horizontal, eyes closed, being tugged along by translucent tendrils of scent wafting in from some delectable source offscreen.[5]

0.32   The word "dabbling," which I hijack from Brian Eno and his own experimentations with scent as a stimulus to make music, is useful here. Eno "played with perfumes" to create his hour-long composition for modular synthesizer, *Neroli* (the name of an essential oil distilled from blossoms of the bitter orange tree).[6] Released in 1993, *Neroli* evolved out of Eno's decades-long habit of buying up oils and absolutes from old apothecaries and perfumeries from all over the world.[7] Subtitled *Thinking Music Part IV*, the piece follows Eno's earlier system-based compositions, such as *Ambient I: Music for Airports* (1978), in which music evolves out of a set of note patterning processes.[8] A loose melody of bell-like tones, spaced out to the point of abstraction, gives off an air that is gently buzzing, mechanical, metallic—an effect that strikes the right "note," so to speak. (Wikipedia describes neroli as having a "somewhat metallic" scent.)[9]

0.321   In an essay titled "The Future Will Be Like Perfume" (an evolution of a lecture on perfume he gave to an audience at Sadler's Wells, London, one year before *Neroli* was released on his own label, Opal Music), Eno described his initial compulsion when working with smells to classify and organize them the same way a classically trained composer or musicologist would think about tone and harmony.[10] However, it quickly became apparent to Eno that the inherited, organizational principles towards sound in the classical tradition, particularly notating sound, were wholly impractical when it came to smell. Eno gives an example of French coriander absolute, a scent he says took on a totally different set of perceptual qualities from one batch to another, and from one year to the next. His attempts to organize odor into some kind of language absolute, then, was abandoned in favor of what he calls "dabbling," a practice Eno suggests has enormous potential for innovation across other disciplines:

> I find myself enjoying [dabbling] more, watching us all becoming dilettante perfume blenders, poking inquisitive fingers through a great library of ingredients and seeing which combinations make some sense for us— gathering experience—the possibility of making better guesses—without demanding certainty. Perhaps our sense of this, the sense of belonging to a world held together by networks of ephemeral confidences [...] rather than permanent certainties, disposes us to embrace anew the pleasures of our most primitive and unlanguaged sense, that of smell.[11]

0.322   Dabbling suggests a superficiality whereby one engages with an idea simply by splashing about at the surface of things without any compunction to go too deep. That's not to say that the results of this "splashing about" are intellectually or artistically shallow; on the contrary, such an approach may yield interesting, if not weird, results. In this case, and given the deviant nature of our project, this is precisely the point.

0.323   What I've set out to do, then, is to dabble in the space of sound and smell. The impression I hope to give is of an amateur perfumer pulling down from overcrowded shelves various numbered vials of scent (Chanel No. 5? Love Potion No. 9?) and mixing up their liquid contents to make experimental concoctions before inviting others to stand over their vapors and sniff the results.[12]

Holes

0.4   If smell precedes the nose, then the nose precedes the body. Wherever you go, your nose goes first. Developmental biology can offer some support for this statement.

0.41   The olfactory system is the first of our sensory systems to develop in the womb.[13] However, our first exposure to odors occurs much later—sometime around four months after conception at which time the plugs in the nasal passages dissolve to allow chemical stimuli in the amniotic fluid to pass into the developing body.[14] Though this appears immediately compelling for our nose-led approach, Toop points out that hearing, not smelling, functions first after birth, quickly overtaken by seeing.[15] But where does this leave touch? What about the skin, what Didier Anzieu calls "the tactile envelope," that delivers within it all the other sense organs into the world?[16] For, even before birth, touch receptors are said to develop around the lips roughly two months after conception, two months before the nostrils have opened up.

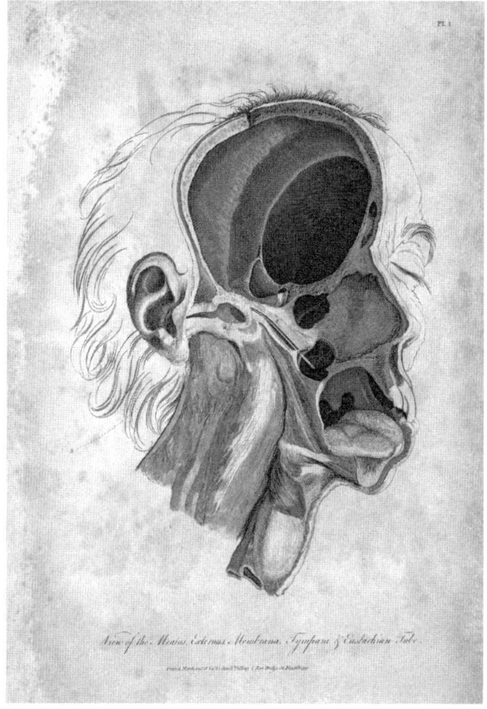

0.411   In purely functional terms, the argument for the primacy of one sense over another appears to be porous, literally full of holes: ear-holes, eye-holes, mouth-holes, nose-holes, skin-holes. What these holes have in common is that their function—both in utero and postpartum—is to allow sensory phenomena to pass through the boundary separating the exterior and interior worlds of the body in space, a space constituted first of liquid, then air.

0.42   When discussing the senses of sound and smell in combination, the reader might be forgiven for thinking that what follows falls within the study of synesthesia. It does not. Synesthesia is broadly defined as a "pairing of the senses" in which one mode of perception of a sensory phenomenon in the exterior world automatically triggers another.[17] Such is the case in incidents of auditory-olfactory synesthesia where, to give a real example, the sound of a vacuum cleaner induced in one listener the smell of vomit.[18] (The same synesthete also reported the sound of drilling smelling like bleach, and the sound of music smelling like food.) The following discussion is concerned less with the neurological co-occurrence of sensory perceptions, however (which in synesthesia is strictly speaking not co-occurrence at all but causation), but with thinking about sound *through* smell.

0.421   In the case of the listener who smells vomit every time they hear the hum of a vacuum cleaner, we might ask: What can the stink of vomit tell us about the qualities of "humming"? Alternatively, in musical terms, what is the timbre, texture, or color of the odor of vomit? What is it about the odor of vomitus that *resonates*? How would we even begin to attune ourselves to such a stink; not to the retching sounds the body makes when ejecting something out the mouth, but to the malodor of the ejecta itself? And what processes and techniques would we need to conceive this as music?

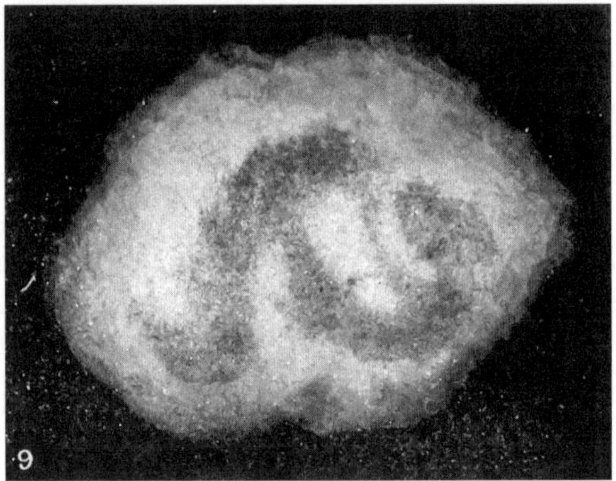

A smelling sound

0.5   It is clear that this inquiry cannot be reduced to a question so pithy as "Can sounds stink?" For, beyond synesthetics, veridically speaking, they cannot. This book starts with a less *terse* (literally "wiped clean") and therefore messier conception of sound and smell, one which agrees with William James's view that the human sensorium is essentially a "buzzing confusion" in which the lines that separate one sense from another are essentially smeared.[19] And so a more fruitful question might be to reverse this thinking to inquire: "Can stinks sound?"

0.51   The aim of this book is to expand and diversify the discourse of listening beyond the auditory to include sonic events informed by smells, particularly "bad" smells. The critical issues concentrate on the concept of stink. Towards the end, I hope to differentiate between two types of stink: stink with a small "s" meaning a powerful and unpleasant smell (the word's primary and literal definition), and Stink with a capital "S" meaning the combined effects in the imagination of a type of *smelling sound* that may induce in the listener feelings of uncertainty, bordering on dread.

0.52   To help orient the reader from the start, a theory of sound as Stink can be summarized using the following five suppositions:

Stink occurs in the real world via *the medium of the air,* which one experiences in the mind as a holistic impression of discrete tonal elements diffused in space.

Stink is *inarticulate.* It cannot be divided into subcomponent parts but appears intensely in the imagination as a unitary meshwork of tones and textures. In this way, Stink is comparable to other seemingly formless sounds, such as moaning and humming.

In terms of its durational aspect, then, Stink is *prolonged so as to be pervasive*—an incensed and incensing static, so to speak—reinforced through reflection and reverberation, and exacerbated by the effects of dissonance. As such, Stink has the potential to spread beyond the auditory to include the olfactory and gustatory modalities, among others, to affect the sensorium as a whole by inducing in the listener strong feelings of discomfort or dread.

Conversely, Stink is *ambivalent,* meaning one can experience it in the mind as being simultaneously pleasant and unpleasant. This is largely dependent on context. For example, we might imagine a Stink that initially appeals to the senses due to, say, its novelty or tonal complexity. After a while it may start to take on some more odious or objectionable qualities. These qualities are not necessarily perceived as being disagreeable, however. The point is this: Stinks, though generally disquieting, are not as a matter of course perceived to be "bad" in every respect. Instead, our responses to them are mutable, producing mixed or contradictory feelings.

꩜ Finally, and though seemingly in conflict with the first supposition, Stink can be *hallucinated*. In other words, Stink can be perceived even when there is no sound-source present in the real word. That is, Stink can be considered a reality because it is *felt* to be real (see chapter five).

0.53   A sound that manifests in the air while also being able to be hallucinated. A sound that is inarticulate yet itself can be distinguished from other types of sounds. A sound that is pervasive so as to produce in the listener feelings of dread, or else, ambivalence. A sound that is perceived beyond the ear to include the nose, the gut, the mind, etcetera. This is the entanglement of paradoxical ideas at the heart of this book and which I name Stink.

Stink music

0.6   Music criticism is an adjectival discourse, wrote Barthes in the opening paragraph to his essay "The Grain of the Voice." "The adjective is inevitable: this music is *this*, the execution is *that*."[20] He goes on:

> No doubt the moment we turn an art into a subject […] there is nothing left but to give it predicates; in the case of music, however, such predication unfailingly takes the most facile and trivial form, that of the epithet. Naturally, this epithet, to which we are constantly led by weakness or fascination (little parlor game: talk about a piece of music without using a single adjective), has an economic function: the predicate is always the bulwark with which the subject's imaginary protects itself from the loss which threatens it.[21]

Stink music. A music that by my own exegesis is ambivalent, moaning, humming, buzzing, ghostly, formless, smeared, thick, muddy, slimy, overripe, pervasive, nauseating. With this slew of adjectives, it seems I have failed unutterably at the parlor game Barthes invokes. And yet the insertion of smell into the practices of thinking, making, and writing about music might afford the philosophical aspect that Barthes is hungry for. Stink—as a stimulus for music composition and improvisation; as critical tool—may reduce the problematic of adjectival discourse. Placing smell in the foreground when setting up this ontology, though it's fragile, may get us closer to the idea of what Barthes describes as the "imaginary in music."[22] For Stink offers a nasal mode for interpreting music as opposed to a verbal one. As such, Stink may be allowed to function as an osmic, that is, *non-linguistic* epithet.

0.61   Stink preserves that which may be lost when one tries to describe in language ("verbal periphrasis," as Barthes puts it) the musical object it predicates.[23] In other words, the nose gets us somewhere inside the music that the mouth, tongue, and teeth cannot. And yet, the nose (as sensory receptor; as tuning peg to the aerated vocal hum) conveys to the listener something of the fleshy, cartilaginous, mucous (literally "slimy, moldy, or musty juice") inner body, what Barthes identifies in vocal music as the "grain" of the voice. I can see my propositions for Stink aligning with many of the ineffable, potentially inexhaustible qualities of Barthes's "grain," or Julia Kristeva's irreducible "geno-text," for that matter. Like Barthes's "grain," Stink affords a tremendous openness or passivity to, as well as being indexical of, the characteristics of the nasal cavity, which unlike the eyes with their lids, the ears with their tympanic membrane, and the mouth with its lips, offers a direct and unimpeded channel of communication and expression in both directions to the very center of the brain.

0.611   Stink furthermore sympathizes with Barthes's other incarnations of the "grain," what he more generally describes as *signifiance*, which can be understood as something like the slippery process or movement of signification—or as Barthes more elegantly puts it, "meaning ... sensually produced."[24] The incarnation most sympathetic to our Stink is probably the "punctum," what Barthes outlines in his book *La chambre claire* (*Camera Lucida*), his treatise on the essence of photography and reflections on personal grief as the feeling that punctuates or "pricks" the general affect of a photograph. (Here, the connotation of the prick as a swollen phallus piercing the dull, monotonous earth so as to violently demand our attention is nothing but a bonus.)[25] Both "grain" and "punctum" hint at qualities (Barthes says of the latter it is like a "sting, speck, cut, little hole") that are particular—or should that be *particulate* in the sense of their describing something extremely small, separate, yet an essential part of a larger whole; like a single spore that miraculously detaches from its former gelatinous mass; like an individual, volatile chemical molecule rising above all others in the general miasma.[26]

0.612   Stink, and by extension the "hum" (see chapter four), offers a critical counterpoint to these traditional theories by proposing a much-needed olfactory dimension to the mostly verbal, orally/aurally fixated ideas in and around music criticism. What's more, Stink offers a practical element for the sound artist or composer engaged in the making of, rather than merely thinking or writing about, music.

0.62   As composer and fellow mycophile John Cage once remarked, "I am not interested in the relationships between sounds and mushrooms any more than I am in those between sounds and other sounds."[27] Let me conclude this section by echoing this sentiment, modifying it thus: I'm not interested in the relationship between sound and smell, or between music, mushrooms, and malodors, for that matter. My interest is in Stink, which is actually, synchronously, an interest in sound and sound ad nauseam.

Pricks up

0.7   The title of this book, *Stinkhorn*, is of course a pun. In case you missed it, as well as describing a type of phallic mushroom, the word is also meant to conjure a magical musical instrument capable of producing a smelly sound that can be heard via the nose.

0.71   My use of the stinkhorn fungus as rhetorical device follows other approaches by authors who have similarly interrogated their subjects through metaphors of mushrooms, animals, artworks, and so on. Most famously *The Order of Things*, in which Michel Foucault devotes his opening chapter to an analysis of the seventeenth-century painting by Diego Velázquez, *Las Meninas*, using the picture as a means to examine changes in ways of thinking between different historical periods in Europe.

0.711   To borrow a line from Foucault's analysis of *Las Meninas*, in order to use the stinkhorn for our own ends, there are certain things that "we must pretend not to know."[28] This is for two reasons: first, to preempt criticism from mycologists, neuropsychologists, material chemists, perfumers, and others who would claim my argument was spurious for being unscientific; and second, in order to create an imaginary space that, by way of a series of mycorrhizal associations and spore-like dispersions, allows us to think through our noses.

0.712   At times we must pretend not to know the structural differences—mechanical and chemical, respectively—of how human audition and olfaction function; that is, the way sound and smell pass through the sense organs and are perceived in different parts of the brain. We must pretend not to know our subjective, collective, and/or cultural experiences of smell; the different ways different groups of humans in different parts of the world agree on what constitutes a "good" or "bad" odor. By extension, we must try to imagine the smell experiences of other animals and organisms to such an extent that their survival and reproductive methods are at stake. In this way, I hope to allay anthropocentric or prejudiced claims about what it means for an odor to be disgusting, dissonant, or whatever. Only in this way can we engage with the world from the lowly position of a mushroom, or indeed from the fly that hums around it.

0.72   In his philosophical treatise on listening, Jean-Luc Nancy implores us to *"prick up the philosophical ear"* and attend to that which presents itself beyond the auditory, beyond the visual, and to the sensorium as a whole.[29] I hear another pun here: "prick up," an expression that figures the ability of some animals to extend and move their ears to better focus their attention on novel sounds; and "prick up," a vulgar intimation of the erect penis ready to fuck.[30] Nancy's phrase also appears to prefigure my own designs on the stinkhorn mushroom as a listening device, a fungus that so resembles a phallus that sixteenth-century herbalist John Gerard named it the "Pricke Mushrum" (see chapter two).

On the turn

0.8   If the battle over "visualism," as Don Ihde puts it, in the field of sound studies is still slowly being fought, this leads me to question why the other senses seem to have been ignored for so long, smell especially.[31] There are some exceptions in the canon, where smell is attended to in relation to sound, but they are fleeting and so quickly dismissed as to be largely inconsequential. For example, Robert Pasnau briefly entertains the analogy between sounds and smells for the way they both fill the air, but he quickly rejects it for being frivolous on the grounds that smell, like other "non-locational" sensory modalities, such as taste and touch, cannot be used to locate the source of the odor the same way that hearing can be used to locate sounds.[32] As Andreas Keller shows us, strictly speaking this is not true.[33] Humans can, and in many cases *do* use smell to locate and navigate towards odorous objects; foraging in the forest for stinkhorns is case in point. Though Keller makes plain that this does not mean that smell is spatially structured, what Pasnau seems to ignore are the more abstract elements of what sound and smell potentially share, not just in the manner of their moving through space, but how this movement affects their *quality*.

0.81   Brian Eno's dabblings aside, we find that until relatively recently any attempt to consider one sense via another by way of analogy, principally analogies that involve smell, have often been disparaged for being too whimsical.[34] My approach to the sound-smell analog chooses to look farther afield, therefore, finding parallels in the olfactory turn witnessed in the humanities over the last couple of decades. This turn has intensified in the last few years, evidenced by an explosion of new titles on the significance of smell in the history of the senses. Several works pick up from where Alain Corbin left off with *Le miasme et la jonquille* (1982; *The Foul and the Fragrant*), his important work in which he outlines historical perspectives on odors from pre-Revolutionary France to the beginning of World War I. Alongside some much broader surveys (such as the six-volume series *A Cultural History of the Senses* [2018], which covers antiquity to the present, a project with editorial oversight by Constance Classen, one of the editors of *Aroma: The Cultural History of Smell* [1994]), this recent crop includes Jonathan Reinarz's *Past Scents* (2014). Reinarz updates some of Corbin's perspectives to consider smell in relation to a range of subjects including religion, race, gender, and class. Katelynn Robinson looks farther back in time in her research on medieval smell theory, *The Sense of Smell in the Middle Ages* (2014), in which, through writings on natural philosophy, medicine, and religion, she tries to identify the various ways the "physical" versus the "spiritual" nose tried to differentiate between sacred and sinful odors.[35]

0.811   Robert Muchembled takes up this good-versus-bad antagonism in *Smells* (2020), his study of the odors of perfumes and plagues from the Early Modern Era in Northern Europe. Significantly, Muchembled notes, people in urban centers were once seemingly oblivious to the smell of sweat, shit, and piss until the start of the seventeenth century when malodors took on a much more minacious feature in the time of epidemics.[36] Andrew Kettler reframes some of the prejudiced perceptions of malodors (which Muchembled describes were attributed to "menstruating, ill, or simply old" women) in terms of racism in his anthropological study *The Smell of Slavery* (2020).[37] Other scholars have similarly narrowed their focus by concentrating on single scents. For example, Karl Schlögel's *The Scent of Empire* (2021) focuses on two perfumes only, Chanel No. 5 and Red Moscow, as a means to understand and connect historical perspectives on the redolent and the rancid in the times of Nazism and Stalinism.

0.82   It's worth commenting on the fact that many of the publications listed above, which represent only a handful of examples of smell studies plucked from the humanities alone, started to appear on (virtual) bookshelves at the very beginning of the COVID-19 pandemic, a plague individuated by the symptom of a lack of taste or smell. Their appearance coincided with a global shift in the way we started to move through odorous space. Forced to work from home, many of us found we had to adapt quickly to new ways of engaging with colleagues, students, family members, and friends over video platforms—which, it should be noted, favor quality of sight and sound at the expense of all other senses. When we *did* venture out into the "real world" of other bodies, for those of us who chose to wear face masks it meant that the smell environments we once moved through so breezily were reduced to the small smell-space of our own mouths and noses. Consequently, it strikes me as deeply ironic that such an accumulation of scholarship on smell has emerged precisely at a period (which one could feasibly narrow down to a matter of months) that we may soon look back upon as being one of the most anosmic in human history.

0.821   Some of the methods I've employed in this study stand in contrast to this fact, engaged as I was during the pandemic in actively seeking out reeking objects from the outside world and bringing them back into my home to sniff. Their stench infuses these pages.

0.83   My approach to foul smells does not seek to replicate or recapitulate the various historical perspectives documented in the examples above. Neither is it intended to be a monograph of malodor, such as that proffered by Dominique Laporte's velveteen-covered book *History of Shit* (1978), though it is this work above all others, with its purposely skittish style and scatological prose, that I feel most strongly resonates with my own. Even more, this book is composed in the spirit of Laporte's textual and conceptual model, and chimes somewhat with his disdain for academic writing etiquette more broadly, what he saw as its impenetrable style that so "launders" ideas of their stench.[38]

0.84   Can a text stink? Can the effects of language on a subject, like the process of translation, shifting sense from one register to another, rot it down, make its meaning more potent? Or can this process, like the actions of voracious maggots feeding from the carrion into which they were born, make a subject more lively than its outward appearance of deadness or stasis?

0.841   Rather than focusing primarily on one tradition or mode of thought—such as phenomenology (and latterly *post*-phenomenology) of sound championed by the likes of Ihde; or on parallel approaches to music and mushrooms witnessed most overtly in Cage's mycological maunders; or on a particular period, such as the "odor of sinfulness," as Igor Stravinsky put it, emanating from the more dissonant elements of early modernism to the postwar avant-garde—I will attempt to show how sound and smell can be conceptualized together by marking out a heterogeneous range of (stink) texts, sensory sources, and fields of study.[39] In no particular order, these include: mycology, musicology, neuropsychology, and philology. I add to these in chapter five where I address the phenomena of olfactory hallucinations, touching upon pathology, philosophy of perception, and psychoanalysis in relation to my own diagnosis of epilepsy in 2020 following several experiences of phantosmia, "phantom smells." This may require of the reader leaps in what Jonathan Sterne calls the "sonic imagination," a willingness to move "across registers, moments and spaces [...] across disciplines and traditions."[40] But, I argue, these leaps are necessary when attending to gaps: gaps in the literature, gaps between the nose and the ear.

0.842   Moreover, there's a weird logic to my employing this range of texts and techniques, designed to parallel the action and ontological experience of the Stinking object itself. As I've outlined above in my five suppositions, one defining aspect of Stink, for example, is that it is pervasive. *Pervasive* means to "spread, or pass through." The effect of this inquiry, I hope, is similarly pervasive in permeating the senses, plural, so as to fill up the space of a thought.

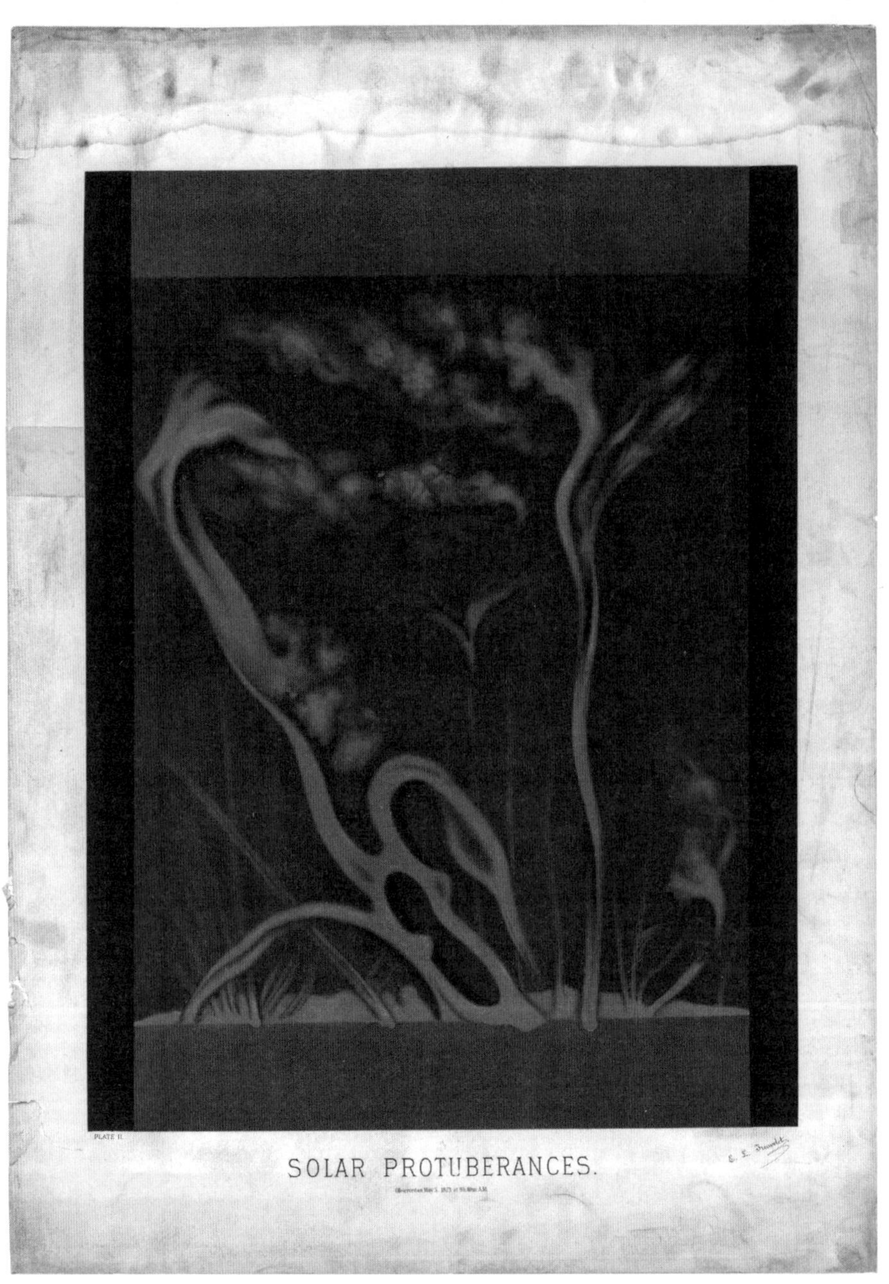

SOLAR PROTUBERANCES.

Observed on May 5, 1873 at 9h.40m A.M.

1. On Stink

A haze of swamps and sewers

1.1   *Stink* describes a smell that is "unpleasant," "offensive." Stink is expansive. It takes up space at various scales, and crosses boundaries, human and nonhuman. An insect secretion on a flower blossom. An inquistive finger. A sick mouth. A tenement stairwell. A stretch of sewage-strewn coastline. A rotting, sun-bleached coral reef. An archipelago. Constance Classen and others describe the temporal and spatial dimensions of stink using the example of the Andaman Islands, where the potent, shit-smelling flower *jeru* of the genus *Sterculia* grows, named after Sterquilinus, the Roman god of manure.[1] This stink, mixed with the sea-salt air and warmed by the summer sun, gives the archipelago the seemingly contradictory moniker "islands of fragrance."[2] Stink is insistent, pervading the mind so that when one is in the place of stink one can think of little else. The stink of sex, for example, sniffing a partner's privates.

1.11   The chemical smell of sex, a 2005 study shows, is hedione.[3] Hedione is one of the most widely used and researched chemicals in the perfume industry, often employed as a fixative, a type of ingredient that stabilizes and prolongs the scent on the skin. According to the study, there is some evidence that hedione is associated with sex pheromones released by genital rubbing. The mix of genital sweat and fresh semen share similarities with the competing fetors of a funeral parlor: indole (lily stamens) and cadaverine (rotting corpse). The intimacy of organs and orifices—tangy, yeasty, honeyed, fecal—repellent in one context, intoxicating in another. For instance, the farmyard-smell of Époisses, a runny cheese famously banned from France's public transport system, shares many volatile chemicals with hog shit. Still, we paste it on our crackers and pop it in our mouths.

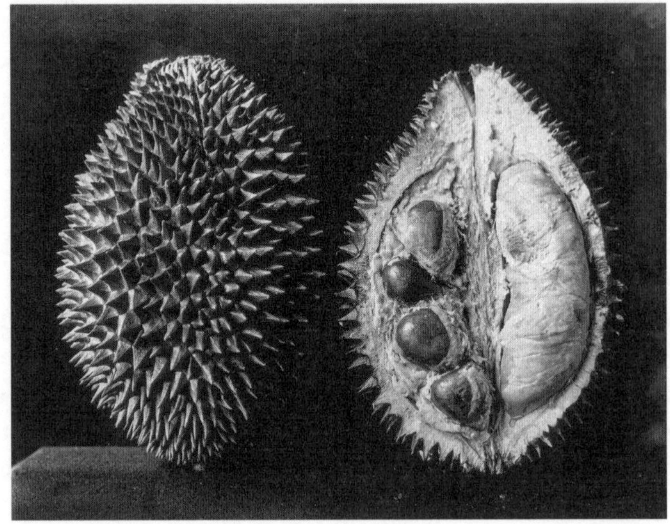

1.111   Durian fruit is similarly banned in public spaces in some parts of Southeast Asia due to its strong odor of turpentine and excrement. One of the compounds detected in varieties of ripe durian pulp is the chemical ethanethiol, a pungent odorant that the human nose can detect in miniscule amounts, a fact that has led to its being added to odorless propane and butane gas to help warn of gas leaks.[4] Stink is a warning.

1.112   Then there's the fermented, ammonia-infused flesh of the Greenland shark, the Icelandic delicacy *hákarl*. To help it survive in the abyssal depths of the High Arctic, the flesh of Greenland sharks contain the chemical trimethylamine oxide, a nerve gas that decomposes to form trimethylamine, the principle odorant in rotting fish. When fresh, the meat is toxic. Sled dogs, and occasionally humans, have been known to fall into a stupor followed by an unshakeable sleep after gorging upon the piss-smelling carcass of a recently landed shark. The intoxicating and hallucinatory effects on the mammalian body is called being "shark drunk." Before it can be safely eaten, the shark's head and main artery are severed, the belly and body meat boiled, boiled again several times more, buried, and fermented for three months, dried for five months, then scraped of its rust-brown outer crust and served in cute little cubes.

1.12   As with most of these foul-smelling foodstuffs, the argument goes that if you can get past the stench, the tongue (a truly dull instrument compared to the nose) can be more easily seduced. As we mature into adulthood, traveling beyond our small worlds to accrue sensory experiences of different cuisines and culinary curios, we may learn to love that which initially disgusts us. As Robert Muchembled concludes in his book *Smells*: "How an individual perceives a given scent is not innate. A brief neuronal flash triggers an initial warning of potential danger, before the sense of smell kicks in, defines the scent as good or bad and memorizes it. Learning the difference is a lengthy process."[5]

1.121   Sometimes there is no difference. Sometimes certain stinks can be perceived as both "good" and "bad" simultaneously. In one context the strong smell of animal excrement is repugnant, whereas the odor of slurry sprayed onto fields to fertilize crops (crops that are, incidentally, then fed back to the animals who excrete it, and so on) might appear nostalgic. In his book *The Foul and the Fragrant: Odor and the French Social Imagination* (1986), Alain Corbin explains how Flaubert's longing for dung was "mingled with the Romantic fascination for the odors of excremental and cadaverous putridity."[6] This agricultural effluvia is clearly not to everyone's tastes, certainly not in the concentrations one finds today as the result of intensive animal farming practices: as the *Guardian* newspaper reported in 2017, for those communities in parts of the United States forced to live in close proximity to open-air lakes of hog shit, the mephitic vapors may be so intoxicating as to make one's eyes sting and one's nose bleed.[7]

1.122   In Europe, since the sixteenth and seventeenth centuries, musk pods, the caudal glands of a type of male deer (*musk* means "small testicle"), have been used to fix perfumes with an animalic heat. Likewise, civet is the powerfully diffusive, buttery scrapings of the African civet's anal glands; castoreum, the piss-yellow seepage from the castor sacs of beavers. Diluted to trace amounts, these glandular secretions give fragrances a base-smell of feces and leather, which, when vaporized and applied to human skin, greatly appeals to the senses. As the cautious perfumier (and Brian Eno) knows, fine fragrance is multitudinous, a complicated mix of numerous plant and animal extracts, tinctures, and fixatives. The prospect of a scent tipping over into stink can be but one-tenth of a percent away. Muchembled:

> Our flexible, adaptable sense of smell alerts us to danger, helping us steer clear of toxins, and to potential sexual encounters, vital for the survival of the species. All human cultures, past and present, have learned to manipulate our sense of smell by associating one end of the scent spectrum with extreme disgust, and the other end with the utmost sense of well-being.[8]

1.13   Stink is durational. It passes time, has beginnings and endings. The complex of chemical compounds in a single fragrance is articulated into "notes," which, like those that constitute a musical chord, decay over time. Stink never lasts forever—save, perhaps, for that of the seventh circle of Lower Hell; but even then, before descending further Virgil and Dante simply pause for a while so as to become "'more accustomed in our sense of smell to this grim belch. We'll then not notice it.'"[9]

1.131   Worse is that emitted by the Bog of Eternal Stench, the inexorably flatulent swampland featured in the film *Labyrinth* (1986), which transfers to the poor soul who steps into its diarrheal slime a stink that will "never wash off."[10] Still, as climate and solar scientists know all too well, one day this bog also will dry up, its stench extinguished by the rising surface temperature of the Earth itself as it is absorbed by the Sun, six billion years from now.

1.132   Spacewalkers have described the smell of the Sun after its fumes have infused their spacesuits. Astronaut Donald Pettit described the smell of space as "a rather pleasant, sweet, metallic sensation" like "the smell of welding fumes."[11] Others have described it as "acrid, like gunpowder," or "sulphurous."[12] Stars shedding a brilliant haze of swamps and sewers. Likewise, there is some evidence that sound also endures in outer space. In 2003, astronomers detected sound waves "a million, billion times deeper than the limits of human hearing."[13] This subaudible drone, an echo of the birth of a Black Hole, is a B-flat, fifty-seven octaves lower than middle C.[14] Infinite space. An eternal eggy stench. An immortal hum.

The nasal imaginary

1.2 Why *stink* and not any other word in the lexicon of smell? Why not just *smell*, for example?

1.21 *Smell* describes both the olfactory sense as well as the olfactory perception of any kind of scent, pleasant or unpleasant. As a verb, *smell* means both the ability to perceive odors via the nose and olfactory organ, plus an object's capacity to emit an odor of its own. The phrase "I smell," meaning to perceive the odor of oneself, conveys what Peter Szendy calls the "reflexive" power of *smell* to loop the imagination back on itself.[15] However, it is a power that doesn't belong to other sense-words such as *see, hear,* and *touch.* (Note, this is different to what Szendy is talking about when he draws from Marcel Duchamp's observation in 1914 that although "one can look at seeing; one cannot hear hearing.")[16] We cannot say, for example, "I see my see," or "I hear my hear," or "I feel my feel"—though I can "feel my feelings"; but I can say "I smell my smell." In the continuous and gerundial form, I can even say "I am smelling my smelling." However, what's not clear in this statement is the quality of my smell. Without an adjective to qualify it—"good" smell, "faint" smell, "foul" smell, and so on—*smell* as a noun by itself tends towards neutrality.

1.22 *Odor* is similarly neutral, though its descriptive range is even more limited than *smell*: whereas you can "odorize" something, you cannot "odor" it. Some have recently expressed a preference to add the prefix *mal-* to make *malodor.* Though to some ears this term may sound laborious and over-egged, there's an efficiency to using *malodor* in locating precisely where a certain scent sits on the spectrum of how pleasant or unpleasant it is perceived to be, what's known in olfactory perception as "hedonicity." My preference for stink deliberately flies in the face of this efficiency, however, in favor of some of the word's more ambiguous attributes.

A sweet stench, or "God and His deliberate finger"[17]

1.3   *Stink* derives from *stench* as *drink* does from *drench*. *Stench* communicates an olfactory sensation that is deep, low down in the frequency range of smell so that it's felt somewhere in the stomach. If *stink* tends strongly towards the unpleasant, then *stench* conveys an odor that is out-and-out evil. Surprisingly, however, the usage of *stench* (originally spelled in Old English without the "h," *stenc*) was historically vague: it appears there was a time towards the latter half of the first millennium when one could encounter a "sweet stench."

1.31   In his *Ecclesiastical History*, written in about AD 731, Bede describes reports from Brie, France, of fragrant vapors (what would later be described by the Catholic Church as the Odor of Sanctity, or more formally "osmogenesia") filling the Abbey of Faremoutiers after the tomb of Ethelburga, an Anglo-Saxon princess and abbess, was uncovered three days after her death: "there came from within the tomb such a sweet odor [*micel swetnisse stenc*], that to all of that household who stood by, it seemed as if a storehouse of balsam and of the most valuable and sweetest spices in the world had been opened."[18]

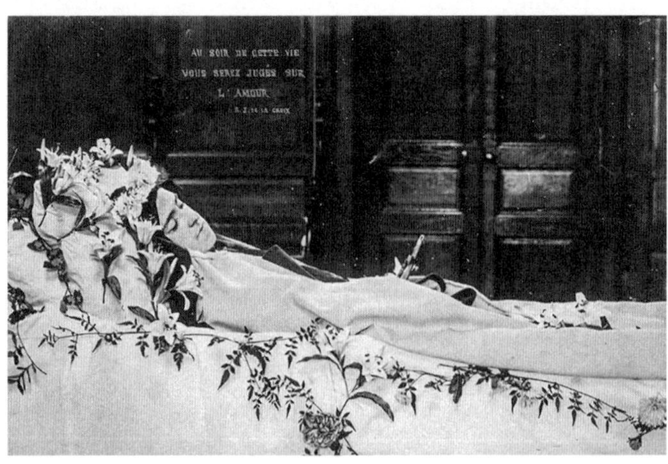

1.311   In the days following her death on September 30, 1897, it was reported that the body of Saint Thérèse de Lisieux, or "Little Flower" as she's otherwise known, exuded a sweet smell of roses. Some have speculated, such as the evolutionist J.B.S. Haldane, that the sugary aroma that oozed from the corpse before burial was probably not the result of holiness but ketosis, the process when the starving body runs out carbohydrates to metabolize and so turns upon itself for nutrition resulting in volatile acetones being released into the air. Acetones have a sickly sweet scent similar to the smell of pear drops, nail polish remover, or bitter almond oil. A parent to a child with diabetes, such as myself, may from time to time detect this frightening fragrance upon their child's breath when they are in a developed stage of ketoacidosis.

1.312   In Middle English, *stink* was equally used to characterize the aromatic odors of the sacred body. Written in the twelfth century and important in showing the shifts in English speech after the Norman conquest, the *Ormulum* describes the smell of the manger into which the child Jesus was born. It notes that in the moments immediately following Jesus's birth, the straw-strewn room "stank so sweetly" [*stunnkenn swiþe swete*].[19] The sweetness of this stink was surely remarkable to the Three Magi who'd travelled such distances to bear witness to this scene, because it must've been at odds with what they would have anticipated emanating from such a place, a place typically used to feed livestock. It was, after all, a manger, and thus likely to be filled with the animalic odors of fodder and dung.

1.313   At several points in the history of the English language, it seems the lexicon of smell, including *stink* and *stench*, were seemingly indifferent to the hedonic character of the olfactive experiences they described. Yet in modern usage they all—as can increasingly be said of *smell*—tend towards the foul. Despite these facts, buried in the history of *stink* is the potential of an ambivalence towards expressing our pleasure or displeasure, or both, upon smelling certain odors. That is to say, the term's evolution of meaning suggests that in *stink* (the smell of a rotting corpse, mold, and shit, and so on) can be experienced in the imagination variably, and sometimes synchronously, as both good and bad. It admits something deeply human in us all: that we can be delighted by stinks as much as disgusted by them, and to such an extent that, more often than we might admit, we actively sniff them out so that we may revere them and revel in them.

1.32   In ordinary language, *stink* is used in several phrasal verbs and multi-word adjectives to suggest behavior or characteristics we deem offensive. An industrialist can be stinking rich. A slighted worker can raise a stink. A comedian can stink out the joint with an ill-judged joke. A parent or partner can come home stinking drunk. The giveaway of public contracts by an unscrupulous politician can stink to high heaven. Almost always the implication is an air of moral or material decay, of something corrupt or corrupting, or of a quality that is just plain lousy.

1.321   In music, *stink* can at times describe a much more positive experience. A jazz drummer relaxing into a collective, improvised flow can "sit in the stink." A "stinky beat" or bassline describes a sound that has slipped from the learned connoisseurship of the brain down towards the gut. It's felt as much as heard. The sound is invariably heavy, hard, perverted—funky.

1.322   *Funk* is synonymous with stink. It means the musty smell of air thick with smoke and sweat. As it applies to a subgenre of jazz, funk describes a type of music that has an authentic, bluesy character, an earthiness. A funk musician can wear a "stank face," an expression of disgust marked by a flaring of the nostrils, squinting of the eyes, and curling of the mouth. But, in fact, the look signals the reverse: an outward sign of an unconscious, uninhibited state, a mind lost to something more powerfully diffusive than music alone.

Stink poetics (dung)

1.4   Language doesn't smell, said Barthes: "Language has this property of denying, ignoring, dissociating reality: when written, shit does not have an odor."[20] I take this to mean that even within the most vile passages, though they may conjure feelings of revulsion or distaste, written language can only ever signify *stink* rather than sensationalize it, in the epistemological sense. And yet there's always a threat that scatological speech may convey something of the real thing. To "talk shit" at someone, for example, is to shower them with invective. As Corbin points out, the phrase "talking shit" has historical links to the act of hurling one's own excrement at an enemy in battle.[21] Whereas Barthes's assertion that when written, *shit* doesn't stink, there still seems to be something about spoken language activated in the oral cavity that embodies sense, both in terms of perception and understanding.

1.41   Socrates showed us that words function best when their sound suits their meaning.[22] *Stink*—rhyming with *tink*, *mink* (Scots slang: "a dirty person"), *skink*; a close cousin to *skunk*, *spunk*, *gunk*, and *funk*; and implied by the phonics of *reek*, *creek*, *shriek*, *squeak*, and *speak*—works well in this regard. The gaseous sound that appears at the beginning of *stink* implies a meaning that hisses; a whiff of something objectionable on its way. Followed at the end by a hard, voiceless *k*, the effect of *stink* spoken aloud (as in the phonetics of the word *cacophony*, etymologically, "shit voice") conveys a dissonance, a not-rightness with the world. Combined in the fullness of the mouth, moving backwards from teeth to nose to throat, *stink* is the sound of fermented air escaping an unlabeled apothecary jar before its glass stopper is hastily replaced to prevent its mephitic vapors from leaking out.

1.42   Classen and others observed that in some cultures, such as the Indigenous Dogon people of Mali, West Africa, the quality of spoken language and its meaning is intrinsically linked to smell because of the way speech-sounds and odors travel through the air. For the Dogon, "good speech is thought to smell fragrant [...]. By contrast, nasal speech, which is associated with witches, is thought to smell of decay, for it sounds stagnant, as if caught between the nose and the throat."[23] According to this view, we can locate the sound-smell meaning of putrefaction trapped at the very center of *stink*.

1.421   The *ng* sound forms the only voiced part of *stink*. The phoneme *ng* (written as /ŋ/ in phonetics) is produced by vibrating the vocal cords, blocking the glottis, and expelling the air through the nose to make a kind of nasal hum. To proclaim "stink is nasal" appears self-evident, tautological. In the manner of the Dogon, to speak *stink* is to emit a malodor from one's mouth. I'm reminded, here, of a joke Eric Idle tells as an aside at the beginning of a Monty Python sketch. Q: What's brown and sounds like a bell? A: Dung.

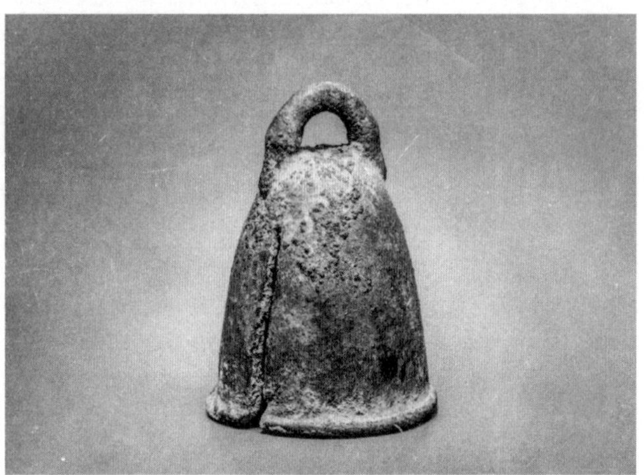

Noise and noisomeness

1.5   There is some discussion about the history of the word *noise* as to whether it derives from *nausea,* literally "boat-sickness," from the rocking and swaying motion of a ship that causes sailors to retch. *Noise* therefore carries with it the potential of inducing vomit, either due to the repeated rise-and-fall motion of a boat in water, or of a mass of undulating sounds in space. Both describe the effects of a type of "wave" (surface, sound) on the body and the conflicting signals sent to the brain by the inner ear. It turns out *noise* was once synonymous with *sound.* That is, at one time either word could be used without prejudice to describe a sonic event of any sort, whether one perceived its quality to be disagreeable or otherwise. The muted flapping of a sail in the wind, for example, as Samuel Taylor Coleridge writes in his poem the "The Rime of the Ancient Mariner": "Yet still the sails made on / A pleasant noise till noon / A noise like of a hidden brook."[24] (As Paul Hegarty usefully points out, *noise* is yet different from *noises*, the latter now needing qualifying the same way the plural *sounds* do: "unpleasant noises, loud noises.")[25]

1.51 *Noisome* is less equivocal when it comes to describing sensory experience. *Noisome* means a "loathsome smell, a stench." In my homeland of Scotland, it seems the word *noisome* did indeed once bridge the gap between the nose and the ear: John Jamieson's *Etymological Dictionary of the Scottish Language*, first published in the early nineteenth century, conflates *noisome* with a description of a sound that's unpleasant or annoyingly "noisy."[26] But in time and with broader usage, *noisome* has come to relate exclusively to the nose by signifying stink.

1.52 In their short history of meaning, one can trace the ways in which these two words, *noise* and *noisome,* used to describe dissonant sounds and disgusting smells respectively, have been confused by their phonetic similarity. But they are nevertheless connected by their implication of annoyance and offence. There is certainly some merit, some etymological foundation, for this mishearing. Perhaps *mis*hearing is the incorrect term for what I'm doing here. Perhaps what I mean is *over*hearing; not in the sense of listening without a speaker's knowledge, but of consciously hearing too much meaning in the collocation of words. Indeed, the same mode of listening may be applied to how I overhear the name *stinkhorn* where the compounding of *stink* plus *horn* is used to imply a synthesis of sound and smell, a *noisome noise,* so to speak.

1.53 I've attempted to show above why *stink* suits our discussion over others in the lexicon of smell due to the word's dexterity, its ambiguity, and because of its "potential" phonetic symbolism, that is, the effect it implies in the imagination by the sound it makes when spoken aloud. Note the air quotes around *potential*; as Steven Connor insists, "phonosemantics may be—no, certainly is—erroneous."[27] And yet Connor himself leaves enough space to consider a certain mode of what he calls "magical thinking" in our approach to language that allows this meaning to remain.[28]

1.54   The pairing of *stink* plus *sonic*—or else, *stink* plus *music*—forces a percussive contraction at the back of the throat, similar to a gag reflex, producing a retching noise that suggests revulsion. Consonant in its rhyming yet dissonant in its meaning, the suggestion of a *sonic stink* is one such sound effect, and a calculated one at that, for it's an attempt to concretize a concept in the hallucinated ear of the reader from the very start.

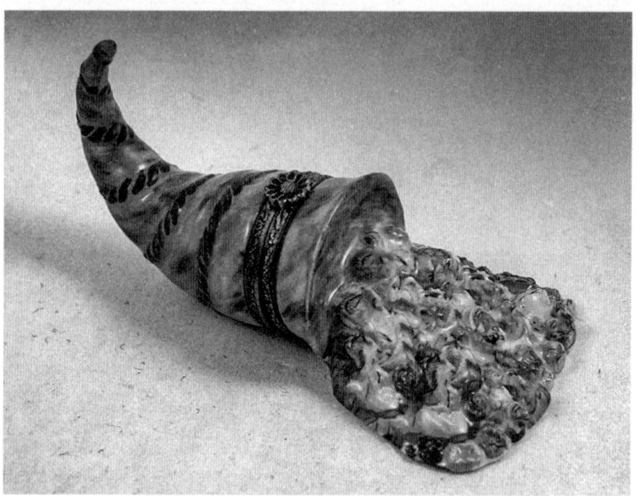

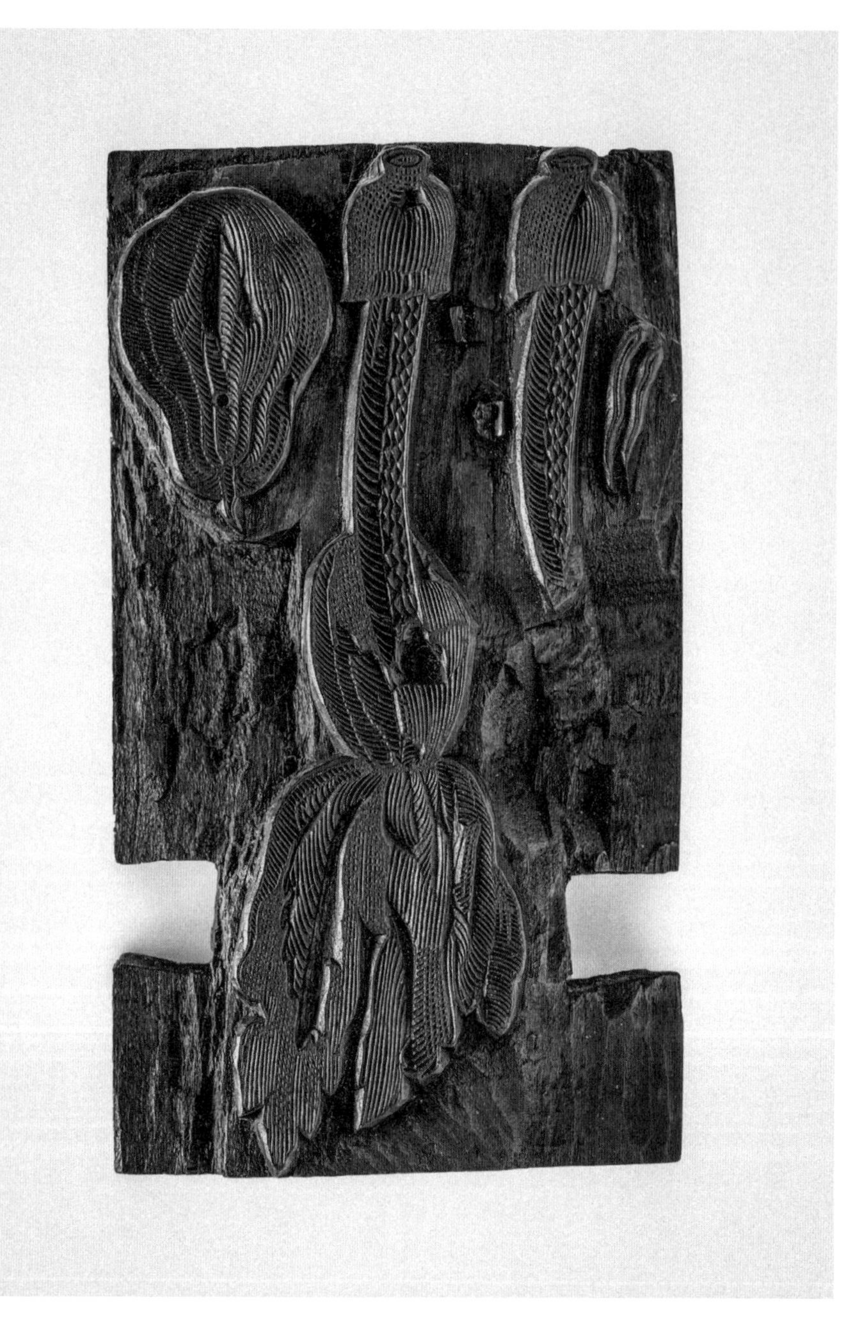

2. The Sight of the Stinkhorn

I like our toadstools for their transience, for the very
reason that [...] they cannot be kept or accumulated;
because they rot; because their images have to be pre-
served in mind and memory. [...] I like them, in short,
as objects of grace.

— E. C. Large, "Pursuits of Mycology," 1961.

A wrapper for long, hard things

2.1   The following three chapters are not meant to be a com-
prehensive historiography or scientific analysis of stinkhorn morphology, odor, or ecology (the same way Vilém Flusser's short book
Vampyroteuthis infernalis is not a scientific study of the vampire squid
from hell, but more a philosophical fiction).[1] Rather, my aim is to
excite the senses by presenting a series of intimate encounters with
stinkhorns from different historical perspectives and sensory modalities. I start here by describing its physical aspects—the sight of the
thing—followed in successive chapters by its smell (chapter three),
and finally its sound (chapter four).

2.11   Before I move on, a word to the reader who may flick through
the following pages and see a profusion of phallic imagery and wonder: What's in this for me? Although the idea for this book has not
been formulated within the discourse of gender studies, that's not to
say that my conceptualization of Stink via the metaphor of the stinkhorn fungus could not easily, and with the slightest modification, be
reframed in a feminist or queer mode. To echo Judith Butler and her
brilliantly titled essay "The Lesbian Phallus and the Morphological
Imaginary" (published in 1993 as part of the book *Bodies That
Matter*), the phallus—almost always conflated with the penis—does
not exclusively belong to a male, heterosexual version of the body.[2]
Rather, and as I go on to address, despite the historical fascination

among early male botanists with the phallic aspect of stinkhorn fungi (what Donna J. Haraway would call "prick tales"), the morphology of the stinkhorn signifies more, not less, than men's bodies, originating as it does from an egg-like primordium—what Pliny named the *volva*, meaning "wrapper, or sheath."[3] Yet even this does not mean to conflate the volva/vulva (from the Latin *volvere*, "to twist or turn over in the mind, ponder") with the feminine alone. Mycologist Nicholas P. Money reminds us that the traditional, male-dominated phallic view of the stinkhorn is a macro one, and mostly superficial:

> The resemblance of some fruit bodies to human genitalia is explained by the necessities of thrusting compacted soil (which gives many emerging mushrooms a somewhat phallic appearance), displaying a head of spore slime to attract insects (augmenting the phallic shape of stinkhorns), and becoming slippery with mucilage to maintain hydration after rainfall (in the more labial-looking jelly fungi). While these similarities are apparent to everyone, the nature of mushrooms as sexual organisms that reproduce after mating requires an imaginative stretch on the part of most readers.[4]

Though I admit that this "imaginative stretch" is what this book delights in, I'm also careful not to anthropomorphize or reduce the metaphor of the stinkhorn, or any mushroom for that matter, to its phallic feature alone. Of course, I could equally replace this surface view of the stinkhorn with a subterranean one, opting instead for, say, Le Guin's "carrier bag" theory, whereby meaning is brought to the surface, not by the penetrating effect of "long, hard things," but by an amorphous sack, pouch, womb, or in our case, the stinkhorn volva.[5] But as Money goes on to say in his next sentence, arguably even this would still be too large-scale and much too shallow a view of mushroom sexuality; for "mating between the fungi that form mushrooms," he writes, "is invisible without a microscope."[6] By choosing to emphasize the stinkhorn's fetid smell rather than its phallic shape, then, we afford ourselves space to consider the ineffable, all that eludes language. (As Butler, writing in 2018, warns about the limits of language in categorizing bodies, human or otherwise:

"I am that name you give me, but I am also something else that cannot quite be named.")[7] And so, though I suspend the question of sexual difference in relation to the body of the stinkhorn, there are certain other areas of my discussion that have gender implications that can, and with very little stretch, afford readers a queer reading of smell, one that challenges the traditional, visualist, heterosexist privileging of the phallus in body-like things in nature to what I believe are the mushroom's more generous, more divergent, yet no less provocative stinking signifiers. But back to the phallic matter at hand.

Lump of earth

2.2   There's always something amplified and overblown about the experience of coming across a ripe stinkhorn in the field, the retelling of which seems to demand an excess of superlatives, adjectives, and metaphors. As mycologist David Arora wryly remarks in his guide to mushrooms of North America,

> When stinkhorns are discussed, the language makes a startling and unprecedented qualitative leap, from monotonous minutiae to half-baked hyperbole, as if the authors were suddenly taking an interest in what they were saying. They are lavish in their praise as they tread the fine line between double-entendre and forthright fungal fact.[8]

Yet surely there's some justification for hyperbole when speaking about stinkhorns, as the words we have for them seem woefully insufficient. Visual representations, startling though they are, may get us closer to conveying the mushroom's true nature. The color illustrations featured in this book are from my own forays into forests near my home on the east coast of Scotland. From these and other finds I've made over the years, I can testify to the same puerile sense of delight whenever I stumble upon a stinkhorn poking up proudly out of the ground. I can testify, too, to the feelings of disgust after carefully transporting an unripe specimen back to my kitchen table to photograph, its intensifying stench filling every corner of our home for days after and continuing to tease out flies from god knows where. The image of the stinkhorn, no matter how magnified or in whatever detail, can never fully explain the intensity of feeling the mushroom induces in the artist or naturalist holding their breath as they try to observe it. As nineteenth-century English natural historian Charles David Badham remarked about the red cage stinkhorn *Clathrus ruber*, "I have found ten minutes in a room with it nine too many."[9]

2.21   The paucity of language used to describe smell might explain why in the history of scientific classification of stinkhorns naturalists have made more reference to their phallic form rather than their fetid odor. But let there be no doubt: stinkhorns look like pricks.

2.22   The most globally widespread stinkhorn, the common stinkhorn *Phallus impudicus*, emerges from the earth first as a cream-colored, leathery-skinned gelatinous sac colloquially known as a "witch's egg." From this egg erupts a long, white, gently curving shaft, also called a stipe. This event happens with such force that it's been calculated that an engorging stinkhorn is capable of lifting over 280 pounds, a weight equivalent to that of an average western lowland gorilla. Stinkhorn mushrooms have been known to break through roads and pavements like miniature pneumatic drills.[10] Despite this Herculean strength, the stipe of a fresh stinkhorn, which is hollow, finely perforated like prawn crackers, and most of its volume made up of air, is extremely brittle. Loosely attached to its tip is a rounded cap called a glans, which, as its name suggests, is remarkably similar in shape and size to the bell-end of the human penis. The cap is completed by a small, round opening like a urethral orifice. Early naturalists believed it was through this hole that the mushroom exhaled its "foul breath."[11]

2.221   The pioneering French doctor and botanist Charles de l'Écluse (1526–1609), better known by his Latinized name Carolus Clusius, was closer to the truth when he observed that the stinkhorn's smell comes from a brownish syrupy substance that develops over the cap itself: "The reeking cap of the mushroom is shaped like a helmet, similar to the acorn-like tip of the penis. The cap is first white in color, becoming brown with age at which time it emits a fetid odor."[12] Clusius's chronology of the mushroom's development is still not quite in the right order, however. When it first emerges from its egg, the smooth cap of the mushroom is covered in an olivaceous gel that darkens as it deliquesces, turning white only after swarms of insects have demolished its runny surface, thus deodorizing it. It is this sticky greenish-black goop, called the gleba, from which issues the stink of the stinkhorn. The word gleba is used in mycology to describe internally produced spores of gasteroid (stomach like) fungi, such as stinkhorns, puffballs, and earthballs. *Gleba* means "clod" or "lump of earth," an appropriate term for the dirt-colored muck that binds the spore mass to the mushroom's tip.

2.23   The lifecycle of the stinkhorn is short, appearing and disappearing like a trick. The mushroom becomes fully erect and ripe in a matter of hours, and its slime is devoured in far less time. The denuded cap reveals a pale skin, reticulated with a series of honeycomb indentations.[13] Thereafter the mushroom becomes flaccid, falling to the forest floor where it rots down to a seminal sludge and is reabsorbed into the earth.

A site of beauty and vomit

2.3   To speak of the sight of the stinkhorn, we must also speak of the spectacle of flies and other insects that invariably swarm towards it, and upon which the mushroom's lifecycle depends to disperse its spores.[14] The synthesized stench of decaying flesh and dung in the air causes antennae to twitch, luring flies with the promise of food or a potential brood site in which to lay their eggs. Corpse-eating flies most frequently found feeding off stinkhorn slime include the large, gray, dung-bred flesh-fly *Polietes lardarius* (which roughly translates as "citizen larderer," or the more pedestrian, yet arguably more sinister, "local butcher"), the orange-bodied *Phaonia subventa*, the greenbottles *Lucilia caesar* and *Lucilia sericata*, and bluebottles *Calliphora vicina* and *Calliphora vomitoria*.[15]

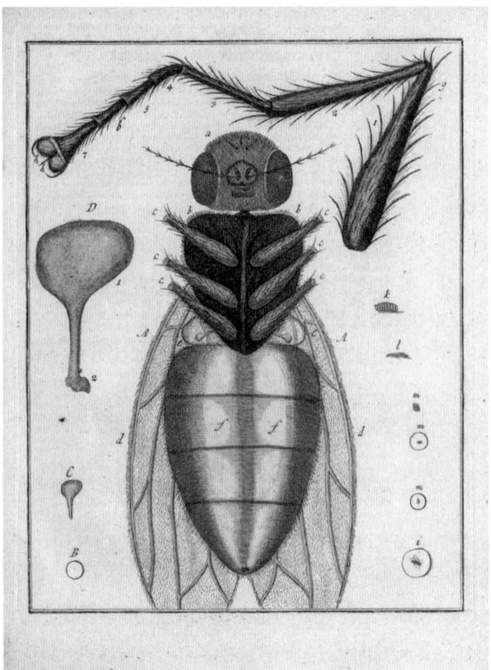

2.31   *Calliphora* means "bearer of beauty," named no doubt for the brilliant metallic blue of the fly's abdomen, handsomely set off by its bright ginger beard; whereas *vomitoria* could mean either an emetic (something that provokes vomiting) or, alternatively, a place where one is sick, such as the vomitoria of the ancient Romans where during feasts they would allegedly make themselves throw up to allow them to devour more food (hence the meaning of *vomitorium* as a passageway in the amphitheater where people would "spew forth"). The scientific name for the orange-bearded bluebottle is thus descriptive both of how it looks and how it eats, heaving up digestive juices from their stomachs to dissolve their food before soaking it up with their spongy mouthparts. The sight of a swarm of *Calliphora vomitoria* bluebottles feeding upon the slimy tip of a stinkhorn, so their Latin name suggests, is beautiful enough to make you want to puke.

2.32   It's true, sometimes we actively seek out such sights for our amusement. In an often quoted passage of her deadly dull childhood memoir *Period Piece* (published in 1953), Gwen Raverat, an English artist and great granddaughter of Charles Darwin, recollects a curious ritual carried out every summer by her formidable Henrietta "Aunt Etty" Lichfield who, with her "little monkey hands," would every year gather basketfuls of stinkhorns growing in a wood at the end of Burrow's Hill in the English village of Gomshall, Surrey.[16] Raverat:

> In our native woods there grows a kind of toadstool, called in the vernacular *The Stinkhorn*, though in Latin it bears a grosser name. The name is justified, for the fungus can be hunted by scent alone; and this was Aunt Etty's great invention. Armed with a basket and pointed stick, and wearing a special hunting cloak and gloves, she would sniff her way round the wood, pausing here and there, her nostrils twitching, when she caught a whiff of her prey; then at last, with a deadly pounce, she would fall upon her victim, and poke his putrid carcass into her basket. At the end of the day's sport, the catch was brought back and burnt in the deepest secrecy on the drawing-room fire, with the door locked; *because of the moral of the maids.*[17]

2.321   For someone so tormented by the impertinent image of stinkhorns, one can only imagine the gruesome spectacle, and choking stench, Aunt Etty endured—no, *chose* to endure—in the closed confines of her drawing room as bundles of freshly plucked phalluses sweated and sizzled on the fire.

Adriaen's phallus

2.4   Whereas the sight of a crop of ripe phalluses was enough to offend Aunty Etty's virtue, it is almost always the physical manifestation of the stinkhorn that so captivated early male (for they were almost exclusively male) naturalists ever since it was first described by Pliny the Elder in his *Natural History*. The American microbiologist Elio Schaechter, among others, claims that Pliny was one of the first writers to mention the stinkhorn, though this is far from certain.[18] Pliny's lexicon of "eggs," "slime," and "rotten earth" appears to suggest as much, but his language is still too vague to be sure that he's describing a species of stinkhorn:

> Like the yoke inside the egg [...] the baby mushroom is just as fond of eating its coat as is the chick. The coat cracks when the mushroom first forms; presently, as the mushroom gets bigger, the coat is absorbed into the body of the foot-stalk, two heads rarely ever springing from one foot. The first origin and cause of mushrooms is the slime and the souring juice of the damp ground.[19]

2.41   A hundred years after *Natural History* was first printed in Europe, a Dutch doctor and botanist by the name of Adriaen de Jonghe (1511–1575), Latinized as Hadrianus Junius, produced a sixteen-page dissertation, as they were then known, titled *The Description of the Phallus*. Published in 1564, the pamphlet details in vivid, eccentric prose, and even wilder poetry, a single species of mushroom that grows in the sandy coastal regions of the Netherlands, what we now know as the dune stinkhorn *Phallus hadriani*. I have reproduced Junius's original dissertation here in both scale and type, translated for the first time in its entirety directly from Latin to English. This is firstly to allow you, the reader, the chance for a little more intimacy with Junius's subject, to help you understand how amateurs (in the original sense of the word) perceived plants and fungi at what was a significant moment in the history of art and writing about nature; and secondly, to show some of the ways in which past perceptions of mushrooms were infected by other nonvisual forces: mythological, cultural, sensual.

2.42   *The Description of the Phallus* is widely considered to be the first illustrated publication dedicated to a single species of fungus. The original pamphlet features two wonderfully detailed woodcuts by Dutch artist Maarten van Heemskerck (1498–1574), which appear over two pages near the front of the pamphlet and then again over another two pages towards the back. It seems Junius was so proud of the picture he commissioned that he printed it twice! The illustration shows the stinkhorn in various states of maturity, including its egg stage and gloriously ripened whole, as well as separated into its anatomical parts.

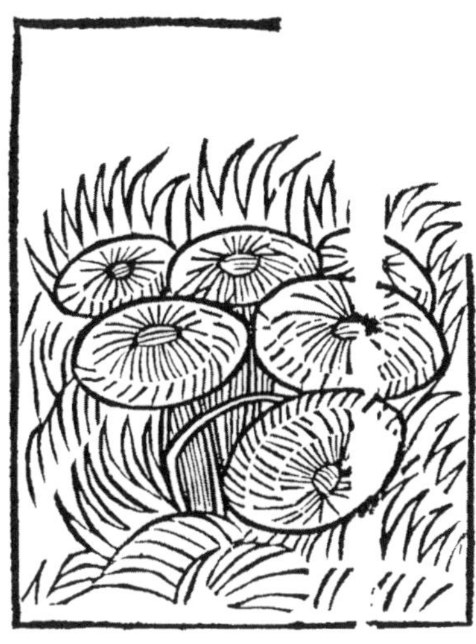

2.421 Speaking about firsts, the first printed illustration of a mushroom appeared in the *Hortus sanitatis* (The garden of health), published in 1491 by an anonymous author.[20] The image, which shows a bunch of nondistinctive mushrooms described as "agarics," like Heemskerck's picture of the phallus, was similarly produced using the woodblock printing method. This technique involves tracing onto a wooden block the image of the subject in reverse before removing the areas to be left blank with a sharp carving tool such as a gouge. (See the figure at the start of this chapter). When the raised level, called the relief, is rolled with ink and pressed onto paper, the print it makes is most striking. However, due to the lack of detail you can achieve with this process, it's often difficult to tell from early mycological illustrations precisely what species the artist was trying to convey. That's why Heemsckerk's woodcut is so extraordinary, in that it manages to accurately express several distinguishing features of the stinkhorn's anatomy. As such, we might say that Heemskerck's magnificently observed drawing together with Junius's detailed account of the stinkhorn's habitat, color, texture, and form presented to the world for the first time an autopsy of a mushroom.

The act of seeing with one's own eyes

2.5   *Autopsy* means "the act of seeing with one's own eyes."[21] Junius mentions twice in his pamphlet that he has seen the stinkhorn for himself. Even the extended title of his dissertation stresses that the picture of the mushroom has been "drawn from life" ("*ad viuum expressa pictura*"). His emphasis on empiricism shows throughout the rest of the text also, as does his penchant for colorful analogy. For example, at one point he mentions the stinkhorn's resemblance to the "sea penis," a priapulid spoonworm (one of many organisms named after the phallic god Priapus) which Junius observes is "just like this one of ours [which] swells while it lives, detumesces in death, and is full of holes."[22] The insertion of the penis worm into the narrative feels weirdly out of place; but then so is the mushroom he is describing.

2.51   After having to wade through some Greco-Roman mythology in the first half of the text (which, though largely tangential and a bit tedious to present-day readers, is typical of such booklets by Renaissance writers), when you finally get to the meat of it, Junius's description of the stinkhorn is remarkably precise and based on observation—even more remarkable because it was written at a time when it was unusual for plantsmen to rely on empirical research.[23] Dutch historian Dirk van Miert points out that this approach marked a shift in early modern Europe for philosophers, apothecaries, and doctors who sought out plants and fungi for their medicinal or magical properties.[24] It was difficult to visualize plants solely from their descriptions by others, writes van Miert; you had to go out and see them for yourself:

> Drawings of plants were not reported in the manuscripts if they had ever been there before. To cope with the confusion, humanist botanists attempted to associate ancient descriptions with the flora they could see around themselves. [...] The center of gravity began to shift from classical literature to modern nature: it turned out to be easier to make accurate descriptions yourself than to clear up the confusion in the old descriptions.[25]

2.511 Junius combines his notes, made in the sand dunes of the Dutch province of Gelderland, with details of his minor experiments carried out back in his study in Haarlem—presumably where Heemskerck made his drawing from life, no doubt having to work fast before the choking smell halted his efforts entirely. Junius's whole approach to documenting the stinkhorn is the very definition of empirical research: the physician guided by experience.[26] As a writer, he's also hot on metaphor. Take for example the following sentence, where we read a description of the netted texture of the mushroom's cap after its slime has been removed:

> On top of [the shaft] there stands [...] a helmet or a little pointed capital, something like a turning post in shape, removable, resembling in other respects the glans of the penis, except in having a chequered skin, as in descriptions of the hide of an elephant, or like a sea urchin, or beef tripe, is observed to be endowed with diamond-shaped squares.[27]

You can hear just how hard Junius is trying to bring to life this strange organism by drawing upon images of multiple other organisms from the menagerie of his mind; or, more accurately, via specific *bits* of other organisms. It shows Junius's enormous encyclopedic learning together with his capacity for field work and his knack for simile. Lacking the right names for things (there weren't any yet) he presents to us his mushroom in layers, different slithers superimposed on top of one another to form a membranous filagree of peeled animal tissue: the smooth, unsegmented skin of a penis worm; the wrinkled hide of an elephant; the honeycomb lining of a cow's reticulum; the dermal bumps of a sea urchin after its spines have been removed.

2.512 Junius's description borders on an abuse of metaphor. Even "phallus" is a catachresis, like the tongue of a shoe, the arm of a chair, the leg of a table. Straining to compensate for the proper referent for his fungus, Junius puts something else in its place: "the glans of the penis," the phallus of the earth.

Gelre! Gelre!

2.6   Is there something about the place in which Junius discovers the stinkhorn, Gelderland, that infuses his thinking? Gelder, from the German *geld*, means "to castrate" or "cut," such as a gelding, a castrated male horse (different from a Gelderlander horse, a type of warmblood carriage horse bred in the Dutch province from the nineteenth century onwards). The word is derived from the old Norse *geldr*, meaning barren. Both etymologies refer to a lack or loss of vitality: potency in men; the inability to become pregnant in women. The former is apposite for the sandy, windswept region of southwestern Holland where we find Junius crawling about the dunes on hands and knees, probing just below the ground for immature balls before plucking one out, "still intact and uncastrated."[28]

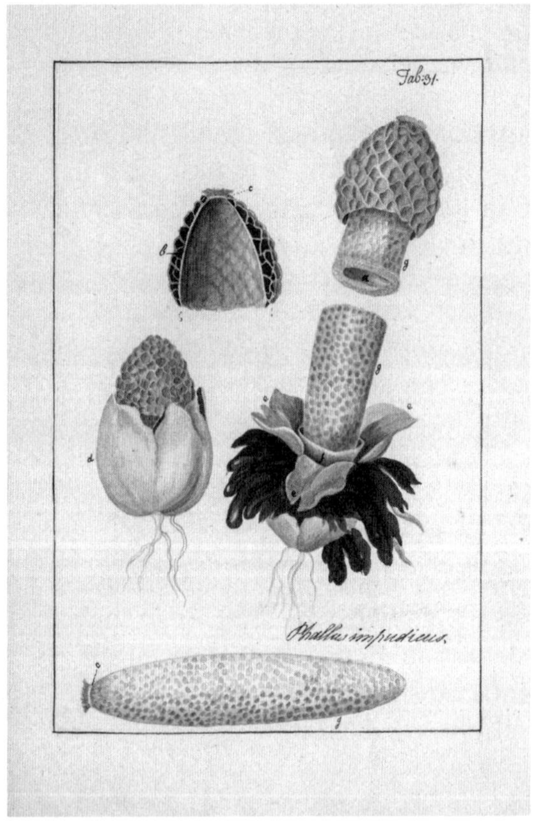

2.61   Fabulous as this all sounds, the derivation of the name Gelderland is much more prosaic, having been inherited from the nearby German city of Geldern. According to folk legend, the city was named after the guttural roar of a dragon who had made its lair beneath an old medlar tree (a type of rose shrub, the hips of which were once named in parts of southern England "open-ass" fruit because of their resemblance to a gaping anus).[29] There, the dragon "shouted and screamed persistently in a raw voice: 'Gelre! Gelre!'"[30] So it was that the old town was named after the rasping voice of the dragon "whose breath ruined the region" until it was silenced by a couple of local noblemen called Wichard and Lupold von Pont.[31]

2.611   Junius famously stammered throughout his life, a speech impediment that was said to have scuppered his ambitions as a professor of medicine in Copenhagen, a post he took up the year *The Description of the Phallus* was published.[32] I hear something of the same impediment in the involuntarily sounds stuck in the throat of that ill-fated dragon—"Gelre! Gelre!"—a stuttering that gave its name to the land about which Junius later made his pronouncement, and with such clarity and insight that it gently resounded for the next five hundred years.

2.62   I'm sure Junius the lexicographer, etymologist, philologist, and poet would've enjoyed this blusterous backstory, elements of which, whether knowingly or not, seem to influence his word choice and imagery. In one of only two phrases used to express the stinkhorn's smell, Junius explains how, like the dragon of Geldern, his mushroom exhales a "foul breath." Further on he describes an "aura" emanating from an overripe mushroom concealed in his study to be "so virulent as to be able to pervade the air of an entire room."[33] A foul breath, a virulent aura; his metaphors are befittingly atmospheric, halitotic even.

2.63   But metaphors are not descriptions. Junius is much better at describing the dune stinkhorn's color, which is varied and shifts kaleidoscopically over time as the mushroom matures. Specifically how, after it has been yanked from the earth, the stinkhorn egg miraculously changes hue, darkening like a bruise from "brilliant white" to purple to blue to black:

> When it is first plucked from the ditch, it is rather pale, but soon it gradually grows purple, from the flowing here and there within of something like veins of blood. The color of the fibers differs somewhat from this, being an intense lead-blue, which gradually dies away to the black color of congealed blood.[34]

The egg's violet tinge, which is only visible after it's been exposed to the air, is what makes the dune stinkhorn so easy to distinguish from the more common *Phallus impudicus*. That plus its distribution typically in sand hills near the sea, or in the grassy dunes of Gelderland. Junius is cautious about calling his newfound phallus a fungus—how can it be! For it emerges from somewhere dry and fresh as opposed to damp and sour. Yet here it is, out of place, gifted inside a bag bearing its own miserable conditions to the surface of the earth. And it's inside this leathery sac that the fifty-three-year-old doctor discovers "Nature's gift" to the world.[35] It is the gift of the "piercing cold" gelatinous load that protects the nascent phallus within.[36] It is the gift of slime.

2.64   From the sixteenth and well into the twentieth century, stinkhorn slime was considered a soothing topical treatment for rheumatism and gout, as well as being used to treat other ailments (discussed in chapter five).[37] Junius cites this as evidence of Nature's benevolence to those afflicted with aching joints, and at first this seems to be his primary interest in the mushroom: Junius the doctor seeking to ease the inflammations of his patients. But for Junius the herbalist, it is the bold and bizarre manner of Almighty God's gift-giving—that is, of the resemblance of the mushroom to the erect penis—that provides "proof of Nature's playfulness."[38]

Good short rude names

2.71 Junius called his mushroom "phallus" on account of the way it appeared to the elderly doctor at a single point in what was a similarly late stage in the stinkhorn's lifecycle. The name assigned to the fungus by French botanist Étienne Pierre Ventenat in 1798, and which is still accepted today, is *Phallus hadriani* (literally "Adriaen's phallus") in homage to the Dutch doctor.[39] Gerard called it the "Pricke Mushrum."[40] Parkinson, the "Hollanders Workingtoole."[41] The taxonomical name for the common stinkhorn *Phallus impudicus*, designated by Carl Linnaeus in 1753, means "impudent" or "shameless phallus." The epithet for the beautifully veiled bamboo fungus *Phallus indusiatus* means "phallus with an undergarment." Other names are more generous to gender. Described as new to science in 2005, *Phallus atrovolvatus* translates as "phallus with a blackened womb" on account of the gloomy gray color of the immature egg. But this is a rare deviation from a largely phallocentric tradition of naming. In the entire history of fungal nomenclature, none of the scientific names ascribed to any species of stinkhorn reference the fact that they stink. Instead, they all talk about their resemblance to the phallus.[42]

2.72 The prioritizing of sight over smell in the scientific naming of stinkhorns is at odds with the colloquial names Europeans have for them. For example, in Germany and Russia, the common stinkhorn *Phallus impudicus* is known as the "stinky morel," a reference to the mushroom's likeness to the latter's brain-like cap. In the Netherlands it's the "big stink fungus." In the Czech Republic and Slovakia, it's the "stink snake." In Finland, "the skunk." In Bulgaria, the "stinking sponge." In Bosnia it's known as the "stinking singer" (my favorite). The French call it "the stinking satyr" (*le satyre puant*), a name that captures both the sight and smell of the mushroom along with the mythological allusion early naturalists so enjoyed.

2.721 As author and self-confessed amateur mushroomer E.C. Large said in his Presidential Address to the British Mycological Association of March 1961:

> We want names for the fungi that young lips can pro-
> nounce. Not long names with awkward Latin plurals,
> like 'Lactarii' or 'Lactariuses,' but good short rude
> names, like 'puff-ball' and 'stinkhorn.' [...] Common
> names may last for centuries if they are good enough to
> win their way into the vernacular. Scientific names, as
> we have seen, change with every fashion in taxonomy.
> [...] The problems of nomenclature will be no less vex-
> atious then than they are now; but a stinkhorn will still
> be a stinkhorn, and a puff-ball a puff-ball.[43]

Almost three hundred years of diligent work by both classically trained and amateur mycologists (the latter group to which Junius, Large, Cage, and I proudly belong) has no doubt helped bring about something of the divine order throughout the natural world that Linnaeus dreamed of in 1753. But in an effort to avoid everyday linguistic variations between places and peoples, something funda-mental is lost in this system of naming things. To focus on the stink-horn's phallic shape is to ignore its more shameless feature, its raison d'être. That is, to stink.

2.73   It's hardly surprising that the author of the first ever myco-logical monograph chose for his subject the stinkhorn. For to look upon the stinkhorn fungus is to witness nature at its most brazen.

2.731   To human eyes, the sight of the stinkhorn appears vulgar because it pertains to low or common things: sex, genitalia, but also viscera, offal, piss, shit, spunk, vaginal discharge, and so on. Sure, the scientific words we continue to apply to each of the mush-room's component parts—volva, stipe, glans, gleba—come close to the "good, short rude names" E. C. Large calls for. But even when bound together in the totality of the name *phallus*, they're each still too veiled in the literary language of Latin to truly convey the eve-rydayness of both human and other-than-human sexuality and its slimy prerequisites. The stubbornly crude, yet by far more euphoni-ous *stinkhorn* works just fine.

Inversions

2.8   After the publication of Junius's *Phallus* in 1564, Heemskerck's woodcut of the stinkhorn became the archetype for scientific illustrations of fungi in early modern book printing. For the next hundred years and beyond, traces of Heemskerck's original drawing can be seen in many of the major botanical publications coming out of central Europe, including works by Matthaeus Lobelius, Carolus Clusius, Rembert Dodoens, John Gerard, John Parkinson, and Franciscus van Sterbeeck. What's peculiar about the history of Heemskerck's fungal image is how, through the process of being repeatedly copied and remodeled, something weird happens to it. It deforms, sprouts strange beasties, and in one famous case is turned completely upside down.

2.81   In Lobelius's *Kruydtboeck*, first published in 1581, a woodblock illustration made for renowned publishers Christophe Plantin (the namesake of the typeface you are reading) mirrors Heemskerck's original style and composition of the anatomized dune stinkhorn separated into glans, stipe, and volva. (The original woodblock, stored at the Museum Plantin-Moretus in Antwerp, is pictured at the start of this chapter.) But with no explanation as to why, the illustrated version of the phallus commissioned by Plantin adds to these elements two small squiggles as if creatures crawling towards the margin. These squiggles feature in all later reproductions of the stinkhorn in other printed works, including one by English herbalist John Gerard (1545–1612) in a revised and corrected version of his famously unreliable and largely plagiarized book *The Herball, or Generall Historie of Plantes*, published in 1633. It's here that we find the peculiar picture of the inverted phallus.

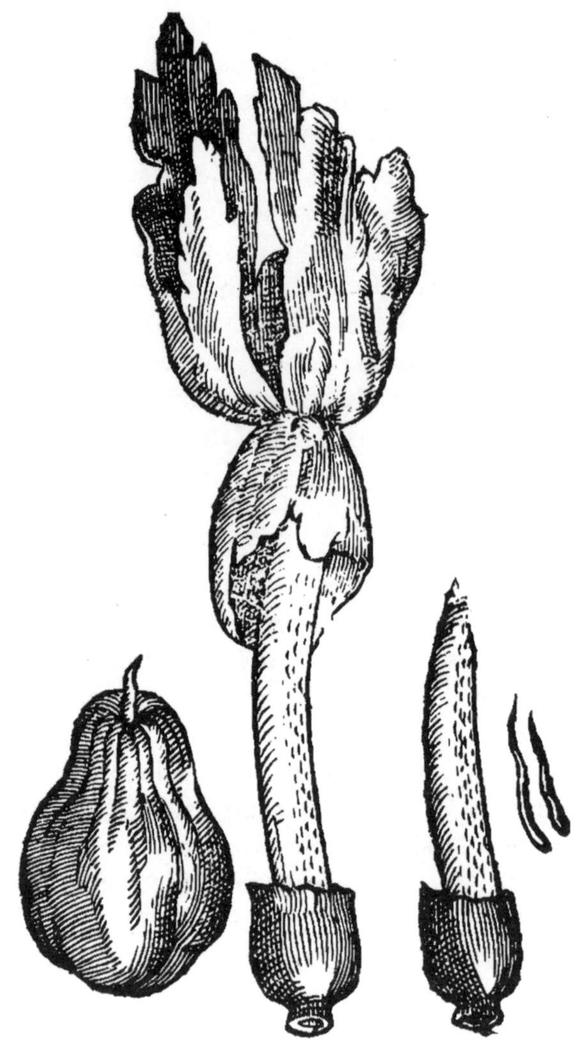

2.811   Unlike Junius, Gerard was not an empiricist. He rarely left London and therefore it was extremely unlikely he'd ever seen or smelled a stinkhorn for himself. As Anna Pavord points out in her book *The Naming of the Names: The Search for Order in the World of Plants* (2005), most of the woodblocks that made up the nearly two thousand illustrations that appeared in the first edition of Gerard's *Herball* were rented from a publisher in Frankfurt called Nicolaus

Bassaeus.[44] Many mistakes were made in the first publication, with several plant descriptions placed next to the wrong illustration.[45] The second edition, published in 1633, twenty years after Gerard's death, was "very much-enlarged and amended" by a thirty-year-old apothecary named Thomas Johnson. Although considerably more experienced in field work than Gerard, it's conceivable that Johnson, without ever having seen a stinkhorn either, would've taken one look at the woodblock borrowed from Plantin's workshop and decided that gravity would surely have caused such sour fruit to droop down rather than stand erect. So it was that the London printers' mistake made the phallus appear flaccid, and the swollen lump more like a wrinkled pear. The error is still there in the 1636 reprint, including the vermiform squiggles.

2.82   On page four of his now out of print book *Fungi: Folklore, Fiction, & Fact* (1982), W.P.K. Findlay reproduces Gerard's misprint.[46] In his caption to the image, Findlay speculates: "One might fancy that the worm like things were supposed to be spermatozoa, were it not for the fact that these were never seen until the discovery of the microscope long after these drawings were made; so what they represent remains a mystery."[47] These "worm like things" appear to me more like early kinds of stink lines, the sort of adornments you might see in a comic book illustration of a steaming turd or overflowing garbage pail. In the language of comics, these lines have a name: wafterton, a form of *emanata*, a word used to describe the types of pictorial elements issuing from a character or object, such as a question mark suspended above the head of a confused cartoon character or the faint ribbons of scented vapors rising from a freshly baked pie. Artists have depicted smells, good and bad, in much the same way for centuries. You can see them in abundance in an 1827 engraving by William Blake for the *Inferno*, showing Dante and Virgil (it must be said, resembling a couple of veiny old pricks in flabby foreskins) covering their noses to shield themselves from the mephitic fumes of Hell as mounds of contorted bodies rot and writhe below.

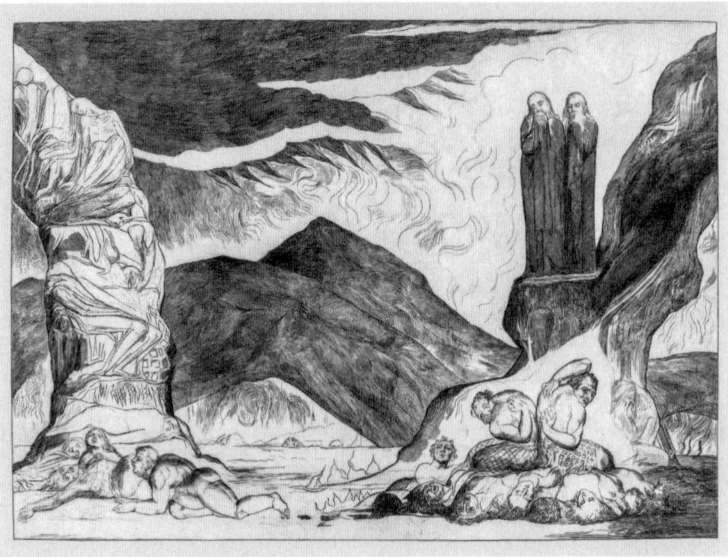

2.83   Rather than stink lines, could these squiggles instead be traces of the erratic flight paths of a pair of flies that almost certainly buzzed about the mushroom as the artist sketched it? Or—and here's a thought—could they be crude depictions of sound waves reverberating from the stinkhorn's bell-shaped cap? It's a tempting idea given the theme of this book. But just as Findlay dismisses the notion of their being oversized sperms (yuck!), likewise the discovery of sound waves had not yet been made around the time Plantin commissioned the woodblock of the phallus. That would come fifty years later with the classic bell-in-vacuum experiment, first described by Athanasius Kircher in his book *Musurgia Universalis* (1650), and subsequently refined by pioneering experimental scientist Robert Boyle.[48] The experiment involves a bell being sealed inside a glass jar, its clapper made to strike, originally by means of a magnet, while the air around it is pumped out to create a vacuum. As the air is removed, the sound inside the jar slowly gets quieter, disappearing altogether if a vacuum is achieved. The experiment helped pave the way for the discovery of how sound travels through the medium of the air and not, as some believed, the result of particles becoming detached from the sounding object itself, the way smelly chemical compounds do from stinking things.

THE DESCRIPTION OF THE PHALLUS

From a genus of fungi
which grows widely on the Dutch sand dunes
and a picture of it drawn from life
by

HADRIANUS JUNIUS[1]

Doctor of Medicine

A new subject and one unknown to earlier generations

DELFT
at the house of Hermann Schinckel[2]
on the corner of Scholar Street near the old church
1564

NOTES ON THE TEXT: ¶ 1. The Latinized name of Adriaen de Jonghe. ¶ 2. SP: Hermann Schinckel (also Schinkel or Schenckel) was a publisher and bookseller in Delft, the Dutch city where he was born. He was beheaded on July 23, 1568, aged thirty-two (four years after the publication of *The Phallus*) for having printed a series of religious works that angered the city's aldermen. When being led to court to receive his death sentence, Schinckel apparently passed to his friend Hadrianus Junius a note advising the correction of a single word he identified in the forty-second line of Seneca's *Octavia*. The word was "*Tanais*" (now the Don River), which Schinckel advised be amended to "*Thamesis*," the Latin word for the River Thames. See J.L.C. Jacob, *Aanteekeningen over het geslacht en de drukwerken van den Delftschen boekdrukker Hermanus Schinckel* (Delft: Jacob, 1843), 28–29.

N.B. These pages carry a facsimile translation
of Adriaen de Jonghe a.k.a. Hadrianus Junius's
pamphlet, first described elsewhere in this volume
on p. 52. Its modest format is embedded in the
larger page, indicated by the grey margin, with
its three texts loosely typeset according to the
original document. Translator's notes have been
added by Caroline Spearing, along with a few
by myself (marked "SP").

TO HIS MOST LEARNED FRIEND
JOHANNES SAMBUCUS OF HUNGARY,[3]
FROM HADRIANUS JUNIUS, DOCTOR

It is not unwillingly that I yield to the authority of Anaximander of Miletus,[4] who proposes the theory of the infinity of the universe and of nature, from which all things come into being, most learned Sambucus, when I see all the limitless riches of that parent coming forth more and more every day from the darkness, in which they lie submerged, and new things springing forth, being investigated by the intelligence of humankind, and illuminated by their skill. To which subject I judge that everyone who has acquired a somewhat piercing intellectual acuity, a rather skillful practice, and (as in the stories of the poets) a more purified form of that Promethean clay[5] should earnestly apply every endeavor and resource. Petrus Matthiolus,[6] something of a pentathlete in his knowledge of the field of botany, most favorable to your rulers,[7] who most accurately sowed that fertile but fallow field of the botanical crop and brought it triumphantly from the darkness—he considers me the champion among these men, and what's more (let envy be far from my words) the supreme champion. While I was reading his medical letters[8]—which you recently sent to me by way of a gift—I came by chance on the description of the Deer Fungus, unknown to Italy (as he himself attests).[9] There, at that point there came to my mind, how I recalled that I once had some fun with the Phallus, certainly a member of the fungus family, but unknown in other regions beyond the sand dunes of Holland. As I turned over the matter more deeply in my mind, and reflected with myself more closely on the meticulous care of our ancestors in having due respect for posterity, I thought to myself that I would set the price of the task as making the topic not unworthy of the scrutiny of the public court. And so I considered nothing more important or more in the ancient tradition than not only to bring forth my description and analysis in rather plain language in writing, but also to present it with appropriate illustrations. Pythagoras of Samos[10] used to say again and again that the Muses should be given priority over the Sirens,[11] by which he wanted to show that a simple statement of truth was better than groomed and decorated speeches: no wonder he likened a decorated rhetorical structure, blackened with

¶ 3. The Latinized name of János Zsámboky (1531–84), a Hungarian humanist and physician. ¶ 4. Anaximander (c.610–c.546 BCE) was a philosopher from modern-day Turkey, who postulated that all things arose from the indefinite *apeiron*. ¶ 5. Junius alludes here to the Greek myth of the Titan Prometheus fashioning the first humans from clay. ¶ 6. The Latinized name of Pietro Andrea Gregorio Mattioli (1501–c.1577), a physician and botanist, and author of a monumental edition of the Greek botanist and pharmacologist Dioscorides (c.40–90 CE). ¶ 7. Junius seems to allude here to the fact that both Sambucus and Matthiolus were in the service of the Habsburg court. ¶ 8. Mattioli's Epistolarum Medicinalium Libri Quinque ("Five Books of Medical Letters") were published in Prague in 1561 by Jiri Melantrich. ¶ 9. SP: The description of the deer fungus to which Junius is referring is the subject of a letter addressed to an apothecary named Julio Moderato living in Rimini, Italy. ¶ 10. As well as devising his eponymous theorem, Pythagoras (c.570–c.495 BCE) was a philosopher and mystic. ¶ 11. In Greek mythology, the Muses were the nine goddesses of the arts; the Sirens, supernatural females whose singing lured sailors to their deaths.

verbal bawdry, to the Sirens, as a he did an unadorned style of speech, dosed up with no gaudy display, to the Muses. I could have used up the ointment box of the Greeks and Latins on the subject, and all the pots of the cosmetics dealer, by burdening equally both the pages and the ears with the riches of varied discourse, and with piles of commentary from all over the place, on fungi, mushrooms, and other things which serve this purpose, but I did not want to be an intellectual hog, and to gather my harvest mindlessly from other men's hard work, or to acquire glory from kidnap. Then I was also keen to provide illustrations drawn by the hand of the most outstanding artist, with a more generous spirit, than that shown once upon a time by Hipponicus.[12] He, when he intended to erect a votive statue to his native land, was advised that he should enhance the status of the work by commissioning the very great sculptor Polycletus to make it. But he rejected the advice, saying again and again that he did not want an image whose glory would redound to its maker, on the grounds that the greatness of the craftsman often obscures the name of the commissioner. But as for me, I fear nothing of such a kind, and do not gaze open mouthed at the incense smoke of petty glory, but am intent upon growing and spreading the knowledge of this subject, irrespective of the common people, whom I despise as an incompetent judge, because it is overly affected by the things that resemble itself, and because perchance it will complain that my efforts have been spent on a trivial subject. And I wanted that offspring to go forth into the public realm. To whom might I more properly offer this labor of mine than you, my honorable friend Sambucus? The greatness and liberality of your spirit towards the undeserving has stood out to such an extent that I would appear destined to incur the slur of ingratitude and even become bankrupt in my debt to you, if I didn't strive to repay you with some little good deed of slender substance. And this very deed will go off splendidly invested, as long as the renown of your name wins the most abundant commendation for our little work among learned readers. Farewell, and judge this inconsequential gift with a kindly face, and keep it safe from the venomous bite of rivals. Soon I will answer your prayers by giving you Nonius Marcellus, because I see that you are willing to receive him, interpolated in infinite places and cleansed of his filth, if God favors my efforts.[13] Haarlem, first of March.

¶ 12. This story about the Athenian military commander Hipponicus (c.485–422/1 BCE) appears in the work of the third-century writer Aelian. ¶ 13. Junius's edition of the fourth- or fifth-century Roman grammarian Nonius Marcellus's *De Proprietate Latini Sermonis* (On the character of Latin speech; also known as *De Compendiosa Doctrina*) was published in Prague in 1565.

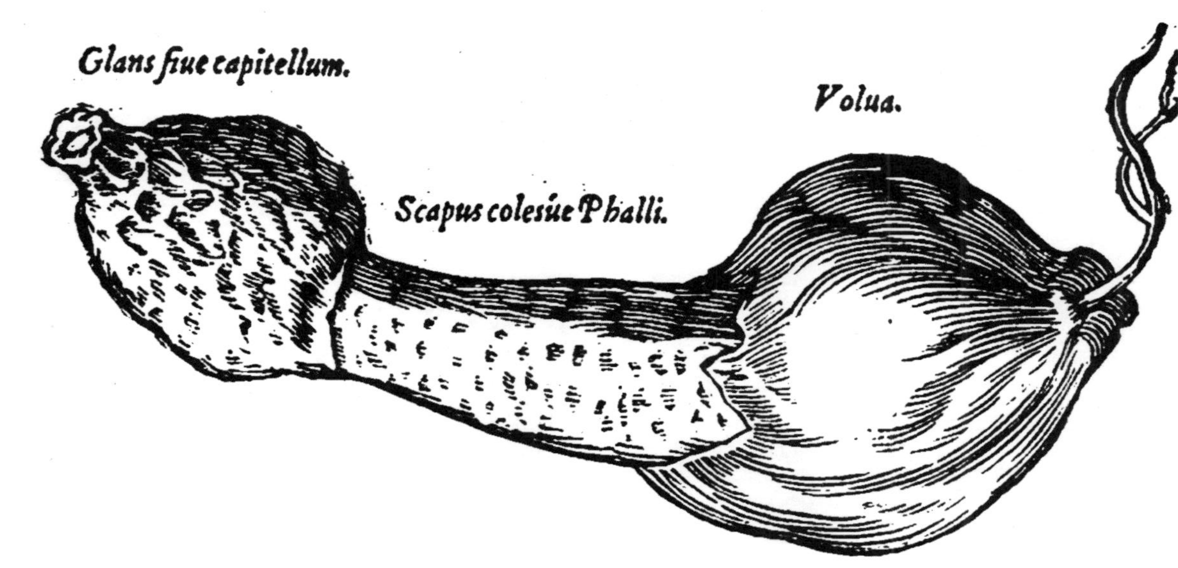

Glans fiue capitellum.
Scapus colesue Phalli.
Volua.

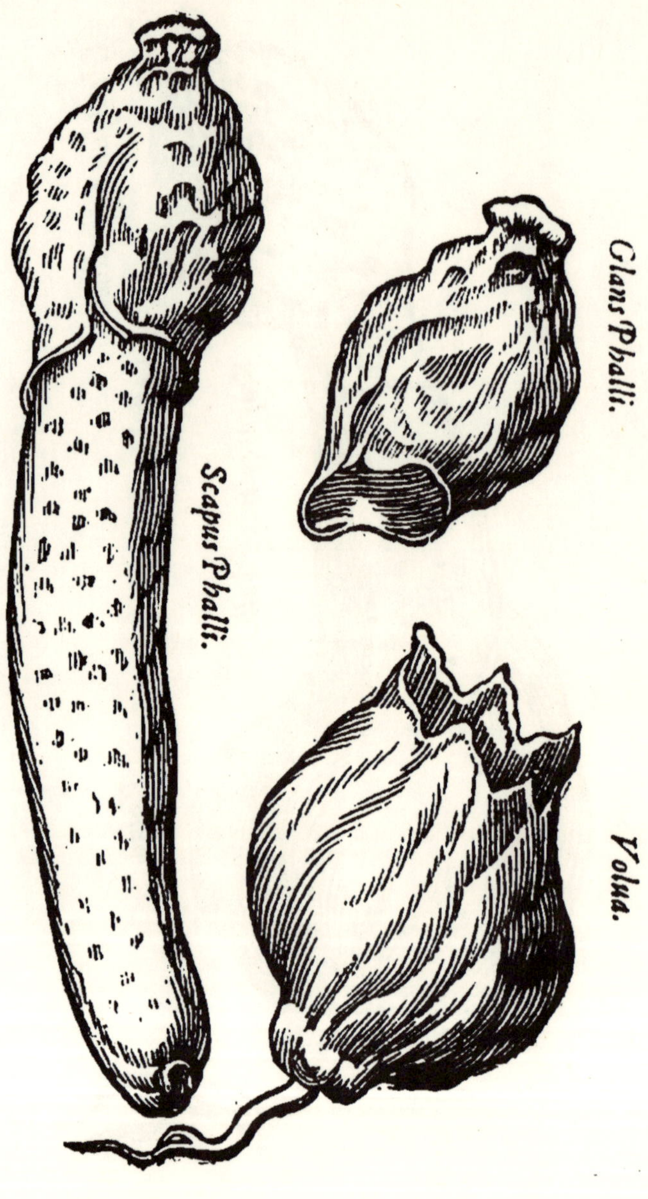

Glans Phalli.
Scapus Phalli.
Volua.

THE DESCRIPTION OF THE PHALLUS

*A species of mushroom growing widely
on the Dutch sand dunes by*

HADRIANUS JUNIUS
Doctor of Medicine

No one should be in any doubt that the fertile power and majesty of Nature, and Earth, sacred parent of all things, have provided abundant cause to wonder at them, when one reflects upon the infinite kinds of shrubs, herbs, and fruits destined to be useful to humans just as much as they were born to give pleasure, all the more so given that Almighty God clearly gives us confidence that nothing is produced without some more hidden cause from the cosmos. Each, however, although they have consistently thus far dedicated themselves to human convenience and necessity, has incurred from the majority of mortals (albeit ungrateful ones) the charge of exhaustion, not to mention bankruptcy—as if the resources of her first abundance were used up and exhausted. But in fact the generosity of each knows no bounds, and as much spontaneously as compelled by cultivation, bestows its gifts to all with great abundance, holding back from no one, everywhere industrious and even subservient, unless perhaps the seeds of poisons, which germinate less readily, redound less to its credit.

To prevent even us from appearing to lack their bounty, I wanted to bring to the monuments of literature and to dedicate to posterity a gift which those matriarchs caused to grow on our native sand dunes. This gift is known to few mortals, described in the works of no ancient or more recent writers (at least as far as I know). Whether it is as the joke of a playful nature that it resembles a penis, or whether it is a remarkable act of kindness undertaken for the use of humankind (especially in these times, in which as a result of unbridled lust and luxury, from which licentiousness has taken all moderation, podagra and gouty diseases oppress us in great quantity), so that the availability of a useful remedy, which is reckoned to be extremely powerful for the intolerable burning agony of the joints, should no longer lie hidden and undiscovered.

Not surprisingly, the extraordinary play of Nature in creating variety shines most brightly in the array of herbs, which is so great and so hard-working. There is no one whom she has not filled with copious admiration for her, while she imitates cymbals, helmets, slippers, goblets, hats, the tails of scorpions, fingers, white spots on nails, the rays of stars, and even hairs. In the kingdom of fish, she has also depicted nettles, fleas, stars, reeds, grapes, cucumbers, lungs, little paint brushes, and she has even supplied the sea penis, which just like this one of ours swells while it lives, detumesces in death, and is full of holes, and which grows abundantly around the Stoechadian Islands of the Gallic sea.[14]

But so that other nations should admire, observe, and as far as possible enjoy this child of Nature, and indeed that learned men, who have more expansive leisure time for all kinds of reading, and who benefit from a more productive vein of intellect, may consider more carefully and may weigh up the character of its strengths for themselves, I decided to bring it into the public domain by issuing a written account.

¶ 14. The present-day Îles d'Hyères, lying in the Mediterranean approximately forty-three miles east of Marseilles.

And I decided that it should be illustrated with appropriate black and white drawings, and depicted by the hand of that outstanding artist Maarten van Heemskerck[15] (the fame of whose artworks reaches the very edges of the earth) and described by me both in the free discourse of prose and the constrained one of verse, just as more than once it was seen by my own eyes, examined, and plucked from amid the reedbeds. Nor indeed do I think the folly of Niger should be passed on as an example by a man who is educated and eager for the truth, and who wants to avoid slander in the future— Niger whom Dioscorides accuses of having daubed his texts, on insufficient authority and with over-hasty judgement, with many things, drawn from the gossip of men and women and the traditions of other times.[16] But to the matter in hand.

It is well known that the more westerly parts of Holland, which was once equivalent to Batavia, which adjoin the Atlantic, piled up great masses of sand through the action of the river Rhine, and the tides of the sea when the winds blow.[17] The course of that most noble river has even been blocked and diverted. It seems that God set up these mounds as barriers and flood defenses against the tempests of the Ocean which would otherwise inundate all the land far and wide: but since those shifting sand dunes, driven by storm winds, began to threaten the chance of the land becoming barren, in almost the same way as the sea itself, the providence of Nature, as if adding a brake, controlled the flow of sand, which is vulnerable to the mocking play of the winds, with a generous growth of sedge, such as I call the toughest and sharpest kind of rushes, which the native tongue names Helm.[18] Now indeed from the central mound of the reeds, but especially the older ones, rarely more fruitfully elsewhere, springs forth that shaft which is the subject of my treatise, defended by a dense rampart against injury from the

¶ 15. Maarten van Heemskerck (1498–1574) was based in Haarlem, where he produced large-scale religious paintings and was an early adopter of the practice of creating drawings for commercial reproduction as engravings. ¶ 16. Sextius Niger (thought to be active between c.50 BCE–40 CE), a Roman writer on pharmacology, criticized by Dioscorides for failing to carry out proper investigation of his proposed remedies. ¶ 17. SP: Now modern Betuwe, situated in the southwest part of the province of Gelderland, which includes inland sand dunes. ¶ 18. SP: Dutch helm is otherwise commonly known in English as marram grass. Its scientific name *Ammophila arenaria* is somewhat tautological, meaning "sand-loving friend of sand."

trampling boots of travelers, just as a rose is fortified by an army of thorns.

The first of our countrymen in recent years, at least as far as I know, to observe this origin of that plant was a certain wagon driver, a man with a limping gait and crooked limbs, not unlike that Vulcan of myth, when, his efforts supported by Diana, he would often eagerly hunt out hares making their homes among the reedbeds.[19] When he had brought away evidence of the object, he displayed this most entertaining spectacle to me and to Johannes Gallus, a doctor of no mean reputation.[20] I have very often subsequently tracked down this miracle of nature with certain not unlearned companions, and I will explain its nature, as clearly and at the same time as concisely as I am able.

As I have said, in the central navel, as it were, of the sharp reeds, just beneath the topmost layer of sand, you can find a white, rounded lump, resembling a handball or an onion both in appearance and the brilliant white of its color. Beneath, it has a twofold sinew or a twin fiber instead of a root, through which, I think, it takes up moisture: it is full of thick, viscous mucus, dense like congealed broth or pap, and so heavy that it surpasses the weight of water and nearly equals that of molten lead; and this same substance is so cold that when the mass (which it will not be wide of the mark to call a *volva*, in the term coined by Pliny) is applied to the palm of the hand, it conveys a sensation of piercing cold. When it is first plucked from the ditch, it is rather pale, but soon it gradually grows purple from the flowing here and there within something like veins of blood. The color of the fibers differs somewhat from this, being an intense lead-blue, which gradually dies away to the black color of congealed blood. But the mucus, which I have mentioned, once the volva is plucked from the earth, very rapidly liquefies and

¶ 19. Vulcan (Greek Hephaestus) was the lame smith-god of Greco-Roman mythology; Diana (Greek Artemis) the goddess of the hunt. ¶ 20. This probably alludes to a member of the prominent Haarlem Galle family, of whom Philips Galle (1537–1612) was a publisher known to have worked with Junius.

flows away: and indeed the shaft itself detumesces not long after. It exhales an aura so virulent as to be able to pervade the air of an entire room. In the months of autumn, this volva, earlier or later in accordance with the varying appearance and temperature of the year, will burst open and split like an abscess. At this time the erect stalk or shaft then springs up, and can be removed without damaging the volva. Then indeed the swollen mass of the volva almost gives the illusion of a scrotum.

Nor moreover should I keep shrouded in silence something which I believe to be by way of a miracle, not to say even more than a miracle: it is indisputably the case that when the mass or volva is plucked from the ditch while still intact and uncastrated, before it has sent forth its shaft, if it chances to be put away in a cupboard, or even set aside in some corner of the house, after one day and then another have elapsed, it will throw up an erect shaft of the right and proper size. When I had received evidence of this from one and then another man of impeccable honor, I wanted to carry out the experiment for myself, and so having secreted two volvas of this kind in the innermost recess of my study, I saw it with my own eyes and as witness myself made proof of their testimony. The shaft is made of fungal matter, fine and lighter than a feather; it is speckled, like ash in color, porous with an accessible opening, which is smooth as though deliberately hewn, broader inside, narrower at the exit, soft, attaining two palms in length. There are even those who claim they have found specimens nine inches long. On top of this there stands, not a spreading cap as on a mushroom, but a helmet or a little pointed capital, something like a turning post in shape, removable, resembling in other respects the glans of the penis, except in having a chequered skin, as in descriptions of the hide of an elephant, or like a sea urchin, or beef tripe, is observed to be endowed with diamond-shaped squares. The tip of its apex, where the wrinkles are closer together, possesses an opening, whence issues a foul breath, for which reason it is densely surrounded by flies. That little cap is the same color as the shaft, but I have also seen on numerous occasions, before I printed this, a black cap on a completely snow-white shaft. However, it should be reported that this is understood to be attributable to age, for it changes from white to a coal-black color when it is mature. From time to time that little cap even takes on a green color instead of ash-white, and not much later turns black.

Thus far I have described the appearance of the plant however it might be, just as it appears with the volva, the shaft, and the acorn-shaped tip. Why indeed I have given the name as Phallus, the reason is easy to explain, nay, obvious to anyone who has even a nodding acquaintance with Greece. This was caused by the similarity which it bears to the member of leather and fig wood, which the ignorant heathens used to carry around when they sang the mysteries of their sacred rites, and superstition had called the latter Phallagogia, the former the Phallus and Ithyphallus.[21] But why forbid us to use a new word for a new thing? when the great diversity of fungi has also found many different names, some of which may be called "spongioli" from their resemblance to a sponge, others are called "ovate" and "digitate" because they are like an egg or a finger in appearance: some even, from their smooth, round shape, might be named "little plums" and "sloes."

Besides, whether that Phallus of ours ought to be admitted into the order of fungi, I would not rashly dare to assert it as something thoroughly tested and established, since I would not want to make a pronouncement in advance of others who are more learned of opinion. To be sure, the

¶ 21. Junius alludes to the ancient Greek rites of Dionysus, called the *Phallagogia*, which featured the carrying of erect *phalloi* (*Ithyphalloi*).

fineness and smoothness of its substance, and (which first gives rise to fungi) the sour moisture of the damp ground, where it grows, provide evidence that it is of the order of fungi; and yet the rows of gills, which are entirely absent in this case but which are visible in mushrooms, argues against it. Nor is there here even any trace of the broad hat clinging to the base, inasmuch as the little tip which it has instead of a hat can be removed without harm. Moreover, its birthplace argues against it, since indeed only sandy places generate that plant of ours, and not all of them, but only those located on ancient reedbeds. Yet writers have said that it is widely acknowledged that it is usually places that are slimy, rancid, squalid in location and next to the roots of oak trees which generate fungi.

I had proceeded thus far, when by chance there arrived some letters of Petrus Matthiolus, a leading man in the study of plants, sent to me by Johannes Sambucus of Hungary, a man of unrivalled learning combined with equal culture and refinement. While I was reading these all too eagerly, I chanced upon a mention of the Deer Fungus and I was trans‑fixed on the spot, captured by the novelty of the subject.[22] Having seized upon the hope of a description similar to my own, I read more eagerly than attentively, because although at first sight it seemed to match ours in several respects, when, after devouring everything too hastily, I read it for a second time, the fungus seemed different from ours. Hunters report that his fungus is born beneath the earth in oaken animal pens, from the generative sperm of a deer, spilled (as one says) while the female frustrates the attack of the male by running away; while ours appears on sandy mounds at the furthest edge of the beach, in the thicker sedge plots, which are the preferred sleeping places of hares. He says that it is sought out for stimulating the sexual appetite;[23] ours is judged to

¶ 22. SP: The description of the Deer Fungus (*Fungus cervinus*) to which Junius is referring can be found in book three of Mattioli's *Epistolarum Medicinalium Libri Quinque* (1561), 418–19. This is likely the deer truffle or false truffle *Elaphomyces granulatus*, which is sometimes parasitized by another fungus, *Cordyceps capitata*. The long yellow stem and (odorless) glossy brown bulbous cap that grows out of underground truffles gives it the common name drumstick truffle-club. You can see why Mattioli was uncertain about this being a single species of mushroom rather than a complex of two, and why, without seeing it for themselves, later herbalists and folklorists continued to confuse it with descriptions of stinkhorns. ¶ 23. SP: The traditional use of deer truffles as an aphrodisiac in some parts of Europe is discussed in chapter five.

be able to extinguish the stirrings of desire at once, by means
of its more powerful coolness. His is described as being of
spherical appearance, like other tubers; ours is slender. His
has a blackish outer skin: ours is speckled and ash-colored.
He does not however shrink from the fact that the author
writes that the appearance of an erect male penis is represented
in several of his own plants; but in that on one side he has set
forth an uncovered glans, on the other little balls like testicles
in appearance, it is completely different from ours. I would
like to add, by way of a final flourish, that that lump or volva,
at the point when it is born or lies hidden in the reeds, is called
in the local idiom, from the round shape which it presents,
ungers eijeren, which means "eggs of Ghosts or Demons."
Now let us append the poem which our slender Muse has
poured forth.

THE PHALLUS

The cabbage was hymned in the writings of Cato, schooled in rhetoric: [1]
Betony was described by the Doctor whose name comes from the Muses: [2]
The son of Maeon sang of Moly in his divine poem. [3]
Who has not told the tale of the flowers inscribed with Oebalian blood,
And which bear witness to the cruel wounds of Ajax? [4]
And who has not told of your revelries, sounding Echo? [5]
My task will be to describe an unsung stem, [6]
Which I may be permitted to call the Phallus (if only chaste Thalia [7] *assents)*
Since its shoot resembles no other shape
Than the infamous penis of Hellespontian Priapus. [8]
My task is on a trivial matter, but, mother and inventor of all things,
In case you are accused of exhaustion in your declining years,
I am happy to dedicate this, such as it is, to you who create everything. [9]
There is an island which the Rhine divides with cloven flood, [10]
Held once by the battle-hardened people of the Batavi,
When Civilis shattered the Latin axes in war, [11]
Where the Titan buries his gleaming head in the waves of the western sea, [12]
And where the furthest part lies over against Caledonian lands. [13]

NOTES ON THE POEM: ¶ 1. Marcus Porcius
Cato (234–149 BCE), whose *De Agri Cultura*
(c. 160 BCE) is the first extant work of Latin prose.
Chapters 156–57 present a fulsome encomium of
the cabbage, celebrating its powers as (for example)
an aid to digestion, as a laxative and purgative, as a
treatment for colic and for difficulty in urination,
as a poultice for wounds and swellings, particularly
suppurating ones, to ease headaches, eye aches, swollen spleen, pain in the internal organs, and insomnia.
Bathing in the urine of habitual cabbage eaters
is particularly recommended for babies. Cato suggests a number of cabbage recipes, of which raw
cabbage chopped with dried coriander, rue, grated
asafoetida, vinegar, honey, and sprinkled with salt is
one of the less immediately repulsive. ¶ 2. Antonius
Musa was physician to the Emperor Augustus
(63 BCE–14 CE), and, according to tradition,
gave his name to the botanical genus that includes
the banana (*Musa*). A treatise on the herb betony,
now known as *Stachys officinalis*, is attributed to him
(*De herba vettonica*), which extols its multiple powers,
including as a remedy for gout. ¶ 3. Homer, who
in book ten of the *Odyssey* describes how Odysseus
is able to protect himself against the witch Circe
with the herb moly. Renaissance botanists identified
the herb with *Allium moly*, a yellow-flowered and
pungent-smelling member of the onion family.
¶ 4. Ovid, *Metamorphoses* 13.382–98 conflates the two
myths of the origin of the hyacinth: first, that it grew
from the body of Apollo's favorite Hyacinthus, son
of king Oebalus of Sparta; and second, that it sprang
from the blood of Ajax, who committed suicide
after failing to win the arms of the slain Achilles.

This island rises from sand-bearing dunes, which horned Ammon [14]
Has shaped, helped by Aeolian blasts, [15]
And which watery Thetis [16] *first spews onto the shore from the lowest depths.*
But to prevent the sterile sands from further covering the fields beyond,
Mother Nature planted them with spiky sedge,
So as to bind in position these mounds which flow like water in the breeze. [17]
She also commanded to rise in the middle of the reedbeds,
A shape like the one which Greece displays at the crossroads, hanging from a taut thong
When the wild revels resound with cries,
A shape similar (yes, truly) to the Great Todger of Lampsacus. [18]
The lowest part lays false claim [19] *to the appearance of a scrotum,*
Issues forth from a pair of fibers, and swells into a loose belly,
Bulging with a pregnant stomach, and exits to a narrow cervix,
Like a cupping glass about to drink up the effluent of the human body.
At first it is pale, but soon, little by little, there rises a multitude
Of little veins, distinguished by the crimson color of cinnabar. [20]
And the fibers grow livid like the color of congealed blood.
It swells with sticky, clotted gore, like clinging birdlime in appearance,
Which is the equal of pliant lead in weight,
But which emits a vile and unappealing juice,
Like the miasma [21] *breathed out by fetid swamps.*
The mushroom itself, torn from the furthest edge of the land,
Strives to rival icy crystal in coldness:
Hence it is thought that the savage heat of stubborn gout
Can be either soothed by its application, or removed.
Before helpful Lucina [22] *opens the womb,*
And it has not yet split, forced to make a fissure,
Where it may grant a space for the genital shaft to burst forth,
The mushroom takes the shape of an earth-born onion, or a loose purse,
To which the maker's hand has not yet added the shape of a mouth: [23]
After this earlier stage has passed,
It splits, like a festering boil bursting.
From here a mushrooming [24] *shaft rises to the air above,*
Fine, even lighter than a feather, with a hole bored through, gaping open,
Like in the middle of a pipe, pale, and with the color of ash:
Smooth on all sides, rounded, it stands erect in perfect cylindrical form.
Covering it there is not a broad-brimmed hat, [25]
A cap like the one the priest once wore, [26] *or the one which a former age gave*
To Helen's brothers, [27] *but an elongated one, like the tip of a turning post.* [28]
It is devoid of blood, deeply ploughed with wrinkles,
Which run criss-cross between themselves,

According to classical writers, the petals of the flower were in some way inscribed either "Ai ai!" (alas) or "Aias," the Latin form of Ajax—an assertion which caused much head scratching among early modern botanists. See Abraham Cowley, *Plantarum Libri Sex* (1668), 4.229–54, with the author's footnotes. Junius refers somewhat disparagingly here to Ovid's ubiquity as a sourcebook for classical myth. ¶ 5. The myth of the indiscreetly garrulous nymph Echo appears in Ovid, *Metamorphoses* 3.359–401. ¶ 6. The Latin word *caulis* denotes both the stem or stalk of a plant, and the penis. (C. T. Lewis and C. Short, *A Latin Dictionary*, Oxford, 1969). ¶ 7. One of the nine Muses, patron goddesses of the arts. Thalia was particularly associated with comedy. ¶ 8. The grotesquely well-endowed fertility god, patron of vegetable gardens, whose cult was introduced to Greece from Lampsacus at the eastern end of the Hellespont (Dardanelles). ¶ 9. Junius alludes to the Lucretian identification of Venus *genetrix* (mother) with a creating natural force (*Natura daedala rerum*). He refers to his own "belatedness" in comparison with Cato, Musa, Homer, and Ovid: although his work is slight, he says, he dedicates it to Venus/Nature so that her creative force should not be thought to have dried up altogether. The image depends on a conflation of the poem with its subject matter. ¶ 10. Batavia, an island on the Rhine delta, where the river divides into the Waal and the Lower Rhine. The Batavi, described in Tacitus, *Germania* 29, were appropriated by the Dutch as cultural ancestors as they began to evolve a national identity in resistance to Spanish rule. Junius's own *Batavia*, a disparate history of the region and its people in

As on the back of the Indian beast,[29] *or like the pattern*
Displayed by the chequered tiles of mosaic floors.
On the top of its head it proffers a narrow orifice,
Greedily thronged by black swarms of flies:
From this opening a stench redolent of venom floods the air.
But after you pull out the shaft buried in the ground,
That sticky pulp, which lay hidden in the pregnant belly,
Does not cohere for long, but soon liquefies,
Dissolving into a watery flux, and following the example of a flower,
The shaft droops, withered, with falling neck.
At the beginning of autumn, when Libra makes the nights equal to the days,[30]
And the grape-harvest teems with fresh must,
Until the months arrive when harsh Boreas,[31]
From the Thracian north, strips the woods of their green adornment,
This shaft rises erect beneath the airy light.
They believe that Orthanes,[32] *the charge of ruddy Priapus,*
While he happened to lust after mountain-dwelling Icmas[33] *in violent lechery,*
But was unable to get his hands on the fleeing Nymph,
Dashed against the ground a life-bearing stream of stinking sperm
And brought the stiff †ice† to life.[34]
There are those who think that it drew its poison from the loins of Heaven
When Saturn harvested his father's shaft with the curved sickle,
And the fertile offspring leapt forth.[35]
Thus they believe that a new offshoot of heaven, and new buds sprang forth.

Latin prose, was completed in 1570 and published in 1588. ¶ 11. In 69–70 CE, the Batavi, led by their hereditary, Romanized prince Gaius Julius Civilis, revolted against Roman rule, destroying two legions before being crushed by Quintus Petillius Cerialis. See Tacitus, *Historiae* 4–5. The axes (Latin *secures*) are an allusion to the axe carried by a Roman magistrate as a symbol of power. ¶ 12. The Titan: Hyperion, the sun god. The Latin *Iberos* properly refers to Spain, but is used more generally to denote the far west (Lewis and Short), where the sun sets. ¶ 13. Junius seems to suggest that the island lies due east of Scotland. In fact, it is significantly farther south. ¶ 14. Ammon is the horned North African god, a development of the Egyptian Amun, worshipped across the Roman empire. Junius appears here to conflate him with the Rhine, often described as "horned" due to its division around the island. See Virgil, *Aeneid* 8.727. ¶ 15. Aeolus: Greco-Roman god of the winds. ¶ 16. Thetis: a Greek sea goddess, mother of Achilles. Here used metonymically for "the sea." Junius periphrastically but accurately describes the formation of dunes from sand thrown up from the seabed and shaped by the combined action of wind and river currents. ¶ 17. The common name of the dune stinkhorn is by reason of its preferred habitat. ¶ 18. Junius conflates the Greek custom of displaying herms (male busts with large erect phalli) sacred to Hermes or Priapus at crossroads with the Italian ritual in honor of Liber, the Roman god identified with Dionysus (hence the "wild revels," or *orgia*) and described by St. Augustine, who in turn cites Varro as his source (*City of God* 7.21.2–4). The Great Todger of Lampsacus (*Lampsacio*

Ithyphallo) is of course that of Priapus. ¶ 19. False, because this swelling is the residue of the immature egg-like stage, so, in Junius's taxonomy, is female rather than male. It's properly known as the *volva*, a variant spelling of the Latin *vulva*, womb. (Lewis and Short) ¶ 20. Cinnabar: a mercury ore with a bright red color. ¶ 21. Latin *Mephitis*, an Italian goddess of noxious exhalations from the earth; also the name of a genus of skunk. ¶ 22. Lucina: Roman goddess of childbirth. ¶ 23. The stalk of the mushroom appears from an egg-like sac, which is either completely underground or just visible on the surface. ¶ 24. Latin *fungosus*. ¶ 25. Latin *petasus*, the broad-brimmed hat worn by travelers and particularly associated with the god Mercury. ¶ 26. A close-fitting cap topped with a point of olive wood. ¶ 27. Castor and Pollux, brothers of Helen of Troy, were often depicted wearing the *pilos*, a conical cap made of leather or felt. ¶ 28. The conical posts used on the Roman chariot racing track. ¶ 29. The elephant. ¶ 30. I.e. when the sun is in the zodiacal sign of Libra, the Scales, from approximately September 23rd to October 22nd. ¶ 31. The north wind. ¶ 32. A Greek phallic fertility spirit, whose name means "Erect One," companion of Priapus. ¶ 33. The nymph Icmas is the personification of life-giving moisture. Junius seems to have invented the story, which replicates the myth of Athena's pursuit by Hephaestus and the generation of the Athenian ancestor Erechtheus. ¶ 34. The text reads *gelebamque*, which is meaningless. ¶ 35. Saturn (Greek Cronos) castrated his father Uranus (Heaven) with an adamantine sickle, engendering (among others) the Furies, the Giants, and the goddess Aphrodite.

2.822 A more plausible explanation for these squiggles is that they are simplified or stylized snakes or slugs. In antiquity, the prevailing view was that mushrooms grew in rotten, poisonous places where slimy things thrive, mating animals spill their seed, and where serpents may infect the developing fungus with their venomous breath.[49] (This standard belief of mushroom ecology is encapsulated in a woodcut featured in a sixteenth-century book by Pietro Andrea Mattioli, reproduced below and in detail on the following page, cropped and greatly magnified to show the smiling snake that threatens a young crop of agarics growing next to a decaying tree stump. The simple form of Mattioli's serpent is not unlike the wavy shapes adjoining Plantin's woodblock illustration of the stinkhorn, published forty years later.)[50] Written in English, the couple of lines of text that appear directly beneath the image of the inverted mushroom in Gerard's *Herball* relays as much in the editor's description of where to find such "bastard plants."[51] But whether worms, sperms, vipers, or vapors, what we see in these versions and inversions of the same image of the phallus are some of the earliest artistic attempts (informed by the beliefs of the ancients) to render *more than* the sight of the stinkhorn alone—more than their association with the "lower" animals on earth, even, but mushrooms more generally as symptoms of rank and discordant atmospheres.

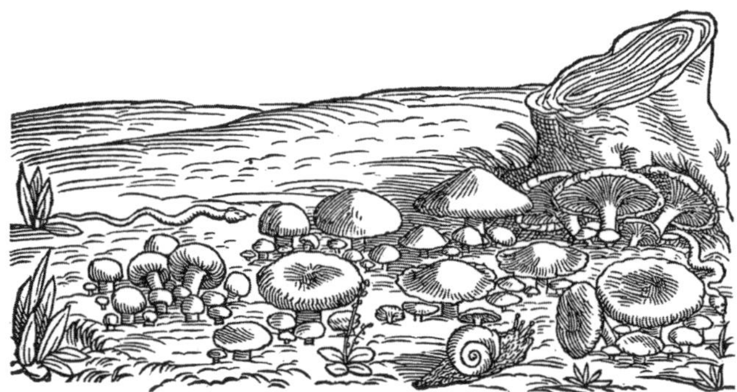

2.823 But here's my honest take on the mystery of the squiggles, admittedly duller, yet much more likely than any of the above interpretations is this. Inspired by Heemsckerck's meticulous attempt to reflect the true nature of the dune stinkhorn in his drawing from life, one of Plantin's draftsmen, possibly Flemish artist Pieter van der Borcht (c.1530–1608), found lying loose upon his desk a couple of fungal radicles, which, because of the mushroom's tendency to fall apart when transported, had become detached from the end of a volva. For the sake of completeness—and in the spirit of Albrecht Dürer's famous dictum: "Be guided by nature and do not depart from it, thinking you can do better yourself"—Plantin's draftsman chose to include the modest tendrils alongside everything else.[52] Still, I prefer the more fabulous view of how the fetid smell of a subject, as if from the foul breath of a snake or dragon, can infect how the artist sees things in the world.

The quiet shunt

2.9   The first copperplate engraving of a mushroom in a printed book appeared in Franciscus van Sterbeeck's *Theatrum fungorum*, published in 1675.[53] The book, considered to be the first substantial published study of fungi, includes 135 mycological illustrations, over seventy of which were copied by the author directly from Clusius's *Rariorum plantarum historia* (1601). Among them is a frightening double-page foldout crammed with twenty or so stinkhorn genera, plus one humble anomaly. It's like a "best of" stinkhorns compilation from over a century of mycological illustration.

2.91   The engraving includes a fastidious recreation of Heemskerck's original illustration of the dune stinkhorn (figures marked letters A to D), plus a slightly more embellished copy of Plantin's woodcut, including the squiggles (figs. E to G).

2.92   Things gets weirder towards the right side of the page. Next to a trio of "dog dicks" (fig. I), a volva viewed from above (fig. K) shows what appears to be a puckered anus ready either to excrete something or to receive the curled finger probing around its wrinkled opening.[54] This image (fig. L) is of a fresh stinkhorn that's obviously missing its cap, presumably because it'd been damaged after erupting from its egg while being transported inside the satchel of some mushroom collector called Hislingh.[55] In his narrative description, Sterbeeck relays the story of Hislingh who, "having gone some way, took the fungus out from his sack and found it so changed that the remarkable sight made him laugh in amazement."[56] I agree, the image is pretty funny. However, the depiction of its decapitated shaft only seems to have added to the confusion between scientists at the time about what constituted separate species of stinkhorns that were, in fact, malformed versions of the same fungus.

2.93   The intact and fully erect mushroom on the far right (fig. M) is no less absurd in that it depicts a fleshy volva, "pierced from both sides."[57] The figure has the look and latent energy of a half-pumped shotgun. Or, to stick with the violent theme, of a popped eyeball or testicle impaled on a blunt railing spike after a night of misadventure. (Barthes's *punctum* incorporate: an image of an eyeball pierced with its own stalk.) Without irony, Sterbeeck describes its odor as "very sharp and penetrating."[58]

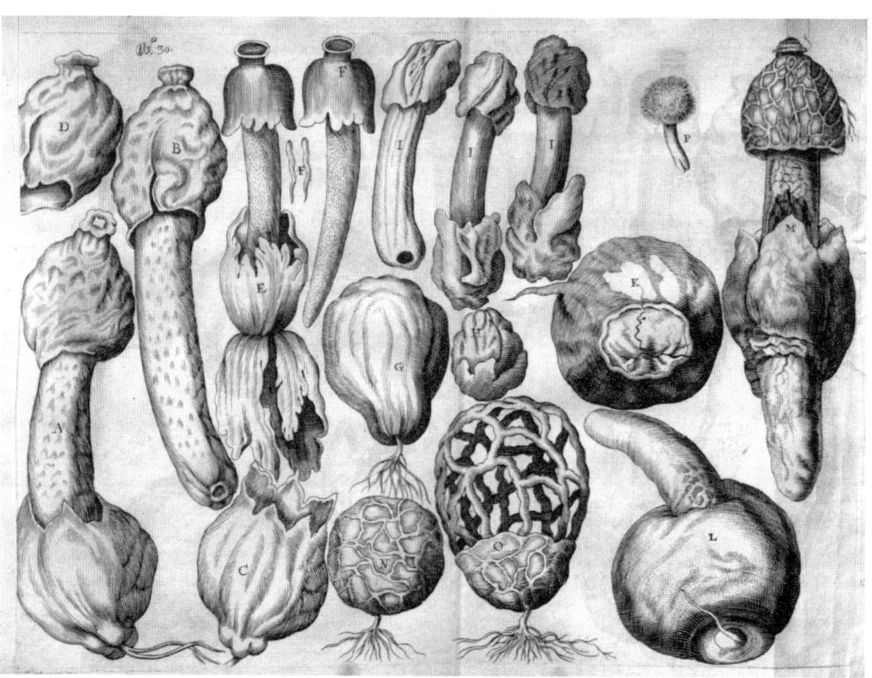

2.931 *Penetrating* pertains to several of the senses. An expression in the eyes that seems to gain access to another's thoughts. A smell that cuts through the air. A sound heard above all other sounds. The idea is of an element that, either due to subtle difference or sheer intensity, passes into the imagination where other sensory phenomena have been rebuffed for being too dull. Leaving aside the figure's more obvious allusion to sexual intercourse (arguably any kind of penetrative sex that involves inserting a penis, dildo, or digit into some orifice), Sterbeeck's goring phallus is a wonderfully succinct visual metaphor for the stinkhorn's various piercing effects on the mind.

2.94 The two figures at the bottom of the engraving in the middle (figs. N and O) are clearly the red cage stinkhorn *Clathrus ruber*. (This mushroom appears as a bright, coral-colored geodesic orb with the slimy, smelly spore mass on the inside; it looks like it was modelled by Buckminster Fuller then half melted in a microwave.) Less clear, however, is the final fungus (fig. P), which is probably the most eccentric among these grotesqueries. Not because it is any more freakish than the rest, but because its size is smaller and exceedingly ordinary by comparison. Sterbeeck names it "Indian cotton fungus." A fuzzy little thing, not unlike the dense, feathery seed head of an anemone flower or dandelion blowball, the figure is one of only a few specimens drawn from life by Sterbeeck himself rather than copied from other artists' illustrations. What on earth is it doing here?

2.941 In his accompanying narrative, Sterbeeck explains how a small, dried specimen was sent to him by a Doctor Syen, a professor of herbs at Leiden, Germany. Sterbeeck writes how he received the item on October 2, 1673 (a Monday) inside a box along with a letter from Syen: "What is enclosed here is unknown to me. It was translated from Indian with the name 'fungus.' Whether it should be referred to as such I leave to your judgment."[59] Likely a plant, possibly a fungus, but most certainly not a stinkhorn. Its encroachment into the land of such monsters is no accident, but is intended by Sterbeeck as a reminder to the reader of the enormous diversity and often bizarre sports of fungal life, which, as he points out, includes cute, cotton-tailed poufs as well as misshapen globules sprouting deviant fingers in want of a comforting hole.

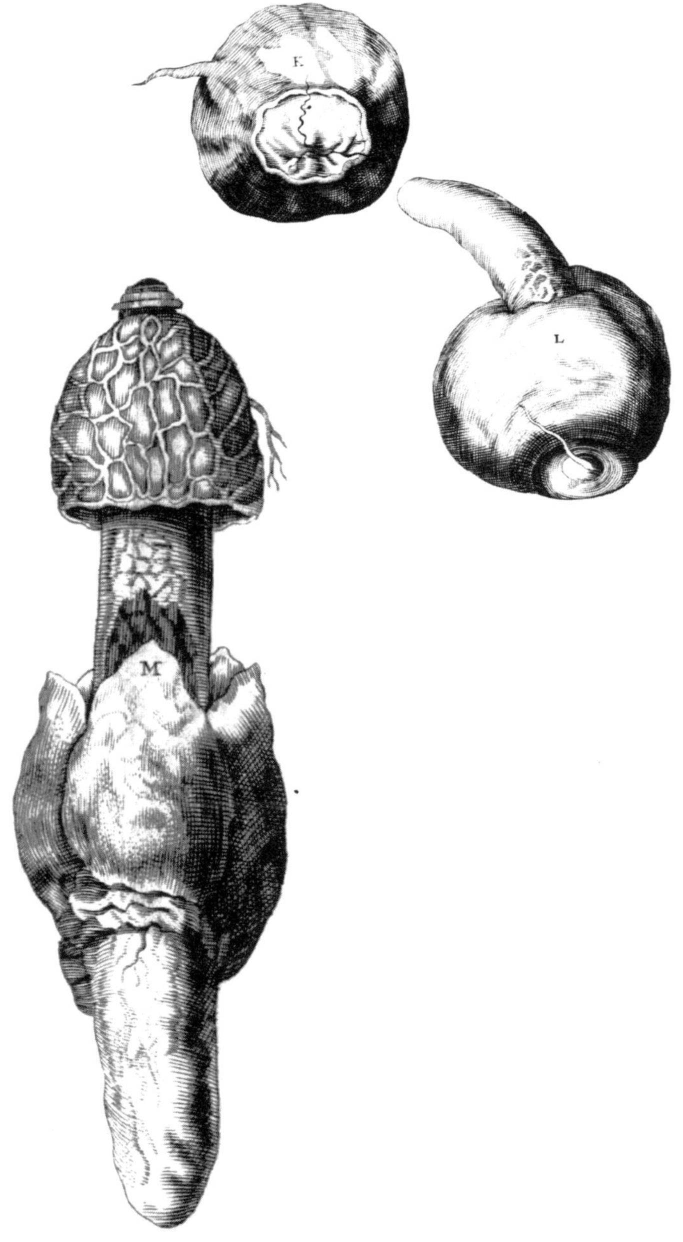

2.95 Viewed altogether, Sterbeeck's crammed composition of stinkhorns shown in various states of engorgement brings to mind the final orgiastic scenes of Brian Yuzna's body-horror film *Society* (released in 1989).[60] In a fantastic fifteen-minute sequence known as "The Shunt," the humanoid nobility of Beverley Hills soften, deform, and invert their brilliantine bodies to feed and fuck themselves on the living room floor while Billy, the spunky, fresh-faced outlier played by actor Billy Warlock, looks on in terror. The film's writhing, anthropomorphic mess, brilliantly designed by visual-effects and makeup artist Screaming Mad George, is prefigured by another mycological illustration featured in Sterbeeck's book and which appears in the pages immediately before the stinkhorn engraving.[61]

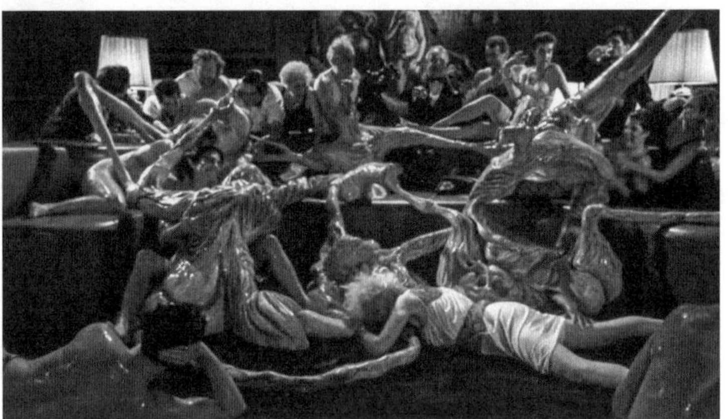

2.951 The image shows a group of gooey-looking people bursting out of a round mushroom fruiting body. The one in Sterbeeck's fungi book is a reproduction of a fanciful illustration, first published in 1671 by the German author Georg Seger (or Segerus, in its Latin form), showing a close-up of a *"Fungus anthropomorphus"* or "geaster," an earthstar fungus similar to the puffball.[62] Seger's early imagining of life oozing out of a more-than-human meat sack wouldn't be out of place in the sketchbooks of that other "Mad" George and their own surrealist fantasy of shunting bodies.

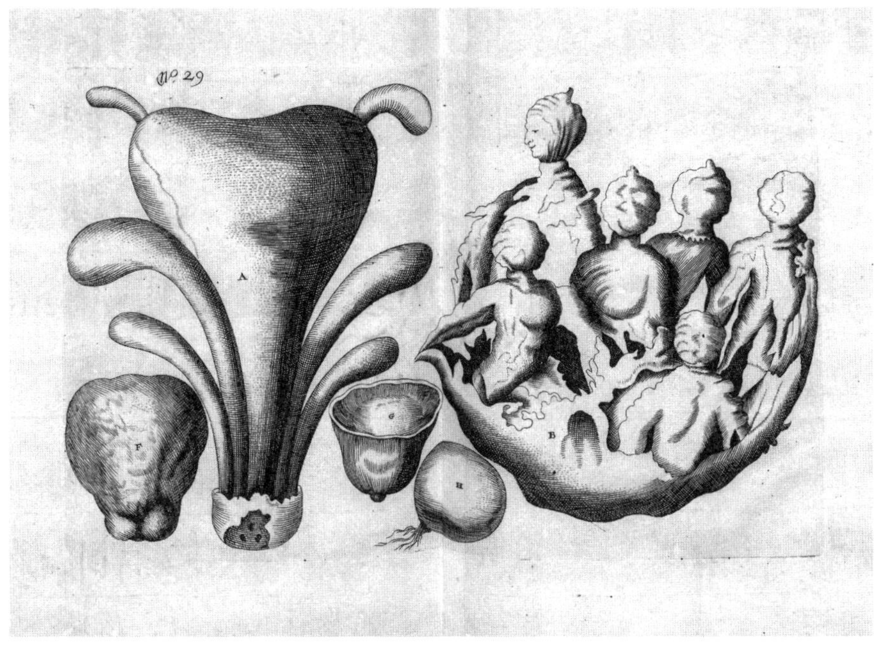

2.952   The scene (which features waiters bearing crystal serving platters of live slugs as if to drive home the movie's core message: that the class system is icky, and the rich are *actual* parasites that "have always sucked-off" the lower classes) plays out almost entirely in one red-lit, smoke-thick room under a soundtrack of squelching noises and an out-of-tune synth version of the even more sickening Eton Boating Song. There's a definite whiff about it: cheesy, over-egged; but this only makes its sensational effect more potent. As the libidinous host Judge Carter says to the gathering elite in the moments before they meld into one another and begin feasting on (and fisting) the low-born interloper: "I do love the smell of the hunt … and the taste of The Shunt."[63]

3. The Smell of the Stinkhorn

The scent of the fungal world

3.1   In Roger Phillips's photographic identification guide, *Mushrooms*, the British author uses seventy-six different words to describe the scent of fungi.[1] Often, he emphasizes the intensity of their smell over their character. These descriptions span from neutral or subtle ("non-distinctive," "faint," "mild," "sweetish"), to pleasing ("fragrant," "aromatic," "scented," "perfumed"), and also encompass less favorable attributes ("strong," "heady," "pungent," "nauseating," "offensive"). Elsewhere he is more specific to the point of being esoteric. On a visit to his home in south London in 2019, two years before his death at eighty-eight, I recorded Phillips reading aloud some of his more explicit descriptions of scent. Many of the words he includes have been gleaned from over five hundred years of writing about mushrooms. The result reads like a list poem, or the ingredients for a witch's brew: aniseed; anise; fenugreek; elderflower; geranium; pelargonium; cocoa; coconut; apples; apricots; plums; rhubarb; overripe pears; onions; garlic; parsley; chicory; cucumber; crushed tomato leaves; bean sprouts; radishes; raw potatoes; boiled cabbage; shrimp; crabmeat; Camembert cheese; rotten wood; rotten cloth; bugs; mold; mice; must; sawdust; sandalwood; cedarwood pencils; pencil shavings; old wine casks; goat moth larvae; tallow; coal tar; soap; iodine; iodoform; ozone; astringent; and ammonia.

3.11   More prosaically, according to Phillips, there are mushrooms that smell "fungussy," and others that simply smell "mushroomy."[2] The mushroomy smell we most commonly know is what the highly-regarded British mycologist and mushroom illustrator M. C. Cooke otherwise calls a "fungoid odour."[3] In his book *Fungi: Their Nature, Influence, and Uses*, published in 1875, Cooke describes this scent as "the faint smell of a long-closed damp cellar, an odour of mouldiness and decay."[4] Mushrooms that smell mushroomy include the butter cap *Collybia butyracea*, the mottlegill *Panaeolus subfirmus*, several species of sulfur tuft *Hypholoma*, and several species of *Agaricus*, most notably the widely consumed common field mushroom *Agaricus campestris*, a mushroom that seemingly smells of itself. "Scent is used for a few mushrooms as a reliable field identification aid," Phillips told me.[5] "Some of them have a spermatic scent, others have a fruity scent. Some mealy, some fishy. Smell is very difficult to describe except by comparison. Sometimes a mushroom just smells like a mushroom."

3.12   In observing the qualities of the smell of a thing in nature, rather than its visual aspects, say, the mycologist is afforded a rare opportunity to deviate from the rigidity of the scientific method. Nature writer Richard Mabey appears to agree with this statement, describing in his book *The Perfumier and the Stinkhorn*,

> smells, unlike sights, are hard to describe. They inhabit an evocative, ephemeral space in our imaginations that is difficult to put into words. They can only be described by comparison with other smells. To be fixed in our imaginations they need to be attached to other memories—of place, moment, feeling—and that needs the experience of age.[6]

This "attachment" of one smell to another, as a means of explication, means that the language of smell can often become laborious, however, relying on a chain of multiple smell encounters that move beyond one's own autobiographical connotations to a collective experience potentially stretching back generations.

A mushroom, a moth, a goat, a ghost

3.2   Take the goat moth wax cap *Hygrophorus cossus*, for example, an all-white and altogether uninteresting-looking mushroom that Phillips describes as smelling like "goat moth larvae." This is a reference by Phillips to an earlier observation made by English botanist James Sowerby, who writes of the mushroom: "The pileus [cap] is covered with a gluten, which constantly gives a strong goat-like odour, exactly resembling the wounded larva of *Phœl. Cossus* [latterly *Cossus cossus*]."[7] Both the mushroom's colloquial and scientific names absorb this smell by taking on the name of the goat moth *Cossus cossus*.

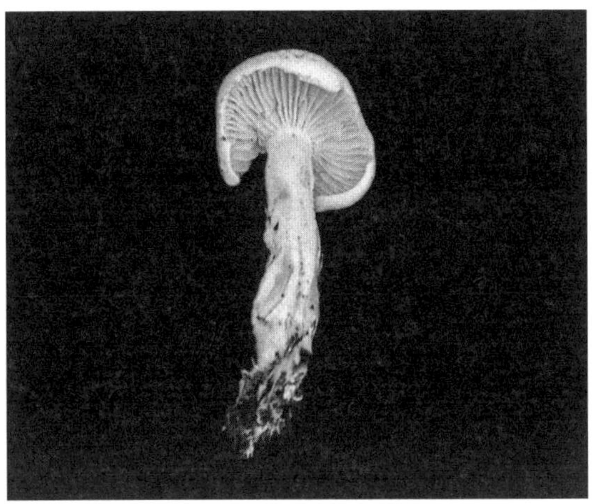

3.21   *Cossus* means "grub," a double meaning that accounts for (i) the caterpillar's large size and voracious appetite for tree bark; and (ii) its function as food for birds, and, it seems, humans. In his *Natural History*, Pliny the Elder describes the culinary merits of *Cossus cossus* as a dish greatly valued by both Romans and woodpeckers.[8] "The birds recognize their presence by the hollow sound of the beaten bark," writes Pliny.[9] Thus, in the percussive Cossus! Cossus! of the woodpecker's beak pounding on the trees we hear the bird's ravenous resolve for Grub! Grub! Food! Food!

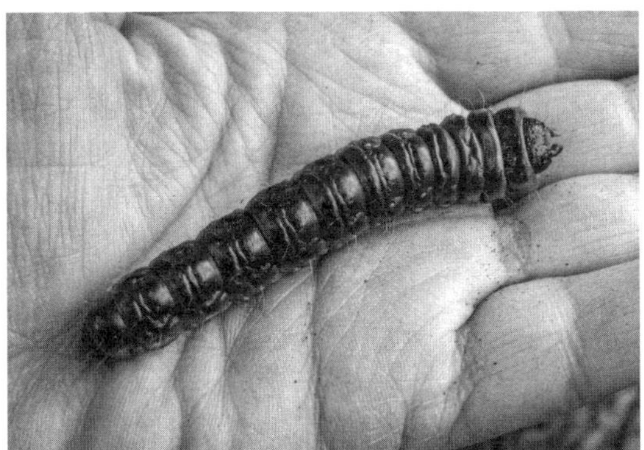

3.211   The goat moth wax cap does not, in fact, smell like the goat moth, nor its caterpillar. Instead, the mushroom's scent is that of the creamy discharge that dribbles out of bore holes in the bark of broadleaved trees from which the enormous, bright red and orange-striped goat moth larvae feeds for four or five years. It's this fermented, fecal excretion that smells like a goat—or to be specific, like the smell of stale piss, head skin, and cornual (from the Latin *cornu* meaning "horn") gland secretions that stain a billy goat's hair. To be even more precise, the smell of a goat is the result of the chemical molecule 4-ethyloctanal, which, when oxidized in the air, results in 4-ethyloctanoic acid.[10] It's this compound that results in the fatty, waxy, lactonic smell that the male goat uses to attract females. Analysis of the volatiles emitted by the goat moth wax cap show similarities in the chemical composition of the mushroom and its namesake.[11] In particular, high percentages of the chemicals 3-octanol and 3-octanone are present in the mushroom.[12] These chemicals are often used as food and fragrance ingredients to give foods a creamy, cheesy, woody, earthy, musty, and—yes—mushroomy aroma.

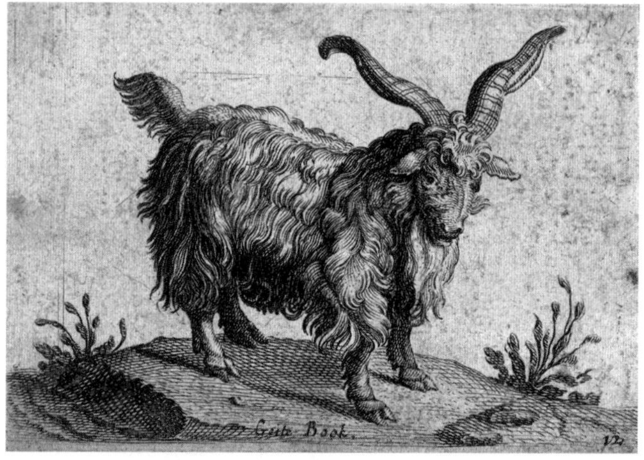

3.22   Let's pull back for a second to consider how this smell appears to us humans, what we collectively understand as the odor of goat. Anyone who has ever encountered a domesticated goat at any distance knows this smell, say, having been near one as a child in a petting zoo or a farm, or less proximately, having sensed its presence in the specter of its feral cousin, its scent trailing behind long after it has bounded into the trees and out of view. In the flesh (in the mouth and on the tongue), we might otherwise only know the profile of goat in our experience of it as food: goat meat, goat's milk, goat's cheese. That full and irrefutable flavor, fragrant yet forever on the verge of tipping over into the foul, a taste and smell that across cultures we describe in a word both succinct and replete: goat.

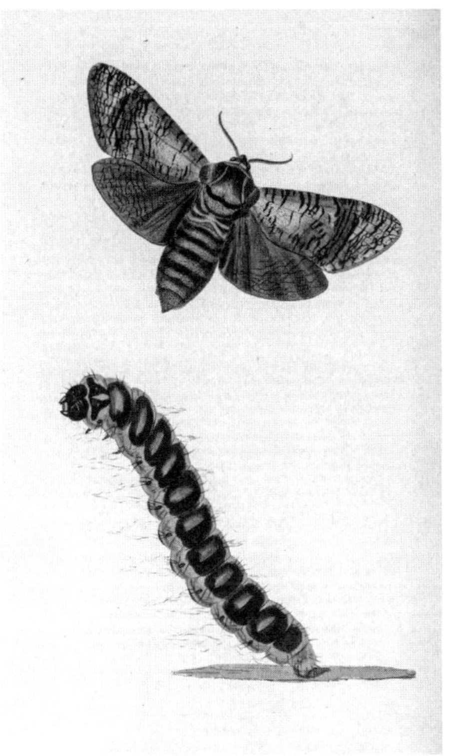

3.221 Now, consider how we might recall this goaty odor in an encounter with a tree in a forest. More specifically, how we might experience the stench of fecal excretions that drool out of and down its bark emanating from a convocation of caterpillars therein. A miasmic mist rings its trunk creating a terrible aura of airborne molecules detached from the tree's fermented sap that has passed through the bodies of worms. And, in this way, the phantom smell that surrounds the tree is precisely that: a ghost, a disembodied spirit. This spirit is so particular and so powerfully evocative of "goat" that we apply the word in the naming of the dull-gray, cumbersome moth (the heaviest in Europe) into which the larva metamorphizes. In other words, the innocuous image of the adult is named after the potent smell of its youth—which in turn is named after the odor of the goat that preceded it. This process of naming both the goat moth and the goat moth mushroom, colloquial and scientific, therefore appears to be contingent upon multiple, discrete experiences shared silently between individuals: that is, the mycologist and their spiritual encounter with a tree riddled with excremental caterpillars; and the lepidopterist and their encounter with the invisible vapors of a goat.

3.222   However, the roles in this ghost (goat?) story are, etymologically speaking, the reverse. Like all lepidopterans—that is, all butterflies and moths, including their caterpillars—though the adolescent goat moth larva and adult goat moth are considered the same species and share the same scientific name, the two creatures bear no resemblance to one another. *Larva* derives from the Latin meaning "ghost." In Roman mythology, the *Larvae* were restless, specter-like creatures that wandered abroad at night, sometimes in the form of skeletons, and striking the living with terror. The term was later applied in zoology by Linnaeus in 1768 to describe the juvenile figure of an animal that "masks" its adult form, or *imago*. Shrouded in youth, so it goes, the moth's true contours are disguised via a winding sheet of segmented skin.

3.223   Though juvenile and adult goat moth are taxonomized as one and the same, there's a controversial theory that proposes that they are in fact two different species coexisting within the same insect, fused together via a process of genetic hybridization that occurred long ago in their evolutionary heritage.[13] In an attempt to explain the incongruous appearance between the immature and mature stages of some creatures, marine biologist Donald Williamson in 1992 proposed the larval-transfer theory, which he describes as a process of radical metamorphosis; or, as Bernd Heinrich more bluntly puts it, "death followed by reincarnation":

there are indeed two very different sets of genetic instructions at work in the metamorphosis of some insects and some other animals, and these are as different as different species, or even much more so. They thus represent a reincarnation, not just from one individual into another, but the equivalent of reincarnation from one species *into* another. How the two coexist in the same organism without creating a garbled creature that is 'neither fish nor fowl' is a potential problem regardless of how those two genetic instructions originated. The solution is that most of one body dies and the new life is resurrected in a new body.[14]

Within the goat moth chrysalis, all the organs and nearly all the cells of the larva die only to be reformed and renewed in the guise of the adult moth. According to this view, the winged moth that the caterpillar transforms into is the wraithlike manifestation of its erstwhile living self. Emerging muted, its mouthparts erased, it cannot eat and so floats silently, clumsily, but for a few days or weeks between willows, compelled to those wounded trees in which it might be reborn in the body of another.

3.224   As we can see in the example above, the naming of the goat moth wax cap *Hygrophorus cossus* presents us with an extraordinarily complex matrix of biographical attachments, weaving together multiple esoteric elements and subjective smell memories. In sequence, the lineage of these discursive experiences and its resulting nomenclature looks something like this: the smell of a billy goat and its similarity to → the smell of the fermented excretions of a species of large, wood-boring caterpillar and its similarity to → the smell of a species of woodwax mushroom.

3.225   Imaginative as the naming of the goat moth wax cap may appear, scratch its surface and it shows up the shoddiness of the language of smell. There are other mushrooms whose common names characterize their scent much more efficiently, however.

Peculiar to itself

3.3   In the natural world, we ascribe the word "stink" as a prefix to a great many plants, animals, and fungi that mimic or emit various rotten smells of decaying proteins as a means to repel or attract other organisms: stink badger, for example, a sort of skunk in the family *Mephitidae*, squirts an oily, yellowish liquid from its anal glands to deter predators; the stinkbug *Halyomorpha*, a type of shield bug, smells of rancid almonds; stinkweed, any foul-smelling plant, such as pennycress *Thlaspi arvense*, whose crushed leaves release a strong cabbage smell; stinkwood, of various trees, especially *Ocotea bullata*, a South African tree which by all accounts smells horrid when felled; stinking cedar *Torreya taxifolia*, a type of yew tree whose leaves give off a strong odor of turpentine when bruised; stinking iris, the "beefy" smelling *Iris foetidissima*; stinking smut, the common bunt fungi *Tilletia tritici*, a plant pathogen used as a biological weapon in the Iran-Iraq war during the 1980s, and which produces in affected wheat an odor of rotting fish. The list goes on. Then there's the stinkhorn, which synthesizes the smell of carrion and dung to attract flesh- and shit-eating flies and beetles to help disperse its spores.

3.31   Stinkhorns stink. In their book *The Romance of the Fungus World*, R. T. Rolfe and F. W. Rolfe describe the smell of the common stinkhorn *Phallus impudicus* as "intolerable," "evil-smelling," "fetid."[15] W. P. K. Findlay describes them as "abominable," resembling "that of a fox," or "defective drains."[16] Phillips says their smell is "strong, sickly, offensive [...] reminiscent of rotting meat."[17] Others have variously characterized stinkhorns as smelling of "damp earth," "spent incense," "sperm," "rotten Limburger cheese," "scorched linen," "burning bricks," "bones," and "the fumes of hartshorn manufactories" (salt of hartshorn is a traditional baking agent used in the seventeenth and eighteenth century made from the shavings of red deer, or "hart" antlers, distilled to make ammonium carbonate, a key ingredient in smelling salts). And when sensational adjectives fail, writers have reached for more emotional language, describing the stinkhorn's effects on the mind and body as being "powerful," "pervasive," "provocative," "infectious," "aggravating,"

"nauseating," "obnoxious," "odious," "insupportable," "madden-
ing," "evil."[18]

3.311   In one of the longest passages dedicated to fungal odors I've
found, Charles Badham, in his book on the edible mushrooms of
England (published in 1863), amplifies this claim of the malevolent
power of stinkhorn smells on the human body, pointing to a belief
held by some communities in southwest France that the mushroom
was pathogenic. Under the heading "Odours and Tastes," Badham
writes of the red cage stinkhorn *Clathrus ruber*:

> Its infective stench has given rise to a superstition enter-
> tained of it throughout Landes, viz. that it is capable
> of producing cancer—in consequence of which super-
> stition the inhabitants, who call it Cancrou, or Cancer,
> cover it carefully over, lest by accident some one should
> chance to touch it, and become infected with that horri-
> ble disease in consequence.[19]

To the common stinkhorn, and frequently the stinkhorn-adjacent
red cage fungus, are ascribed the superlatives of stink. In terms of
intensity, their smells are what all other fungal odors are measured
against. In his breath-taking illustrated volumes, *Coloured Figures of
English Fungi* (published between 1797 and 1803), James Sowerby
gives the best description of a stinkhorn I've read, writing that "the
smell is peculiar to itself."[20]

3.312   Some have described the much rarer dune stinkhorn *Phallus
hadriani* (an image of one collected by me features on the cover of
this book) as smelling "pleasant, like liquorice," or of having a "sweet
smell of violets when fresh," though this impression strikes me as
incredible and utterly at odds with the mushroom's fusty character,
a chemical trick it has evolved to help disperse its spores.[21] In his
book *British Entomology* (1823–40), John Curtis includes, alongside
his picture of an oversized dung fly (the toothed fly *Borborus hama-
tus*, now *Crumomyia nitida*), a brilliant yet anemic-looking illustration of a mature dune stinkhorn found near the beach of Lowestoft,
England. Pictured without any of its oily slime about its cap, Curtis's

slimeless, beige-colored illustration renders the dune stinkhorn sterile, presumably having come across the mushroom late in the day when the flies had had their fill. In a note, he describes the mushroom as having "a scent somewhat like violets at a distance, when growing, but was very offensive when dried."[22] In 1836, Miles Berkeley, arguably the founder of British mycology, calls it *Phallus iosmos* (Greek: *io*, "violet" + *osmós*, "smell") after Curtis's observation, though even Berkeley is skeptical of Curtis's description of the dune stinkhorn smelling sweetly of violets, writing "this is so contrary to the general nature of these fungi, that the matter certainly requires confirmation."[23] Around this time, but as late as the mid-1980s, writers about mushrooms can often be found repeating claims for the dune stinkhorn's "sweet violet" or "non-fetid odor."[24] These descriptions are often made in comparison to the much more prevalent common stinkhorn *Phallus impudicus*, which, being common, could be more easily found, smelled, and disliked firsthand. But by this weak comparative method, so are most other things "non-fetid."

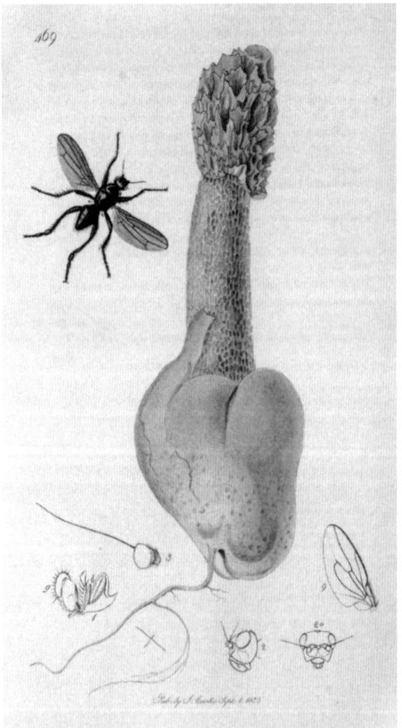

3.313   Maybe it's to do with expectation, finding out that a legendary stench is really not that bad. Or maybe, like Dante and Virgil pausing to hold their noses while standing on the ledge above the seventh circle of Hell, it's to do with acclimatization. But Berkeley is not convinced by this theory either, writing, "The observation that if one has courage enough to hold the [dune] stinkhorn near enough, the odour loses much of its character, is not confirmed by my own observations."[25] This is true of my own experience, where I've had to hold my breath when photographing close-up the dripping pileus of a dune stinkhorn before periodically moving away from the viewfinder to retch.

3.314   My feeling is that Curtis's detection of the sweet fragrance of violets was influenced by the pinkish, lilac color of the dune stinkhorn's egg, reminiscent of a violet plant's bluish-purple blossoms. But who am I to say? Maybe some dune stinkhorns do smell sweetly of violets. (They don't.) One notoriously acerbic American mycologist, C.G. Lloyd, wrote in 1907 that references in England to a violet-smelling stinkhorn variety must've been described by someone with "defective olfactory nerves."[26] The epithet "iosmos" was dropped soon after.

Ass plants

3.4   To less faulty, more sensitive noses, stinkhorn odor is so powerfully diffusive that it's been said a "bitch in heat" can pick up its scent from up to three miles away.[27] In olfactory terms, the space a single stinkhorn occupies above ground is enormous.[28] This is by design.

3.41   In the right conditions, carrion flies can detect the smell of rotting flesh from distances up to several kilometers.[29] By some evolutionary quirk it shares with other sapromyophilic plants (foul-smelling plants pollinated by blowflies), the stinkhorn fungus has managed to become attuned to the phenomenon of synthesizing the stench of a third party, thus ensuring its place on Earth.[30] Other plants pollinated this way include the corpse flower *Rafflesia arnoldii* (the heaviest inflorescence of any single flowering plant in the world); the titan arum lily *Amorphophallus titanumarum* (another misshapen phallus, this one truly massive); or the dead horse arum lily *Helicodiceros muscivorus* (otherwise known as the "ass plant" for its resemblance both to the hairy anal opening of a horse or pig, and the sulfureous smell of its rotting hole).

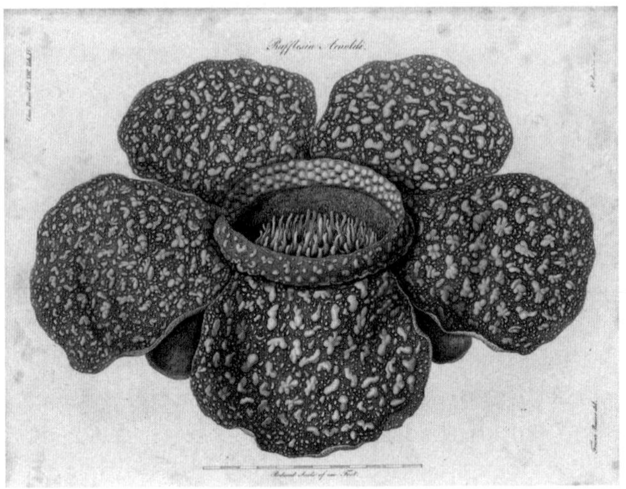

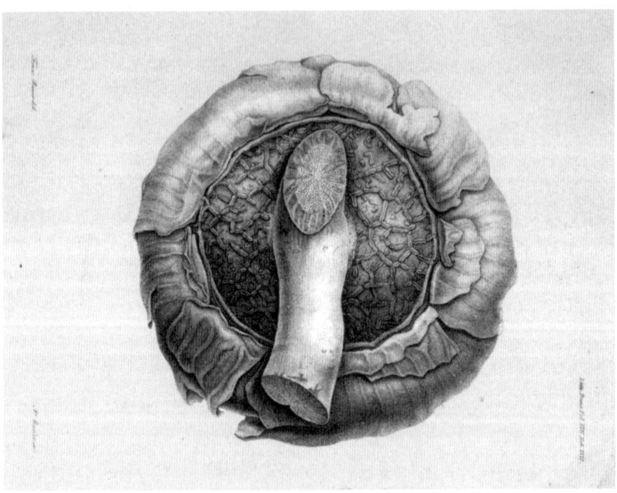

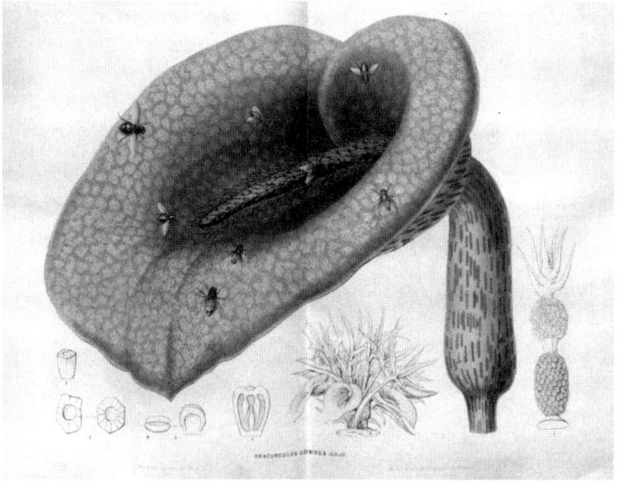

3.411   Stinkhorns can often be found growing in clusters around the entrances to badger setts. A study from 1997 speculated that this stinkhorn-badger association could be attributed to a high population of blowflies during the period when stinkhorn fungi begin to fruit, a time which coincides with high birth rates—and correspondingly high death rates—of badger cubs below ground.[31] The growth of stinkhorns in forests and coastal regions, where the occurrence of decaying animal carcasses is more common, therefore helps constitute a rich ecology of insect-fungi-mammal interrelationship, one that begins and ends with stink. This makes sense when the smell of the stinkhorn is experienced en plein air around the openings to badger setts and rabbit burrows. However, when relocated to a more confined space for observation, such as one's study or kitchen, the stench quickly intensifies to become insufferable. As Junius himself observed, removed from its original environment in nature to the interior of the human habitat, the stinkhorn "exhales an aura so virulent as to be able to pervade the air of an entire room."[32]

3.42   Stink is relative. To us humans, stink is a signifier of death and disease. Whereas to nonhumans, such as the necrophagous or coprophagous fly, it is the promise of food and fecundity. Stink is also a stratagem. Instead of a protein-rich animal corpse, flies find oozing from the ripe stinkhorn a sugary slime. The flies then carry off particles of spore-rich syrup to other parts of the forest on their limbs (it's been claimed that a speck of stinkhorn slime on the bristle of a fly may contain up to twenty million spores) and in their feces.[33] Stinkhorn slime has a laxative effect on flies, meaning spore dispersal occurs near the mushroom, therefore increasing the mushroom's chance of growth in similarly rich soil.[34] Because of the sheer volume of loose-shitting flies, it's not unusual to find in just one spot several stinkhorns in various states of engorgement poking up through the soil like the dicks of the departed (another folk name for the stinkhorn: "Deadman's cock").

3.43   Stink is measurable. In 2014, a group of chemists at the Institute of Chemical Technology in Prague measured the different compounds the common stinkhorn emits at various stages in its life cycle.[35] A technique called gas chromatography/mass spectrometry -olfactometry (GC/MS-O) effectively affords scientists an electronic nose to analyze the different odorants a solid material releases into the air. It's these volatile organic compounds, or VOCs, that allow a thing to be smelled. What makes the stinkhorn stink, then, is a group of particularly pungent VOCs called oligosulfides.[36] The worst offenders are the compounds dimethyl disulfide and dimethyl trisulfide, odorants also chiefly responsible for the foul smell of the corpse flower, the dead horse lily, and the titan arum lily. (Note, the link between lilies and the scent of death is the odorant indole. The origin of the association of lilies with funeral parlors was functional rather than decorative, as the sickly-sweet scent of the flowers' stamens would help mask the smell of the recently deceased awaiting burial or cremation.) According to the website The Good Scents Company, the odor of dimethyl trisulfide is like "cabbage, raw onions, meaty, fishy, creamy with savoury nuances."[37] Listed like this, it doesn't seem all that bad. However, along with the crudely named cadaverine and putrescine, oligosulfides are the compounds most responsible for the sulfuric, decomposing, cabbage-like stench of a rotting corpse. It's this smell that the stinkhorn uses to deceive flies into thinking its sporacious slime is in fact carrion or carnivore feces.

Hinge

3.5   As I discussed in the previous chapter, to consider the full form of the stinkhorn fungus we must think of it first in bits. Yet, as maggot is to fly or caterpillar is to moth, the stinkhorn is more than the brief appearance of the phallus, which in mycological nomenclature gives its name to the truly bizarre-looking family of fungi called *Phallaceae*. Articulated into volva, jelly, shaft, urethra, glans, gleba, slime, stink, swarm, and so on, we observe a thing made up of multiple yet tenuously connected units—so tenuous, in fact, that each unit can be easily teased apart as if the parts were glued together with spittle.

3.51   On the gesture of articulation, the American philosopher and theologian Mark C. Taylor writes this: "To articulate is to joint. A joint (where only outlaws and the errant hang out) joins by separating and separates by joining. This joint, this threshold, is neither here nor there, neither present nor absent."[38] What joins the stinkhorn's separate parts together into a single phenomenological whole—what makes it feel "present" as opposed to "absent," "here" as opposed to "there"—is contingent upon its smell. Note here what David Toop says about sound: it is a "present absence" and a "deadly lure."[39] Both qualities are equally applicable to Stink.

3.52   Derrida's use of the word "hinge" [*brisure*] offers some nuance as to how we might distinguish between "difference and articulation" at the site of the joint.[40] The hinge, writes Derrida, allows us to connect individual elements in a chain to constitute a whole (language), while still being able to see the separate parts which function therein.[41] *Hinge*, in this sense, means "folding point," the site at which different things connect and which enable them to move or turn, as in the spine of a book or the segmented appendages of a fly.

3.53   Stink is the stinkhorn's mechanism of joining separate species—fungus and flies, for example—into a mutualistic relationship. Stink is the mushroom's means of mobility and self-replication, which is only articulated further under magnification as the spore-carrying speck of slime on the hair of a fly's leg. Stink, and not the mushroom's corporeal form, is the space the stinkhorn occupies above ground. The insistence on the sight of the phallus, or even the volva which births it, is misplaced, therefore, for Stink demands less of our aesthetic faculties, not more.

3.54   Stink is the time of the mushroom, a duration marked by potency and diffusiveness, plus the intensity of feeling it induces in humans (anxiety), and carrion- and shit-loving insects (rapture). In other words, when it comes to the stinkhorn, the Stink is the thing.

Saint Cyrus

3.6   If *autopsy* is "the act of seeing with one's own eyes," then *autosmy* is the act of smelling with one's own nose. Allow me a sudden change in tone from the heady language of the theoretical to the excremental language of the empirical and my own attempt at what might generically be called "nature writing." I have a story to tell about smelling stinkhorns—a dune stinkhorn, no less; the proto-mushroom—and, like Junius before me, I mean to be explicit.

3.61   On Sunday October 2, 2022, I was out with my family in a small wood on the outskirts of Dundee (a horrid wood, the type I generally avoid for the almost guaranteed run-ins with dog shit and golfers) when we came across another group of local mushroomers out on a foray. There were five of us, four of them. We met, peered into each other's baskets, and began to share our finds. Unless speaking about the more highly prized edible mushrooms, such as porcini, chanterelles, and so on, the locations of which folks are understandably keen to keep quiet about, I find these types of short exchanges between mushroom enthusiasts quickly escalate into superlatives with excited show-and-tells of the more recherché ends of the fungal world. The leader of their group, a man in his seventies who had all the accoutrements of a seasoned forager (and who had something lichenous about him in general) said one of their party, a woman, had a few days before found a stinkhorn growing near the beach in a place called St Cyrus, a nature reserve less than an hour's drive from where we live on the Tay Estuary. Unable to hide my excitement, I asked if she had any pictures. On a cracked phone screen, an effect which lent the images an explicitness they deserved, she swiped left through a series of close-up shots of a large, penis-shaped mushroom growing in the sand and sprouting from what looked like a lightly bruised bollock. Unmistakably the dune stinkhorn.

3.62   Two days later, I was driving up the east coast with my nine-year-old son beside me. My son has an extraordinary nose, which, over the course of the last five years of escorting me in my singular pursuit, has been fine-tuned to the nuances of stinkhorn vapors. Perhaps it's conditioning. Perhaps it's the way he stravages the physical world, picking up bits of info from the edges of things. Or perhaps it's simply because his nose is closer to the ground than mine. Whichever, the fact is he's a stinkhorn hound. When out walking in the woods, he'll often stop dead in his tracks, pausing for a second before shouting enthusiastically: "Stinkhorn!" He's rarely wrong, and though it takes us a minute or two of sniffing around, together we're soon able to root one out. Despite the tip off we received, St Cyrus nature reserve covers a large area of almost a hundred hectares, and so I wanted my son's expert snout with me on this trip to help increase my chances of tracking down a fresh dune stinkhorn so that I might smell one for myself.

3.621   I'd only ever smelled a dried dune stinkhorn, which I'd done some weeks previously during a visit to the Herbarium at the Royal Botanic Garden Edinburgh. Desiccated for over a century, the mushroom still retained elements of its oniony odor, though much refined and smelling deliciously fruity, a bit like a chipotle chili. It felt necessary that I should smell a fresh specimen, if even to feel a little closer to Junius's original experience of the mushroom he'd encountered five hundred years and four hundred nautical miles from where we stood looking out onto the North Sea. And so, we parked the car and started out, noses in the air.

3.63   St Cyrus Nature Reserve occupies a long flat coastal plain between the small village of St Cyrus in the far-southern end of Aberdeenshire to where the North Sea meets the mouth of the River Esk. (*Esk* just means "water" or "river." In Scots, it can also be used imitatively to mean "hiccup." To pronounce "River Esk" is thus to regurgitate spasmodically.) The site is bracketed between a three-mile-long strandline on one side, and a seventy-five-meter-high volcanic basalt cliff on the other. These cliffs cup the interstitial land like a protective hand shielding a flame, so that several plant and fungus species can be found growing there that you'd otherwise find a couple of hundred miles farther south where the weather is milder.

3.631   As you move in closer, color, texture, and smell begin to separate the site into four types of terrain that run in parallel to each other. All along the base of the escarpment, there's the gorse scrub with its bilious, dog-vomit-yellow blossoms and sweet perfume of overripe pineapple and coconut. On the farther side, there's the beach, broad but boring, filled with the briny odor of sea salt and rotting seaweed. Sandwiched beneath the two is a swathe of grassland rich in wildflowers, including common restharrow, a creeping pink-flowering plant, which, when bruised, releases a rank odor of old onions, spoiled meat, unwashed feet, and armpits, hence its local name "sweaty oxters." (The root of common restharrow is also said to smell a bit "goaty" when fresh). Where the meadow moves tentatively to meet the shoreline, the solid greens of hardy plant stalks and resinous leaves begin to soften into sprays of bluish-silver where spiky marram grass (*Ammophila*: "friend of sand") helps bind the sand together to form sand hills. From reading Junius's account, I knew I'd find my dune stinkhorn here.

3.64   Mushroom hunting requires a special kind of attention. *Scanning* is the word, and it carries with it that same sense of trying to locate a half-known phrase within a passage of dense text or verse. Quick, systematic, this mode of looking makes one move through space strangely, sinuously, and therefore slower than if you were simply trying to proceed in a straight line towards a clear point of reference. Time, too, becomes slippery. (Orlando in *As You Like It*:

"There's no clock in the forest.") Eyes and nose angled down, a vast landscape is foreshortened so that a space of no more than a few feet matter.

3.641 At this micro level, small things start to pop out. The barred, candy-like shells of lemon snails. Spider holes, perfect *O*s, like a chorus of grease-rimmed mouths preempting the cries of their prey. The crayon reds, greens, blues, and yellows of little viscid waxcaps. All types of animal shit: rabbit, seabird, sheep, cow. ("All excrement spoke," writes Pascal Quignard, who observed that for early humans the spoor was a type of text, a *stink text*, which had to be read in order to make meaning of the landscape.)[42] And all types of dead animal bodies: (bits of) rabbit and seabird, again; but also fish, crab, lizard.

3.642 Here in the sand dunes, smells are harder to pick out than they are in the sheltering forest. Even on a relatively calm day, such as this one, when the wind picks up and blows in off the sea, the mood can quickly turn belligerent. This means that any effort to detect or discriminate between delicate wafts of scent are frustrated. The sight or sound of insects as indicators are no good either, too blown about to trace their trajectory.

3.65 Ahead of me straying off the path, my son, bravely in shorts, is letting off little yelps as the knee-high, needle-like swards of beach-grass prick his shins. Dune stinkhorns often grow in clusters at the dense base of marram tussocks, so they're almost entirely obscured. In this wind, it should've been impossible. But in what feels like no time at all, a cry goes up: "Stinkhorn!"

3.66 There are a couple clumped together, though they're wilted, gone over—so much so that they've started to develop across their surface a furry mold. Searching in the same spot, we quickly find another. It's perfect, ripe and proud. Around it, there are a few more half-buried lumps, like turtle eggs. This one must've hatched a few hours ago, just in time for our arrival. The slimy spore mass has already started to deliquesce. Up close, its smell (in this moment, joyous) is thick and doughy, much more semen-like than its common cousin. It's also strongly savory, like a warm blast of concentrated kitchen fumes as you pass through an alley behind a restaurant.

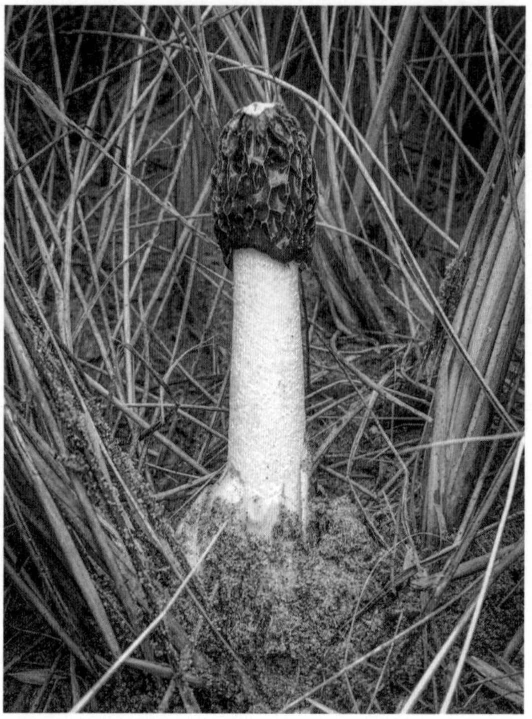

3.661   With a rounded picnic knife, I carefully dig up the ripe stinkhorn, plus two of the immature eggs growing in the same spot. Straight out of the ground, the rubbery eggs are still whitish, though they'll soon oxidize and discolor to take on their distinctive violet hue. Weighing one in my palm, the egg is heavy and disconcertingly cool. Squeezing one slightly between thumb and forefinger, it has the firmness and density similar to a grapefruit, and I can feel the swollen glans of the mushroom beneath as it nears the end of its gestation—dull and threatening like a knuckle.

3.662   I pack them in wads of kitchen paper and seal them in a sandwich box, which I later have to discard. For the sake of completeness, I take the two overripe, furry stinkhorns also. By the time we get home, one of the two immature eggs has started to split, a clear gluey substance like pre-cum starting to ooze out from a thin slit that's developed at its crown, showing the olivaceous tip of the pubescent mushroom grinning through.

3.67   With a sense of urgency, the light beginning to wane, I spend the next two hours documenting my specimens in various ad hoc and improvised fashions: photographing them on my phone; pressing them whole onto a flatbed scanner; smearing some of their slime onto endpapers torn from a book; and, more tentatively, tasting them—stalk only. Sliced crossways into discs, raw and unadulterated, it's innocuous enough, tasting mildly of radish or raw turnip. But the smell—especially that of the overripe pair, which have a post-coital air about them—is truly obnoxious. "Heady" is insufficient, for it too easily separates the experience from the rest of the body, particularly the stomach, where the smell is most keenly felt.

3.671   Partly to chase the light, and partly out of consideration for the rest of my family, I've now confined myself and my mushrooms to the bedroom. It's October, two weeks into autumn. Outside, the wind has picked up and is barreling down the river straight onto the front of our building. The air is cold, and the door and window to the room are shut tight. And yet, from nowhere, two small flies appear, like spirits invoked by fumigation. A miraculous success.

3.68   The scent of the fungal world is, as M. C. Cooke puts it, one that mostly arises as the result of a process of "*eremacausis*," the slow oxidization of organic matter, such as decaying trees and dead animals, in the presence of air and water.[43] In the small, hermetic space of a sandwich box, a car boot, or a bedroom where these elements are diminished, an otherwise savory, "mushroomy" smell can become nonsensical, supernatural even, for how it seems to overspill its volume. Such concentrated smell experiences can leave an indelible mark on the imagination, changing forever the way one moves through atmospheres and making stinkhounds of whomever is close enough to be haunted by its fumes. There are some mushrooms, writes Cooke, whose smells "once inhaled are never to be forgotten."[44] Cooke includes in this list the common stinkhorn (the top spot he reserves for *Thelephora palmata*, also known as the stinking earthfan or fetid false coral fungus, a leathery, hand-shaped mushroom that is said to smell of rotting garlic) a stench, he writes, which is much more intensified in the red cage stinkhorn:

> It is very probable that, after all, the odour of the Phallus would not be so unpleasant if it were not so strong. It is difficult to imagine, when one encounters a slight sniff borne on a passing breeze, that there is the element of something not by any means unpleasant about the odour when so diluted; yet it must be confessed that when carried in a vasculum, in a close carriage, or railway car, or exposed in a close room, there is no scruple about pronouncing the odour intensely fetid. The experience of more than one artist, who has attempted the delineating of the Clathrus from the life, is to the effect that the odour is unbearable even by an enthusiastic artist determined on making a sketch.

3.681   That efforts by artists to depict stinkhorns from life have been stymied by the sheer strength of their stench is something to which I can personally attest. Attempts to represent it must be done fast and in short bursts, so as to draw breath, and using multiple specimens that must soon after be thrown away, wrapped in several sheets of paper, double bagged, and disposed of at a distance from one's home. However, in this haste, something essential about the mushroom is lost. As Cooke suggests, it's because of the intensity of their odor that stinkhorns seem to resist "true," that is, *total* artistic representation. Despite the best efforts of artists such as Heemskerk, Curtis, Sowerby, and others, this will always be the case inasmuch as the inherent power of the stinkhorn—its abject smell—will always be incondensable or entirely absent from the constricted time and space of the botanical illustration or photograph. In order to manifest a more complete, trans-sensory conceptualization of Stink as outlined at the beginning of this book, we must therefore broaden our attention beyond the visual and olfactory to include other, intangible phenomena.

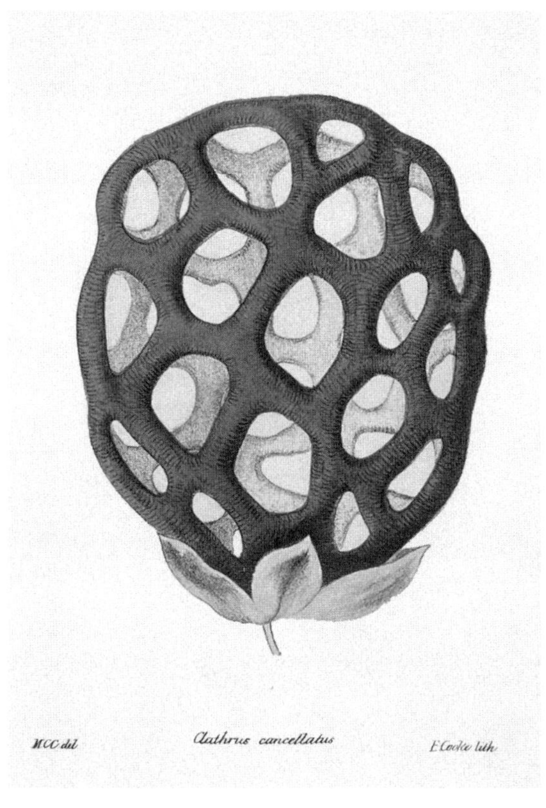

M.C.C. del.
Clathrus cancellatus
E. Cooke lith.

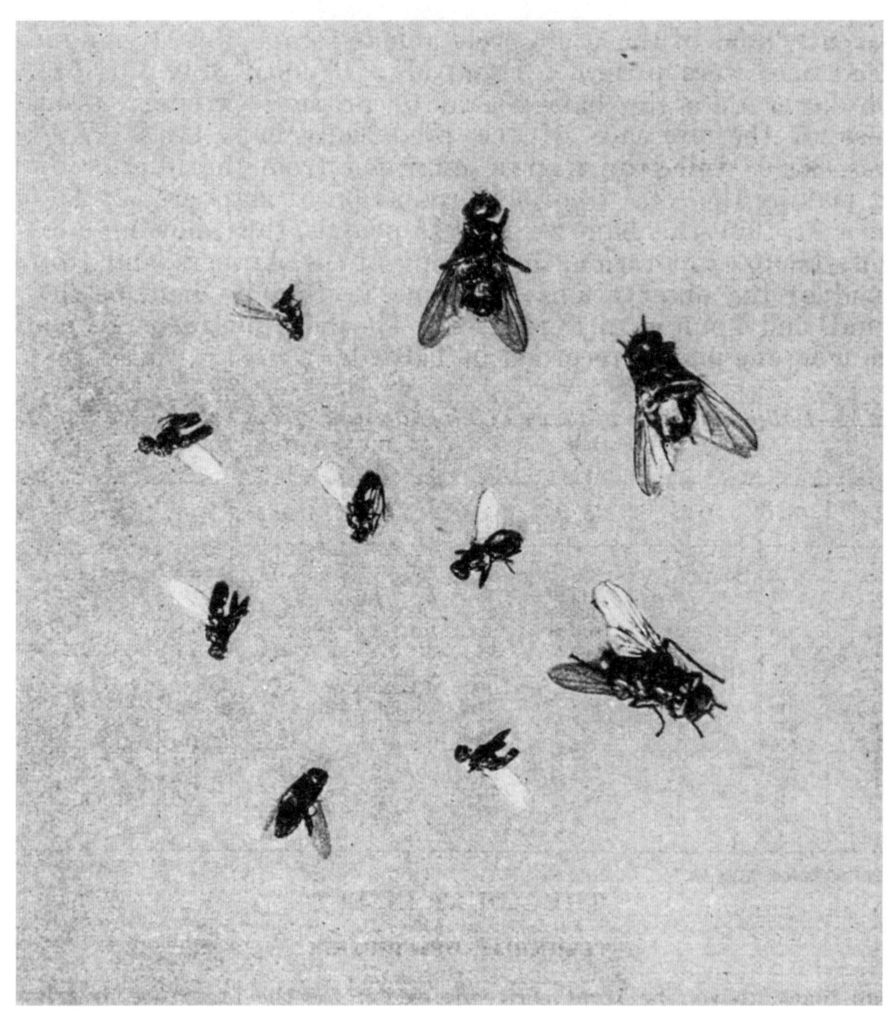

4. The Sound of the Stinkhorn

Composers are continually mixing up music with something else. I prefer my own choice of the mushroom.

—John Cage, *Music Lover's Field Companion*

Mmmm

4.1   Where Cage's penchant for mixing up music and mushrooms was more general, mine is, in the biological sense, specific. In its fully erect and most pungent phase, the stinkhorn appears as a mass of material, texture, and tone: fungal flesh, slime, insect hair and limbs, etcetera, all united together in the air by an invisible, malodorous vapor. As I say in my introduction, even its colloquial name, "stinkhorn," conjures in the mind the sound of an instrument—most certainly a wind instrument—capable of producing a smelling sound. You can imagine emanating from such an instrument the raspberry blow of a trumpet, the flatulent parp of a tuba, or the honking of a bassoon.[1] But this smelling sound isn't a rasp, or a parp, or a honk. It's a hum.

4.11   A quick aside on the hum note. Musicologists have long labored over the problem of determining a single pitch of a bell, that is, how the overall harmonic effect is perceived by the listener after a bell, particularly a large bell, has been struck. Despite its dull form, the bell is a complex musical instrument that sweeps through multiple frequencies, many of which are so low as to be imperceptible to the human ear. A vocabulary of tonality has emerged in an attempt to nail down the harmonic tuning of any given bell consisting of five principles or partial tones. For example, the "strike note" is the pitch we perceive immediately after the bell has been hit with a clanger or mallet. As the sound decays, the lowest tone that lingers—an octave lower than the strike note—is called the "hum note." Despite its careful tuning and temperament, a bell may appear to have several pitches, and therefore be perceived variously depending on each listener's analytical ear.[2]

4.111   Much as different listeners will hear different pitches rising above others in the ringing of a bell, so does my ear pick up on the double signification of the word "hum" in our encounter with the ripe stinkhorn, a multisensory experience compounded in the imagination as the singular Stink. For, though it's often said that you smell a stinkhorn before you see it, many times you'll hear it before you smell it; or at least the two sensations, sound and smell, are synchronous in the air around a stinkhorn in that they occur and are sensed together.

4.12   Humming is the spoor that marks the trail towards the unseen mushroom and helps constitute its sonic atmosphere, its Stink. The audible hum in the space surrounding the stinkhorn does not, of course, resonate from the mushroom itself, but is the sound produced by a swarm of several species of fly that are almost always found about it. The fly we humans are probably most familiar with is the common housefly *Musca domestica*. Save from the Antarctic continent and a handful of islets, *Musca domestica* can be found on every major landmass on the planet.[3] As the epithet *domestica* suggests, the hum of the housefly has been a constant feature in the daily lives of humans as long as we've existed. By speaking the name of the fly, *musca*, we mimic with our lips the vibration of its single pair of wings. Houseflies hum not with their mouths but with the beating of their wings, which they do at a speed of 190 cycles per second.[4] Houseflies hum in the key of F major.[5] The noisier blowfly *Calliphora vicina*, one of the most frequent flies to visit the stinkhorn, flaps its wings at a more bassy 150 times per second.[6] This produces a hum equal to around 150 hertz, a pitch somewhere between D and D sharp (concert D3 and D3 sharp). These three notes—D, D sharp, and F—played together in a rapid, repetitive broken chord or tone cluster comes close to the sonic experience of the stinkhorn and its querulous whine of flies.

4.13   I hear something of this testy (tsetse?) quality in Sallie Tisdale's breathless evocation of the fly as a sum of seemingly contradictory adjectives: "grotesque and frail and lovely and vigorous, quivering, shivering, lapping, flitting, jerking, sucking, panting."[7] I hear it too in the music of György Ligeti, his pieces *Atmosphères* and *Continuum* specifically, and in much of Éliane Radigue's prolonged and impalpable compositions for the ARP 2500 modular synthesizer. (Arguably, a certain odor can be detected in almost all of Radigue's astonishing catalog of recorded works.) Even more, I hear it in Angela Morley's tautly suspended string arrangement for Scott Walker's track "It's Raining Today," a single atonal chord that sustains throughout almost the entirety of the four-minute song to create a sense of simultaneity, or better still, *ambivalence* of several irreconcilable feelings all happening at once.[8] I hear it echoing in the trills rising above Radiohead's song "How to Disappear Completely" (a disorientating and unnerving effect guitarist Jonny Greenwood admits to stealing directly from Walker/Morley), and resounding again in Mica Levi's score for Jonathan Glazer's science fiction film *Under the Skin*.[9]

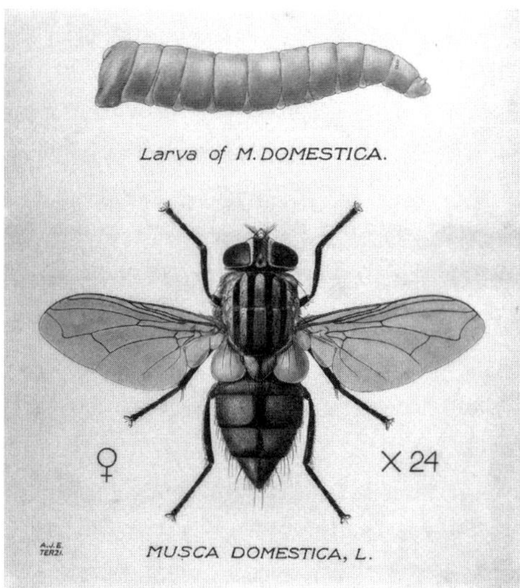

4.14   Cage once joked that his interest in mixing up *mushrooms* and *music* stemmed from the fact that the two words were (at the time) next to one another in the dictionary.[10] We find that the Latin entry for fly, *musca*, is similarly close by.

4.141   Steven Connor shows us examples of how the names for the fly in several languages is imitative of the humming sound the insect makes (unlike the English *fly*, which derives from the way it moves through the air; though Connor points out that we do hear this "sonic principle" in the word *midge*): "The Greek *muia*, an imitation of the fly's buzz (or more precisely perhaps, the hum that Greeks seem to hear), gives us Latin *musca*, Italian *mosca*, and Spanish *mosquito*, 'little fly', and French *mouche*."[11]

4.142   The types of words ascribed to the fly in Romance languages can be described as phonaesthemes. Phonaesthemes are words whose form appears to evoke their meaning directly. The *m* sound used to mimic the humming noise of the fly is called a bilabial nasal, meaning the sound is produced by closing the lips and expulsing resonant air out the nose. *Malodor. Mushroom. Music.* Add to this triad *musca* and a humming sound is formed from their initialism: *mmmm.*

4.15   The phoneme *m* is the least expressive sound one can make with one's lips. Connor goes one step further by saying it is the "primary phoneme," indicative of mother's milk, mammary glands, of a mouth otherwise occupied so that one can only utter out the nose.[12] Think of Stephano's admonishment of Trinculo in *The Tempest* after Trinculo's teasing of Caliban: "Why, I said nothing," protests Trinculo, to which Stephano replies "Mum, then, and no more."[13]

4.151   The wordless *mum* (a silent interjection; a promise to keep quiet) can be heard in other verbs starting with the letter *m*, which similarly signify silence or inarticulation: *muffle, mumble, murmur, mute.* Even when the verb signals an articulating gesture—that is, when the mouth employs the teeth as well as the lips, such as *masticating, mashing, mulching, munching*, and so on—its meaning serves only to break down matter further into smaller and smaller bits until what's left is an indistinguishable and unintelligible *mush*. However, when the *m* sound is doubled, tripled, or quadrupled, the signifier suddenly opens up to become spacious, thus making room for an enormous range of meaning to enter in.

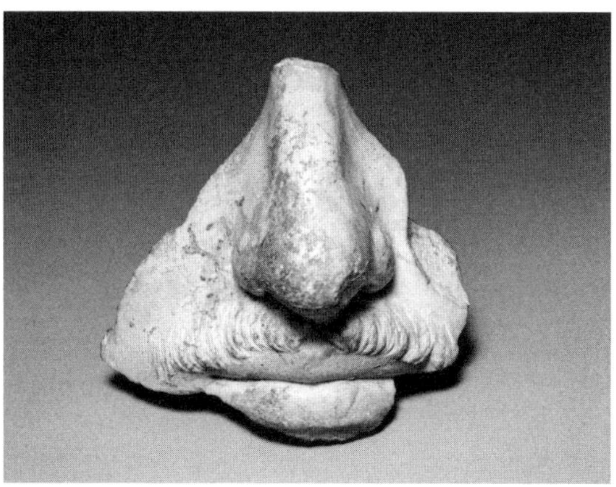

4.152   In his book *Beyond Words* (2014), Connor writes: "If the lungs are the loudspeakers of the speech, the nose is its tuning-dial."[14] Depending on the ways in which the nose "tunes" the hum—how the resonant nasal breath effects dynamics of pitch and modulation—*mmmm* can move from silence ("absent presence") to sound ("present absence"). For example, to pronounce *mmmm* is to involuntarily signal extreme pleasure or satisfaction. Followed by a question mark plus an upward inflection—*mmmm*—the noise notifies others that your interest has been piqued, as if *musing*, literally "to stand with one's nose in the air." (In his *Etymological Dictionary of the English Language*, published in 1910, Walter Skeat tries to explain this analysis of *muse* and its sense of "nosing the air," attributing the etymology to German philologist Friedrich Christian Diez. Skeat: "This is plainly from Italian must, 'a musle, a snout, a face.' The image is that of a dog snuffing idly about, and *musing* which direction to take.")[15] Pronounced flatly before trailing off, the three dots of the ellipsis like fly turds on the page—*mmmm ...*—the sound indicates indecisiveness, ambivalence.[16] When contracted and pronounced emphatically with a downward intonation—*mm!*—the sound signals disgust. With added breath—*mmph!*—the sound is reflexive and functional, designed to obstruct and expulse any small amount of foul air that may have momentarily entered the nostrils.

The atomic hum of meaning

4.2   Like the spontaneous generation of maggots and flies from rotting and foul-smelling things, a belief that continued throughout Europe for many centuries, the stinkhorn seemingly emerges from nothing, like a conjuring trick.[17] The stinkhorn fungus, too, is a timeless, "potentially immortal" organism, immune to the decrepitude of age: mushrooms "die from disease, injury, or lack of resources," writes Anna Tsing, "but not from old age."[18] Corporeally speaking, the stinkhorn is without end. It's neither cock nor cunt but both and more—a genderful rather than genderless organism that emerges from the ground first as an ovum and then a volva from which births a phallus, a phallus covered in a shit-colored spermatic slime that reeks of death. As I described in the previous chapter, in its mature phase and at the height of its potency, the stinkhorn recalls the smell of rotting flesh and vegetable matter. Rot is an excess of life. The stinkhorn is life and death, sex and terror, rolled into one redolent, murmuring entity. The smell of rot presents a threat to those still living, whereas flies swarm to rotting things, helping to fragment them further through the actions of their toothless mouthparts.

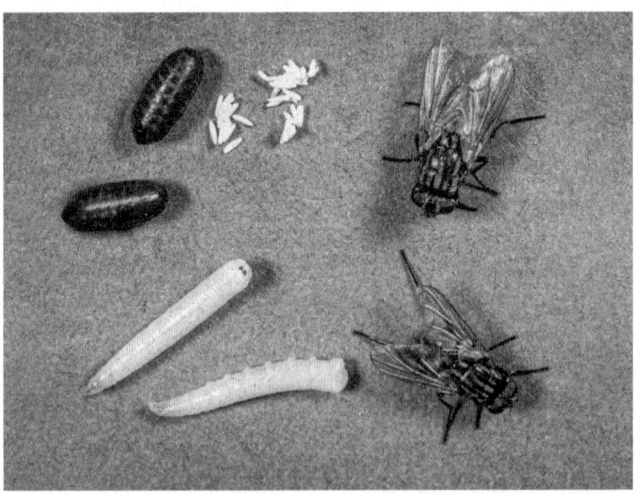

4.21   A couple of lines by French writer Pascal Quignard seem to fit the fly's liquifying gesture as they break down dead and dying matter into smaller and smaller bits: "The molecule decomposes again into its atomic Erstwhile. Etymology is the art that enables literary people (specialists in letters) to dissolve entities into their elements."[19] This is etymology as rot. With these sentences, Quignard is himself engaged in a process of decomposition, in the literal sense, unwriting the etymology of etymology. And like the work of fungi, bacteria, worms, and paramecia in breaking down matter, we can imagine this process—*composting*, shall we say?—lets off a kind of smell, as well as a muted sort of sound.

4.22   Connor points out a link between the words *etymology* and *entomology*, thus:

> There is in fact a significant etymological conversation between the words atom and insect. An atom, literally that which is without a cut, signifies something indivisible. The English word for insect comes from Latin *in-* and *secare*, to cut, which is a more or less literal rendering of Greek *entomos*, meaning with a cut in the middle or the inside. The segmented bodies of insects seem to compromise their unity. Insects, which were often thought to be the smallest possible living creatures, mere motes of life, keep on providing evidence of the further divisibility of the elementary, all the way down, far beneath the threshold of visibility. The atom is always subject to more anatomy (literally, "un-dividing"); there is always more divisibility in the visible.[20]

The fly stands for both the singular and the multiple, Connor goes on to say. The humming of the individual fly therefore promises the chorus of the collective swarm, the same way a single speck of stinkhorn slime excreted out an insect's anus carries with it the possibility of twenty million spores and a multitude more "prick tales."

Background hum

4.3   "In evolutionary terms, human humming came before language," writes Christine Hume in her prose poem "Hum."[21] "Before words, we used humming as a means to maintain contact with one another across space, a vibrational touch and sonic grooming. We hummed to chill out and focus our attention. We hummed because we hear total silence as a warning; an eerie dread runs through it."[22] The humming sound of flies that trace the space around the stinkhorn encapsulates this dread. It's a hum that masks—no, *mingles*—with the stink of an unseen, odorous object. It conveys the possibility of death at the site of a rotting corpse or source of disease. It's a dread, too, that the background hum of the world has somehow poked through the hymen that separates the audible from the inaudible, and, once allowed to be heard, will never cease buzzing in our ears.

4.31   Musicologist Lawrence Kramer offers up a subtle distinction between the audible and the inaudible that may be helpful here, a concept he calls the "audiable." "The audiable is the material promise of sound. [...] The audiable is the precursor of sound yet to come, yet it is also experienced through hearing, as if auditory sensation had a future tense. The audiable is the hum of the world. One has to listen for it."[23] We must attend to that which is present in silence in order for discrete elements at the edge of perception—sounds within sounds—to reveal themselves, writes Kramer in the introduction to his book *The Hum of the World* (2018). He goes on to argue that this conception—the audiable—allows us to consider auditory experiences that extend beyond the capacity of the hearing ear, or even the hallucinating ear, to include touch, language, and (though he oddly omits it from his list) smell.[24] By attending to the audiable rather than the audible, then, the ear, the skin, and the nose may be afforded a set of teeth with which to articulate and divide the background hum of the world into the heard. The stinkhorn as a listening device amplifies this faint signal from beyond, answering in a whisper, a hum, a Stink, the call for an ancient secret to be divulged.

4.311   This secret is inscribed on all things, the residue of a primordial sound—what Quignard calls "sonorous scent" (*odeur sonore*), and in which I hear a close cousin the name of our "stinkhorn" for its compounding of the sensations of sound and smell.[25] We know this sound more colloquially as the echoic emanations of the big bang. The sound of the big bang was synthesized by physicist John G. Cramer in 2003 using data captured by NASA's Wilkinson Microwave Anisotropy Probe, and then again in 2013 using data from the European Space Agency's Planck satellite mission. Both satellites were used to measure cosmic microwave background, the radiant heat left over from the origin of the universe. Cramer produced a low-frequency drone, much too low for humans to hear, which replicates the sound waves that continue to appear every twenty- to two-hundred thousand years apart, and which is the "echo" of the singularity that caused the universe to expand more than thirteen billion years ago. This sound hums interminably at a pitch somewhere around fifty-seven octaves below concert A (440Hz).[26] A sonic descendent of our universal becoming, it's a hum that pervades all space and time, a hum that will certainly succeed our species, if not all living creatures, and thus offers up the auditory future Kramer is so keenly listening out for.

4.312   The background hum of the world is embodied in all human life, resounding through the involuntary buzzing of our nerve impulses, the rushing of our blood in our veins and arteries, the borborygmic groaning of gases in our bowels, and externalized in our constant wheezing, hissing, and pissing out of our body's many orifices. More purposely, we can mimic this sound by activating the vocal folds and forcing the breath out through the nose to make a humming noise. In doing so, we find our bodies in *harmony* (literally "joined," "fixed together") with the originary sound of the universe.

4.32   To *hum* means to sing a low, steady sound with lips closed. In British slang it also means a disagreeable smell. Korean composer and sound artist Suk-Jun Kim picks up on this linguistic anomaly between British and American English in his treatise *Humming* (2019). "What does humming have to do with smelling?" writes Kim before offering a possible answer: "I believe this has to do with the air, caused by the mouth closed; those whose mouth is closed as they hum end up breathing in and out with their nose, hence the smell. But this doesn't really solve the conundrum: why does that smell have to be *bad*, why such negative connotation?"[27]

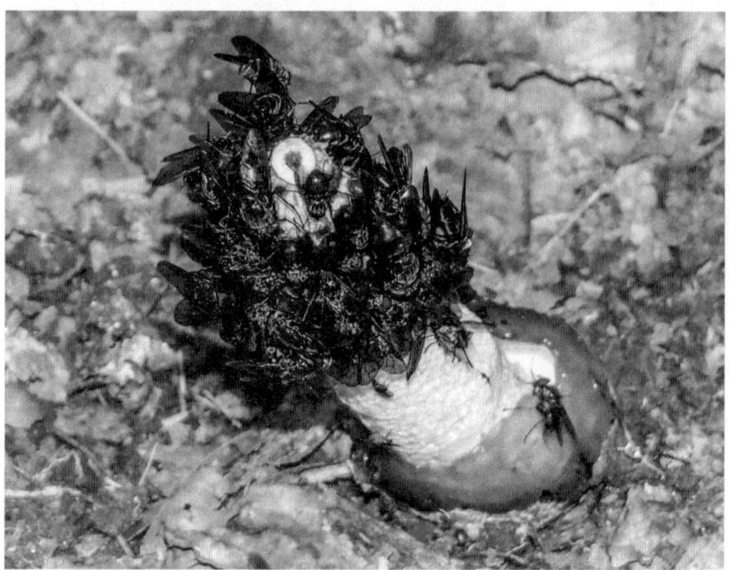

4.321   Kim dwells on this problem only for a short while before offering a vague solution via Steven Connor's descriptions of fetid airs and pervasive fog in Britain around the nineteenth century (similar descriptions by Alain Corbin and Robert Muchembled can be located elsewhere in their respective histories of foul smells in late modern Europe). I agree with Kim's belief that the connection between sonic and osmic humming "has to do with the air," particularly an air that is "suspicious," and thus forces us to close our mouths.[28] For, as I have described above, my choice to mix up sound and smell is predicated on the view that they're both actualized in, spread through, and combine within the air to induce a single unitary experience in the imagination.

4.322   However, I believe Kim's answer to the second part of his question—as to why, in British slang, *humming* connotes a smell that is "bad"—to be insubstantial. The *OED* offers little help as to precisely when the two meanings began to overlap, taking us back to the beginning of the twentieth century only and a description of a piece of Camembert cheese at room temperature ("Lor'! it do 'um!").[29] Perhaps the reason the smell is "bad" is because of the efficient and expressive capacity of *hum* to cut through the air to articulate the inarticulable. As such, the humming smell, though it may be dull, and though it may be slow, pricks us. It is, in the original sense, *pungent*. "What's that sound?" we might ask after a while. "What's that smell?" for that matter. The same answer to both questions is concisely: "A hum."

Fly to flies to form swarm

4.4   Humming is of the air. Flies hum. Bees hum. Hummingbirds hum. The wind hums. Humming is associated with high spirits; the animating breath of life. Humming denotes a sound that emerges in space with every tone all at once, what Kramer describes as a kind of "choral monotone."[30] To hum is to forget to care, to sing absent-mindedly, to speak without saying anything. Humming is inarticulate.

4.41   A humming sound is an apt simile for stink, for the edges of both are hard to define. Unless smelling a single, isolable chemical molecule, which is a rare experience indeed, a pleasant odor, such as a liquid perfume, is typically multi-tonal. In the language of fragrance marketing, a commercial scent can be described as consisting of multiple "notes" that can be detected at different points in time during its diffusion. In this sense, smell is musical. Unpleasant smells, or stinks, on the other hand, either due to their intensity or intrusion, are typically sensed as a single, prolonged, droning mass. That is to say, stinks are *monotonous*.

4.42   If the sonic hum is, as Hume puts it, the "vibrational touch" that connects humans to humans, which in turn leads them to form communities (to commune: "to talk intimately"), then the osmic hum is the odorous adhesive that connects all parts of the tenuously jointed stinkhorn. At the same time, the stinkhorn's *humming* is what connects the words *fly* to *flies* to form *swarm*. As naturalists from Junius onwards have observed, this moment in the stinkhorn's life-cycle is forever at the point of falling apart, a thing that is simultaneously articulate (both in the sense of being composed of *bits*, and of being *bitten* by scavenging, toothed dung flies), and inarticulate (*muddled, murmuring, mushy*, and so on). Even at its ripest and liveliest stage, then, the smelling sound perceptible in the air around the stinkhorn is at the very point of *de*-composing as in its being unmade, atomized.

The Stink of the stinkhorn

4.5   The dynamic principles shared by the twin phenomena of a *humming sound* and a *humming smell* can be summarized like this. Both hums describe immaterial or imponderable emissions taking flight (as vibrating air forced through the nostrils; as pungent fumes from the slimy tip of a mushroom). Both hums describe pervasive yet inarticulate events that exist continuously for a prolonged time and so are perceived as something like static. Both hums have the capacity to induce feelings of ambivalence as a result of their teetering at the threshold of perceptive states between presence and absence. At the same time, both hums move quickly towards inducing feelings of annoyance, displeasure, or dread. In this way, and in correspondence to the criteria I outlined at the beginning of this book, I can conclude, therefore, that not only does the stinkhorn stink, it Stinks.

Decay of decay

4.6   I want to return briefly to the epigraph at the beginning of this chapter and to John Cage, whose music and writing were often inspired by the chance or "indeterminacy" of mycelial growth. In reviewing Cage's oeuvre, I'm struck by what seems to me two unlikely fungal omissions. The first is the ear fungus *Auricularia auricula-judae*. Despite his passion for fungi, both as food and an inspiration for his music and poetry, it strikes me as odd that Cage seems to have never picked up on the ear mushroom in any of his writing or interviews. The ear mushroom is a type of jelly fungus similar in shape and texture to a human or large rodent ear (in the Philippines it's known colloquially as the "rat's ear"). It's also commonly known as the Jew's ear, a mistranslation of Judas's ear on account of the elder tree from which Judas Iscariot hung himself, and from which the ear fungus typically grows when the wood is dead. Though edible, the ear fungus is nonnutritious, almost entirely tasteless, and odorless. Save for its slight cartilaginous texture (a bit like tripe), it's an altogether *insensate* mushroom. In other words, it is an ear that hears nothing and tastes and smells of nothing. It seems reasonable to presume that the innocuousness of the ear fungus would have greatly appealed to Cage for its signification of sound and silence.

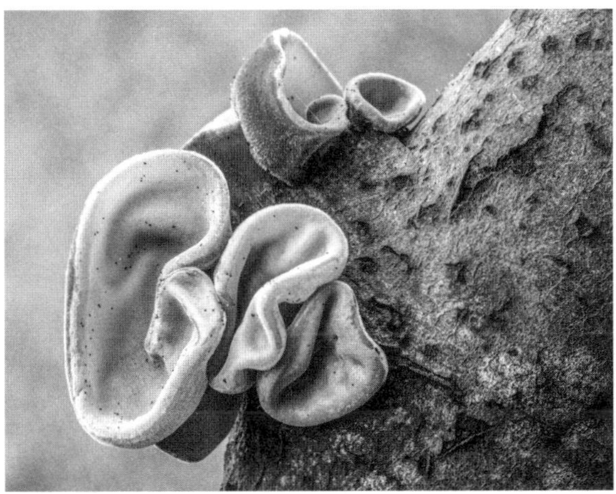

4.61   The second glaring omission in the Cage canon is the stinkhorn. There appears to be only one reference to stinkhorns among Cage's vast collection of mycological ephemera: a postcard dated 1980—not by Cage himself, but credited to Gerry Miller, an artist, mycologist, spiritual healer, Amazon-jungle tour guide, and antique dealer who owned a shop in East Haddam, Connecticut. Cage must've bought the postcard sometime in the early 1980s on one of his trips up from Manhattan to Wesleyan University. (Cage had a long relationship with the music department at Wesleyan, which lasted for nearly forty years.) The postcard is a monochrome photocollage showing the corner of an empty hotel or restaurant dining room. A series of meaty-looking stinkhorns, severed midway down their shaft, have been pasted into the scene so that they appear sprouting out of the pristine white tablecloths like a series of monstrous, bell-shaped shaded lamps. Save for this single image, Cage's apparent disinterest in the stinkhorn and its humming aura appears especially peculiar to me given his fascination with fungi and their sonic possibilities, and his fondness for wordplay more generally. One can easily imagine Cage contemplating the common name of the stinkhorn and finding in it, as I do, a double meaning: an allusion to a magical instrument that can only be experienced by its smell rather than its sound. In an interview he gave with Jeff Goldberg in 1976, Cage had this to say about his encounters foraging (an activity sometimes described by mushroom foragers as "the quiet hunt") in terms of a listening project: "You can stay with music while you're hunting mushrooms. It's a curious idea perhaps, but a mushroom grows for such a short time and if you happen to come across it when it's fresh it's like coming upon a sound which also lives a short time."[31]

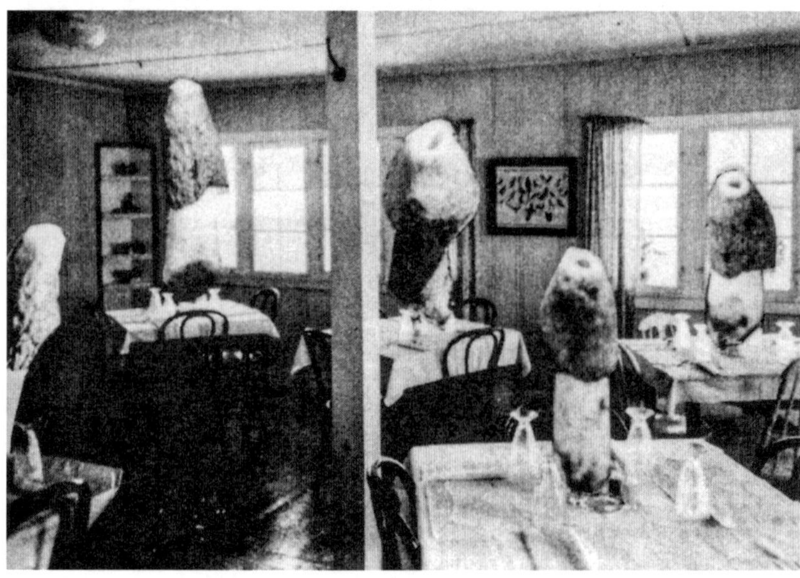

4.611 A fresh mushroom, Cage observes, is like a musical moment: both decay after a short while. The stinkhorn is an extreme example of this momentariness, for when the mushroom is at its most fresh—that is, when it's at its ripest—it's also at its most rank. What's more, with a swarm of humming flies around it, it's also at its loudest. As the stinkhorn overripens and its flesh begins to rot, its stench dissipates, as do the cloud of insects that have been compelled to feed upon its slime. In Cage's musical analogy, the mushroomer who stumbles too late upon the overripe and drooping stinkhorn experiences, simultaneously in sound and smell, a decay of decay.

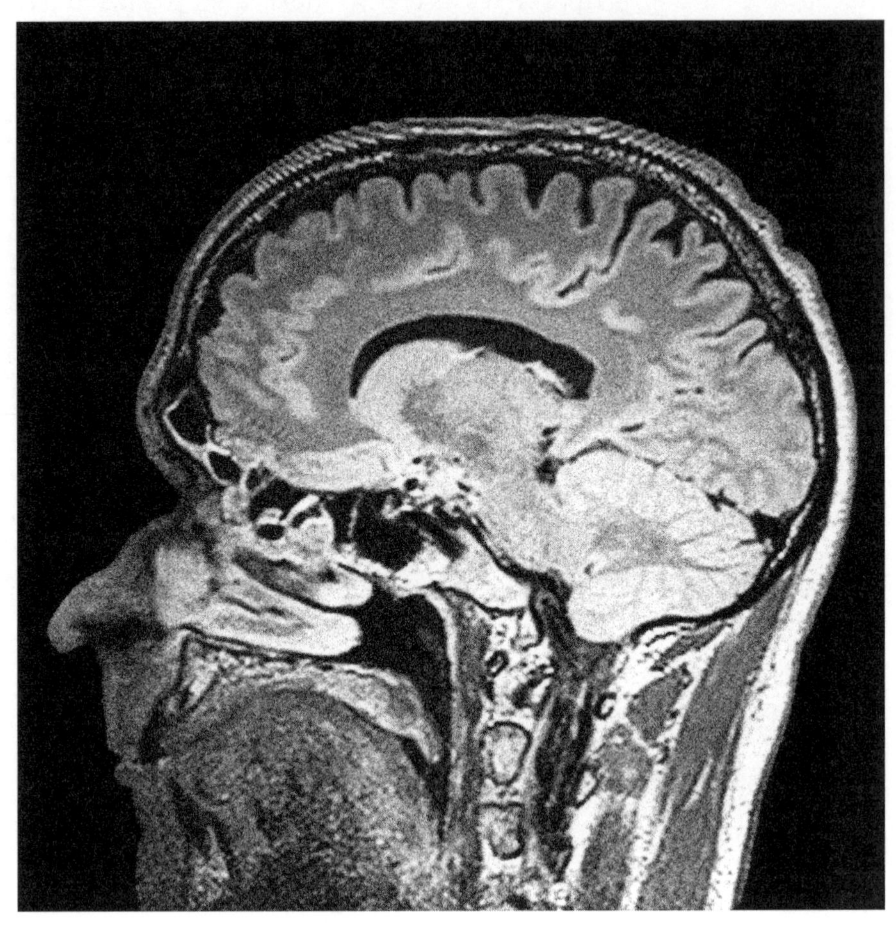

5. Phantom Stink

"What does it matter if it's an illness, then?"

—Dostoevsky, *The Idiot*

Funny turns

5.1   In May 2020, while traveling on a train from Dundee down to York, I experienced an episode whereby I suddenly smelled a strange and obnoxious odor. Cool, chemical-like, pure and poisonous, the smell was intense and so completely unnatural that, even in that moment which lasted no more than ten seconds, I knew it couldn't have come from within the train compartment nor drifted in from the landscape outside; it had appeared spontaneously, like a specter, from someplace else entirely. Immediately after the appearance of this apparition, I lost consciousness.[1] The unfamiliar faces of my fellow passengers looked down upon me as I awoke (*mi ritrovai …*), my body twisted awkwardly in the gangway. The long, rubberized cable from my headphones was still tightly tangled around my neck, for I'd been listening to music when I collapsed.

5.11   The song was "2nd. Body" by electronic musician Sam Annand, from an unreleased EP titled *Four Celestial Bodies* (2019). Each track on the EP was created by Annand entirely on modular synthesizer using four oscillators to produce a series of seemingly static chords. The music was composed using the frequency, or pitch, of one oscillator to control the panning (the movement of the audio signal between the left and right ear) of another oscillator. What emerges is a sound mass made up of four tones that's powerfully dynamic and constantly changing, each frequency moving between the ears at a rate of fifty- to over one thousand times per second. Listening to it on headphones, the effect is rich, harmonically complex, and dizzying.

5.11   "You were having a seizure," said a man sitting behind me. "My sister has seizures. The way your arm was jerking? You looked like she does when she's having a fit." I was shocked. More terrifying than the idea of my having had a seizure, however, was the awareness of a gap having just occurred in my otherwise usual cognitive experience of the world. Or rather, a gap having *not* occurred, for it was not at all like sleep, which still feels somehow bound to time, but total blankness, an erasure. (I'd later read in my medical notes a diagnosis of unexplained *syncope*—a word I'd never come across before. It means a "cutting off" or "cutting out" of a thing that one would normally expect to remain intact or steady, such as a missed heartbeat, or a portion of time excised from the mind; or a sound or syllable struck from a word, like the dropped *o* in the sloppily pronounced "memory.") I managed to get my doctor on the phone, who reassured me by saying that it was probably nothing to worry about. A "funny turn," he said.

5.12   A year of intermittent and still unexplained episodes followed, which I experienced monthly like menstruation. Seizures that occur in women around their period, and at no other time, are called catamenial epilepsy. How could this account for the cycle of my own seizures in that first year, however? Another explanation, though challenged in recent times as myth, can be found in an ancient astrological theory that links the co-occurrence of epileptic seizures with the phases of the moon, especially in the days leading up to a full moon.[2] Mine came on unexpectedly at different times in the day, and in different situations: one while I was out running; one playing squash; another while delivering a seminar to a group of undergrad students; and several while reading to my two younger children in bed. Apart from that first time on the train, all these subsequent episodes had been mild, in that I always knew where I was and could still function to some degree. I could still run, still talk; but even in these moments of semi-lucidity, I had the disconcerting feeling of being separated from myself and my surroundings, as if living in between worlds.

5.13   What finally prompted my diagnosis of epilepsy was the reappearance of the exact same smell I'd first experienced on the train. More than any other quality, it was the potency of the odor that was remarkable and that cut it off from "normal" experience. But this time, the smell was accompanied by other sensory hallucinations: a loud and intensifying droning sound, not quite humming, but more like a choral murmuring. During these latter seizures, I also experienced repeated visions of the same three or four film and TV actors: Olivia Colman, Emma Stone, Daniel Mays, and Ed Skrein. More specifically, their mouths, all speaking at once and shining like the disembodied lips and teeth of Billie Whitelaw's televised performance of Beckett's *Not I* ("the buzzing? ... yes ... all the time the buzzing [...] and the whole brain begging ... something begging in the brain").[3] Coleman, Stone, Mays, Skrein ... figures with no personal significance to me, just scrapings from the sediment of my subconscious. (Though after doing a Google Image search and studying their faces more closely, I can detect something gauche in each of their features that may connect them in my mind: a certain crookedness in the lower lip that curls down left when they speak or smile?)

5.14   A year later, the same day the UK government announced that anosmia, or "a lack or change in taste or smell," would be added to the list of symptoms of COVID-19 infection, I was diagnosed with temporal lobe epilepsy. Speaking over the telephone, the consultant neurologist informed me that the "funny turn" I'd experienced on the train was in fact an episode of phantosmia, a type of olfactory aura that often forewarns a secondary epileptic seizure.[4] The irony was not lost on me. Because it is *weird*, isn't it, that my brain would conjure from itself an odor so foul and frightening around the same time my mind was busy contemplating the ontology of stinks?

5.15   Several weeks later, I was speaking via video with French psychiatrist Alain Sebille about this. Sebille is a psychiatrist for the French Office of Immigration and Integration in Strasbourg. His clinical interest is in schizophrenia and neighboring diseases, such as late-onset schizophrenia (LOS) and the French concept of *psychose hallucinatoire chronique* (PHC), both of which involve occurrences of olfactory hallucinations. After hearing me describe my own experience of phantosmia, he emailed me the next day saying this:

> It's funny that you were thinking so hard about phallic-shaped mushrooms (*Phallus impudicus*: the name speaks for itself!) around the time when you experienced your first olfactory hallucination. This suggests a context of hyper/over-sensorial stimulation. And the duration of the experience of phantosmia, which is roughly the same as an orgasm [...]. All of these elements contribute to mark your whole story of olfactory hallucinations with sexuality. Or let's say, at least your story of hallucinations could be just part of a broader story in which the phallus and sexuality are central.[5]

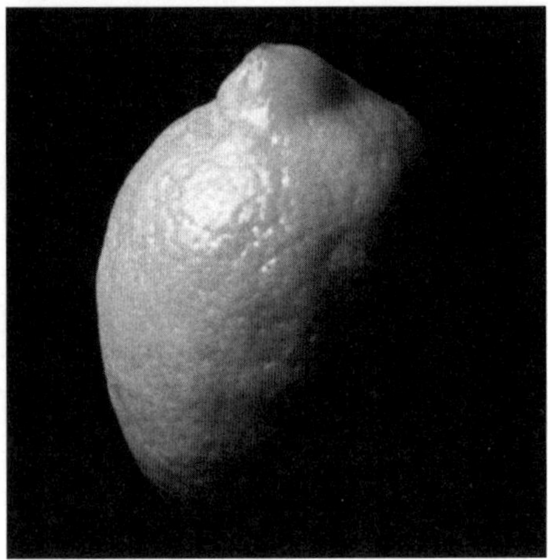

5.16   As Timothy Morton reminds us, *weird* etymologically means "to turn."[6] As a verb, *turn* can mean to move or rotate an object or idea to a different position so that we may consider it anew, much the way artist Hollis Frampton did for the lemon, making the familiar appear strange simply by shifting the way the light reflected upon its dimpled skin.[7] As a noun, *turn* can also be used to describe a short episode of unexplained illness or altered awareness, as in a "funny turn." In this context, where *funny* also means "weird," the language my doctor used to describe my first episode of phantosmia on the train represents a tautology in which "funny turn" is otherwise a *weird weird*. I hear in this echo a reflexive looping of the mind twisting inwards upon itself, sensing (sniffing?) itself in ignorance of any extraneous object or stimuli.

5.17   This chapter presents one last turn from the path walked thus far, a turn that serves both as noun and verb. In this final foray into the forest of the mind, we find our nose-led approach to be redundant, *anosmic*, and therefore incapable of leading us towards the source of the Stinking object in the mind.

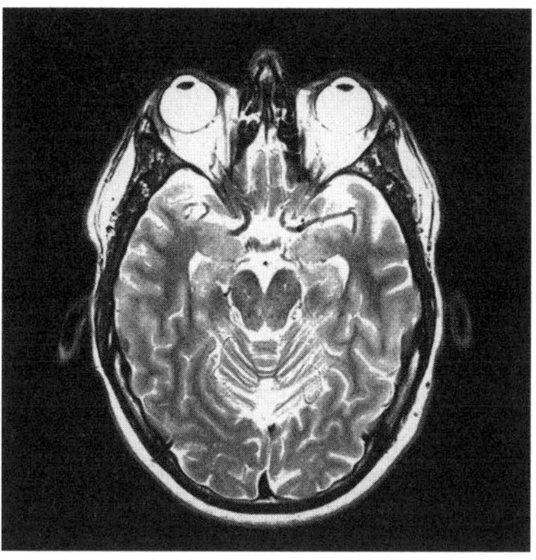

5.18   Because phantosmia describes a hallucinated, and therefore *non-phenomenal* perceptual experience (but, as I will argue, one that is not necessarily "false"), what follows attempts to shift the concept of Stink even farther beyond encounters with smelling sounds in the real world to include neurologic—and psychic—experiences too. I will do this by drawing upon multiple testimonies of sensory epileptic auras, tracing some of the most commonly reported characteristics of smell and sound hallucinations, while also commenting on the circumstances of their onset, particularly those "funny turns" that, like mine, are preceded or triggered by listening to a certain piece of music.

5.19   To reiterate the paradoxical element at the heart of this book: Stink is the combined effect in the imagination of a type of *smelling sound*, which I identify in the previous chapter as a sort of hum, that may induce in the listener feelings of discomfort bordering on dread. Stink is inarticulate, ambivalent. Stink, though pervasive, is also elusive, hard to pick apart and stubbornly resistant to language. Stink occurs in the "real" world via the medium of the air, which one experiences in the mind as a holistic impression of discrete, tonal elements diffused in space. And yet Stinks can also be hallucinated, perceived even when there is no actual stimulus present. This final chapter attends to the latter contradiction, expounding some of the ways in which a phantom Stink can be considered a reality because it is *felt* to be real.

Fugues and fumes

5.2   Phantosmic episodes are often associated with depression, migraine, and epileptic seizures that start in the temporal lobe. But phantosmic episodes can also occur because of other neurologic and neurodegenerative disorders, such as Alzheimer's and Parkinson's disease, as well as disorders of the brain caused by head trauma, tumors, or strokes. There is also recent evidence of individuals experiencing phantosmia as a result of COVID-19 infection.[8] Though the causes vary between individuals, experiences of phantosmia and the qualities of the hallucinated smell are reported in surprisingly similar terms: "unpleasant," "offensive," "burnt," "dirty," "fetid," "rotten," "spoiled," "sulfuric," "musty," "moldy," "putrid."[9]

5.21   George Gershwin described the repulsive nature of his recurring olfactory hallucinations as the smell of "burned rubber," a sensation he experienced on stage during a performance in 1937 of his *Concerto in F* with the Los Angeles Symphony Orchestra.[10] Subsequent and similarly alarming auras experienced months later prompted his medical diagnosis by a doctor in California of "hysteria."[11] It appears, however, that the doctor was unaware that Gershwin had suffered from frequent seizures in the previous months, or that the description of his phantom smell—the smell of burning—is often associated with temporal lobe epilepsy.[12]

5.22   In 2017, a study by a team of Swedish scientists of 2,500 older adults who had experienced olfactory hallucinations showed that, like Gershwin, over half the participants described their phantom smells as "smoky" or "burnt."[13] These acrid qualities have long been associated with phantosmia. The study was noteworthy because it showed some of the ways in which phantom smells elicit autobiographical memories, particularly memories of physical environments, such as rooms or buildings. For example, one participant reported the smell of a childhood home that burned down when they were aged two. Another participant described the odor of a barn in which they played as a child. And another said that their phantom smell recalled the scent of an old house in the forest belonging to their grandmother.[14] In contrast, other participants described their experiences of pleasant odors, such as scented lotions and fragrances, but the connotations were almost always of death: the smell of a dead mother's perfume, the scent of a deceased husband's aftershave, the chemical smell of a hospital ward "associated with the death of a spouse."[15] Whether smoke fumes or perfumes, the phantom smells reported by the majority of participants overwhelmingly confirmed a sensory experience that was incongruous, or "out-of-tune," with their ambient environment. The simultaneous awareness of one's immediate environment and one's hallucinated or warped perception of that environment in the imagination is what pioneering neurologist John Hughlings Jackson called "doubled consciousness."[16]

5.23   Smoke fumes feature heavily in the minds of phantosmics.[17] It's been suggested that the prevalence of an acrid quality in phantom smells may point to an evolutionary quirk that makes our species more alert to the smell of fire smoke, which signals encroaching physical danger and prompts adaptive behavior.[18] Even in our dreams, the smell of burning carries with it an aura of death.

5.24   *Aura* means "breeze." In his definitive history of epilepsy, *The Falling Sickness* (first published in 1945), Owsei Temkin describes the Greek physician Claudius Galen as a young man listening to an account of a thirteen-year-old boy who has experienced an inexplicable rising sensation in his body, starting in the lower leg and climbing "upwards in a straight line through the thigh and further through the flank and side to the neck and as far as the head."[19] When asked what it was precisely that rose up to the head, another observer remarked "that it was like a cold breeze."[20] This "cold breeze," Galen observed, was symptomatic of a type of epilepsy that starts in the extremities, spreads throughout the body, before finally suffusing it totally.[21] The meaning of aura has since been developed by Galen's successors. Today the definition takes in other types of non-motor symptoms, such as hallucinations experienced as part of epileptic seizures. Types of auras now include sensory (auditory, visual, olfactory, gustatory, and tactile), epigastric (a rising feeling in the stomach as if on a fairground ride or traveling fast over a hump in a road), and psychic (typically *déjà vu*, but also *jamais vu* and *presque vu*, respectively the disconcerting feeling of having already, almost, and never seen something).

5.25   Although diagnostically useful, it's rare that the above symptoms happen in isolation or are experienced discretely, for example, the perception of an olfactory aura with no visual or auditory disturbance. Each of these signs may last for different durations or appear at different stages in the development of a seizure. But it's important to point out that it is the combination of these feelings that constitute the overall experience of an epilepsy aura. That is, the aura is a complex of sensory and psychic phenomena that occur either simultaneously or sequentially, ascending throughout the body and pervading all aspects of the mind. The ancient Greek physician Aretaeus appears to have considered the aura much the same way, writing of the moment preceding an attack: "If it be near the accession of paroxysm, there are before the sight circular flashes of purple or black colors, or of all mixed together, so as to exhibit the appearance of the rainbow expanded in the heavens; noises in the ears; a heavy smell; they are passionate, and unreasonably peevish. They fall down then."[22]

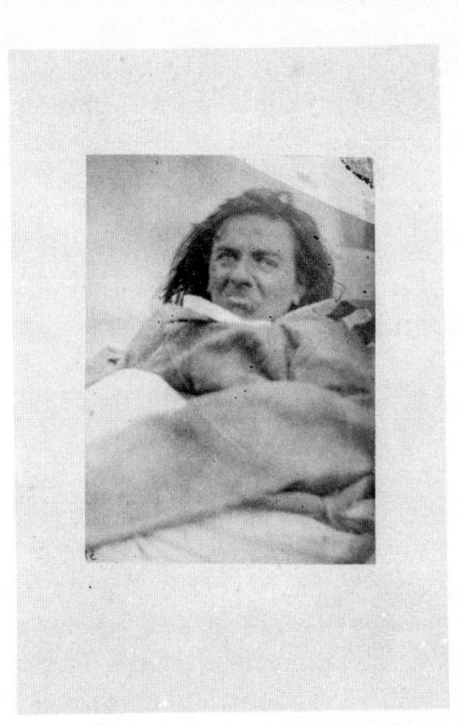

HYSTÉRO-ÉPILEPSIE : HALLUCINATION
RÉPUGNANCE

5.251   Flashes of color in the eyes, noises in the ears, a heavy smell. Visions, sounds, and smells combine in the moment like a chord—like a *discord*—to create in the imagination an overwhelming psychosomatic sense that something is terribly wrong with the world. And with that revolting idea pervading the mind, the body collapses.

Is it a kind of dream?

5.3   Here the musical idea of the epileptic aura as a discord of the senses reasserts the concept of Stink as the combined effects in the imagination of a *smelling sound* that may induce in the listener feelings of disgust bordering on dread.

5.31   If you are subject to musicogenic epileptic attacks, even imagining a certain tune or musical phrase has the power to bring on a seizure.[23] Imagine listening to the suspended D chord that rings out from Bernard Sumner's guitar at the beginning of Joy Division's "Love Will Tear Us Apart," or the oboe's melancholic phrase in the intro to Art Garfunkel's woeful "Bright Eyes." (This is the track my parents assigned to me as my "birth song," so it has a personal resonance to me for its evocation of mother's milk and dead rabbits.) How is it that such a seemingly innocuous sound could give rise to feelings so abysmal that one hears oneself screaming out in terror?

5.311   In his 1937 study, neurologist Macdonald Critchley gathered eleven such cases in which patients described seizures induced by auditory stimuli. Some of the musical triggers reported by his patients included Tchaikovsky's *La Casse-Noisette*, Strauss's *Thousand and One Nights*, and Wagner's opera *Lohengrin*.[24] Others described their triggers in much broader terms, such as "piano music," or "a brass wind instrument playing bass notes," or a "violent noise."[25] In nearly all cases, patients described feeling intense anxiety when listening to certain music while experiencing an epileptic aura. For some, this fear was experienced repeatedly whenever they heard the same particular piece, or a similar type of music that triggered their initial seizure. *Love will tear us apart … again.*

5.32   It's important to point out that the examples of musicogenic epilepsy described above—whereby an actual sound or piece of music heard in the real world induces a seizure—is different from auditory auras in which the sound one hears is not actually there. Examples abound in neuroscientific literature of epileptics hallucinating sounds of "humming," "hissing," "buzzing," "ringing," "rushing," and "swishing" in their ears.[26] This set of sounds might be grouped together in a lexicon of noise rather than music. (To be clear, this is not a negative value judgement of noise, or that noises cannot be constituted as music, as Paul Hegarty valiantly argues in his book *Noise/Music*; just that, in this instance, they are not organized in the mind as such.)[27] That is to say, each of these words is used to describe a sound that is *inarticulate*; of a quality of sound that cannot be further subdivided into distinct tones or phrases but appears in the imagination as a formless, unitary mass. What's more, these sounds (humming, hissing, buzzing, and so on—sounds that could be described as "static-like") imply a certain duration that is prolonged so as to be pervasive.

5.321 Regarding the co-occurrence of olfactory and auditory hallucinations, though their qualities are different, their combined emotional effect on the mind of the epileptic is the same: dread. This feeling of dread is caused by a dissonance between the (non)existence of sensory stimuli perceived within the external environment and the discrete sounds and smells perceived in the imagination.

5.33 Kant pointed out the difference between "the real" and "reality."[28] What this thought sounds like in the mind of the individual with epilepsy during an episode of phantosmia goes something like this: "The stink I'm sensing right now is not real. I know it's not real, and yet it *feels* real all the same." As Morton helpfully illustrates, the difference between the real and reality is that the reality is the "*feeling* that it's real."[29] Following on from Kant, Heidegger showed us how we perceive things in terms of "from where and through which" they originate. So, for instance, it's the fly we hear buzzing and not the "acoustic sensation" or "bare sound" of the buzzing itself.[30] In the same manner of speaking, then, when we say "I smell a stinkhorn," what we're really doing is giving prominence to the visual image of the mushroom itself as the smell-object, and not the cloud of malodorous molecules the mushroom emits.

5.331 As discussed in chapter two (*The Sight of the Stinkhorn*), in his pamphlet *The Description of the Phallus*, Hadrianus Junius demonstrates not only how the figure of the mushroom can be separated from the ground from which it emerges, but how the mushroom itself can be anatomized into its constituent parts: volva, shaft, glans, and so on. What's more, we can do this for other perceptual properties, such as the mushroom's texture, color, and even the quality of its sliminess. Its smell, however, cannot be so easily teased apart—at least, not by the nose alone. Although we know from lab experiments that the smell of a mature, fully ripe stinkhorn is composed of over twenty-two chemical compounds, this means nothing to the human nose when we sniff one out in the field. Even when armed with this information, it's not enough to change our object view of what it is we're smelling. We do not alter our perception to say "I smell a cloud of oligosulfides," for example. No, we still say, "I smell a stinkhorn." Our persistence in perceiving smells in terms of the physical thing the smell originates from is what Andreas Keller calls the "illusion of objecthood."[31]

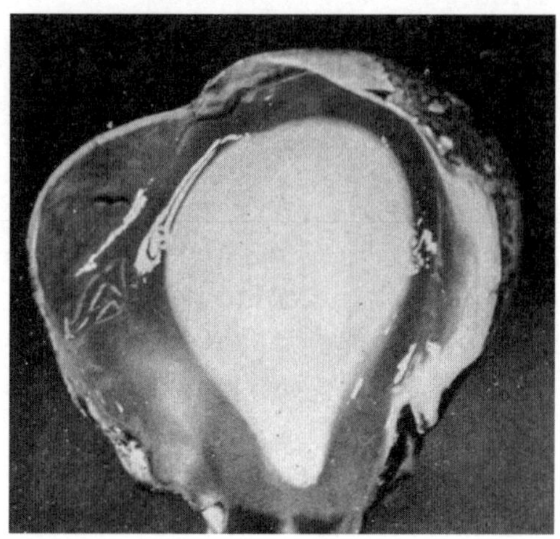

5.34   In his book *Philosophy of Olfactory Perception*, published in 2018, Keller argues that olfaction functions by detecting changes to our smell environment. We become quickly used to constant smells, so that when changes do occur, we become alert to them. It's this change itself, writes Keller, that we perceive as the smell object. But he warns against the usual metaphorical, visuocentric modes of comparing the way we see objects in space to the way we smell odors in the air. Keller: "The constant odor to which we are adapted, and therefore perceive only weakly, can be considered 'background odor.' Any change 'in front' of this background can then be considered an object. Olfactory objects, according to this description, are similar to auditory events."[32] What Keller means by "auditory events" are sounds that can be distinguished rising over and above other sounds. For sound, we call this amplitude, or loudness. For smell, we call it intensity. If a background noise is made up of a mix of frequencies occurring at the same time at low amplitude (a sonic presence, so to speak) then a background odor can be described as a mixture of smells sensed subtly together as a single mass. (As discussed in the previous chapter, the conflation of the sense of a constant sound and a pervasive smell, both background sound and background odor, could otherwise be described as *hums*.)

5.35   The residue of cooking smells, perfumes used in cleaning products, laundry liquids or furniture treatment, the concentration of yeasts or dampness in the air, and so on, most of the time we are oblivious to this mix of smells, so that the sudden appearance of a more intense odor is enough to punctuate its constancy. Someone walking through the room trailing dog shit on their shoes, the vapors of that cheese-smeared cracker as you raise it to your lips, the bad breath of an interlocutor as they move closer to make themselves heard … the stink appears, is observed, then passes through, or is subsumed, into the incessant background hum of the sensible world.

5.36   This phenomenon—where one perceives a change in smell while others remain constant—is what Keller calls the "olfactory perceptual object."[33] However, he warns us to resist the temptation of treating smells as objects. For if a change to a background hum can be said to constitute a "perceptual object," then any change, no matter how small, must also be considered an object. As a result, this definition of olfactory perception at once becomes meaningless. In the case of the phantom smell, however, I can segregate the "olfactory perceptual object" not just from the background hum of the train carriage, but from my entire phenomenology, so that the malodor in my mind appears as if emerging from a completely different external reality.

Uncus

5.4   The *OED* defines a hallucination as an experience "of an external object when no such object is actually present [...] distinguished from *illusion* in the strict sense, as not necessarily involving a false belief."[34] I believe the latter distinction to be significant. For in the case of a phantom smell, even though an external stimulus is not actually there, the reality is the *feeling* that the smell is there. I want to go one step further and say that a hallucinated stink has a source—albeit an internal one—in that the malodor originates, in the Heideggerian sense, "from" and "through" something in the real world.

5.41   So what is the source of the phantom smell, exactly? Let's be clear about what it's not. It's not burned rubber, or charred toast, or putrid meat, or fried onions. (Fried onions is the smell that precedes every seizure—an event also signaled by the ringing of a bell—reported by David Niven's character in the 1946 fantasy-romance film *A Matter of Life and Death*.)[35] It's not plastics or solvents. It's not an object at all, at least not in the material sense. But neither is it an *illusion*, for it does not imply a "false belief" in a thing. There's no spatial dimension to the phantom smell: it does not occupy space in the physical world, nor diffuse through the medium of the air. As such, you cannot move closer to its source and experience an increase in its intensity.

5.411   Instead of the source of the smell, let's try to describe its cause. Admittedly, the difference between the two words is subtle: *source* means that from which something originates, while *cause* means that which gives rise to something, such as an event or phenomenon. In the case of the stinkhorn, the cause and the source of the smell are ostensibly the same. As described in chapter three, these are principally a group of oligosulfides that become volatile when the mushroom ripens and its slimy, spore-carrying gleba begins to deliquesce. In the case of the phantom smell, however, there is no cloud of odor molecules floating through the air, nothing for the nose to smell. Rather, its cause is a surge of neurons misfiring deep in a part of the brain called the uncus. This gives rise to the term "uncinate fits," a type of sensory seizure strongly linked to temporal-lobe epilepsy, and typified by olfactory and auditory hallucinations.

5.42   *Uncus* means "hook," because of its curved, talon-like shape. It also resembles a phallus, or stinkhorn stipe, on its side. The uncus is located within the innermost part of the temporal lobe, just behind the ears. The temporal lobe is the part of the brain that functions to create conscious memories and preserve long-term ones. It's where we understand language, perceive objects, and process smell and taste sensations. The right temporal lobe—the nondominant lobe, and the site of my own seizures—is also where we become aware of music. It's where we process emotion, where we feel things. A disorder of this part of the brain, therefore, can result in momentary dysfunction of the imagination. Hence the sound-smell hallucinations and their weirding effects on the mind.

5.421   In MRI brain imaging, the uncus appears as a clearly defined black shadow with hard edges, easily distinguishable from the tangled mass around it. It's tempting, therefore, to identify the uncus as the source of the phantom stink, and of the buzzing or humming sounds that often accompany it. However, phenomenologically speaking, we know the uncus itself does not emit a cloud of odor molecules; neither does the malodor consist in vaporized bits of brain binding to our olfactory sensory neurons. Instead, the hallucination is the brain's best guess at what is, in fact, a momentary electrical disturbance in the uncus. Think of it like a synthesized stink. The perception of this smell is then measured against one's own autobiography of malodors smelled in the real world (burned rubber, putrid meat, fried onions, and so on). But even if we could trace the source of the phantom smell back to a simulation originating in the uncus, this doesn't explain why the hallucinated odor is perceived to be bad, or why the feeling it induces is so dreadful.

5.43   "What is present in phenomenology in olfaction depends on the background knowledge of the perceiver," writes Keller.[36] In other words, we each smell things differently depending on our own experience of the world. The specific character of the odor of a durian fruit, or fermented shark meat, or a stinkhorn, is therefore dependent on a hierarchy of experience beginning with whether or not we have previously encountered such objects in the flesh. Similarly, the stinkhorn's connotations of death and disease are only available to us if we have encountered the same malodorous matter (rotten animal carcass, dung) that the mushroom mimics. Otherwise, it is just *some kind of stinkiness*. And as Keller reminds us, *some kind of stinkiness* is not an object.[37]

5.44   In his book *Hallucinations*, Oliver Sacks observes how complex visual hallucinations are fueled by what the eyes have already seen: "One has to have seen people, faces, animals, landscapes to hallucinate them," writes Sacks.[38] But in the case of olfactory hallucinations, it appears a phantom can emerge seemingly from nowhere and without suggestion. This implies that either our brains can hallucinate completely novel smells that we have never encountered before in the real world, or, as Sacks suggests, that some smell hallucinations are so complex, so *weird*, that they are unavailable to language.[39]

> Some hallucinated smells may be impossible to describe because they are different from anything ever experienced in the real world, and evoke no memories or associations. New, unprecedented experiences can be a hallmark of hallucinations, for when the brain is released from the constraints of reality, it can generate any sound, image, or smell in its repertoire, sometimes in complex and "impossible" combinations.[40]

As discussed above, one's perception of the stink of a stinkhorn is dependent on whether we have previously encountered one in the flesh together with our knowledge of its ecology, such as its symbiosis with insects, its mimicry of other smells in nature such as carrion and shit, each of which have their own string of attachments. But the phantom smell is potentially free from such attachments, free from the limitations of language even. It therefore offers us the possibility of a pure, uninhibited, unmediated sensory experience.

5.441   Extending Sacks's point further, there is another view that suggests there exists in each of us a bank of smell memories inherited from early on in our species' development and hardwired into

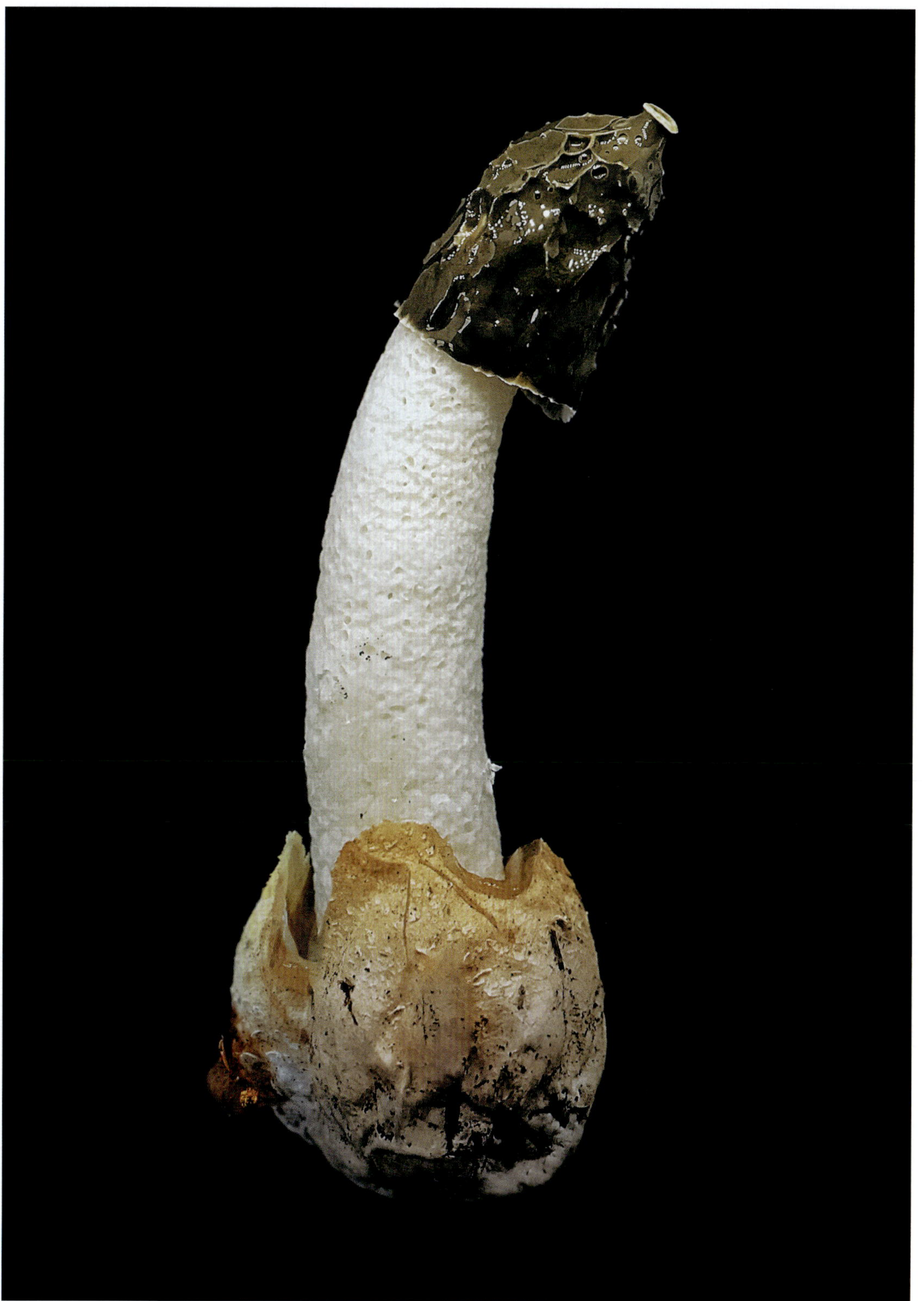

Common stinkhorn *Phallus impudicus*.

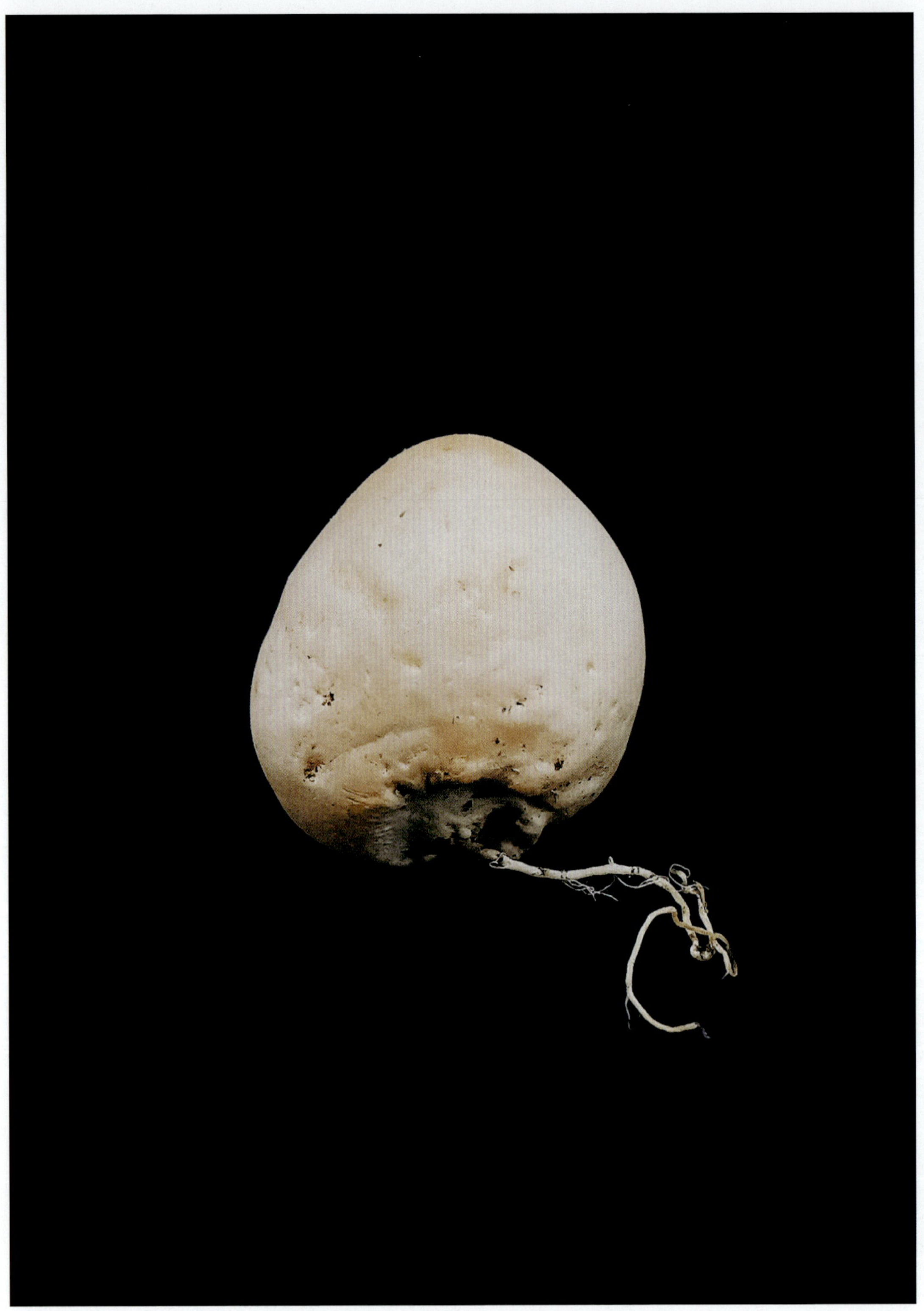

Immature stinkhorn volva, or "witch's egg."

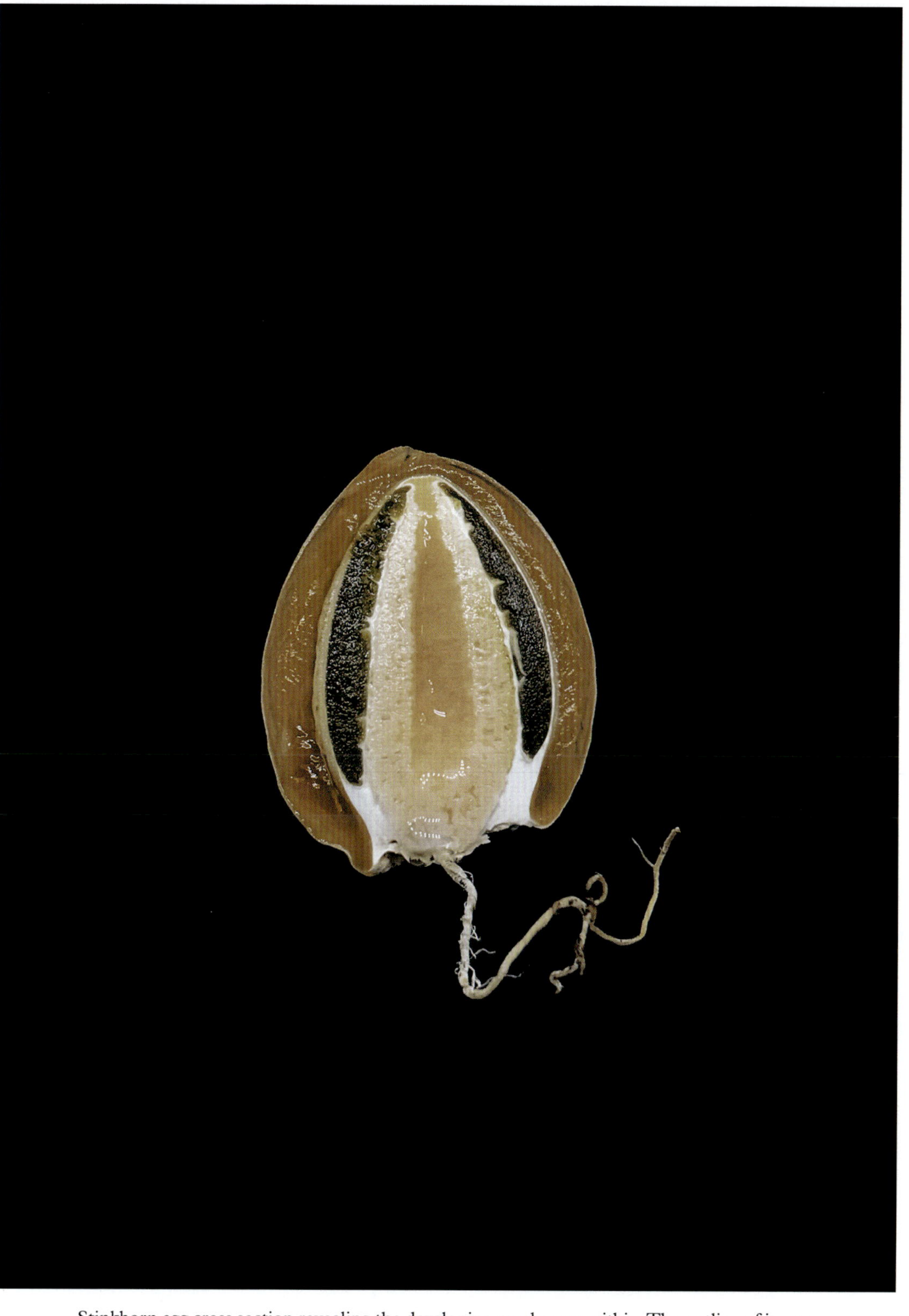

Stinkhorn egg cross section revealing the developing mushroom within. The outline of its cap is visible by the greenish-brown gleba, which is covered in a thick translucent mucus.

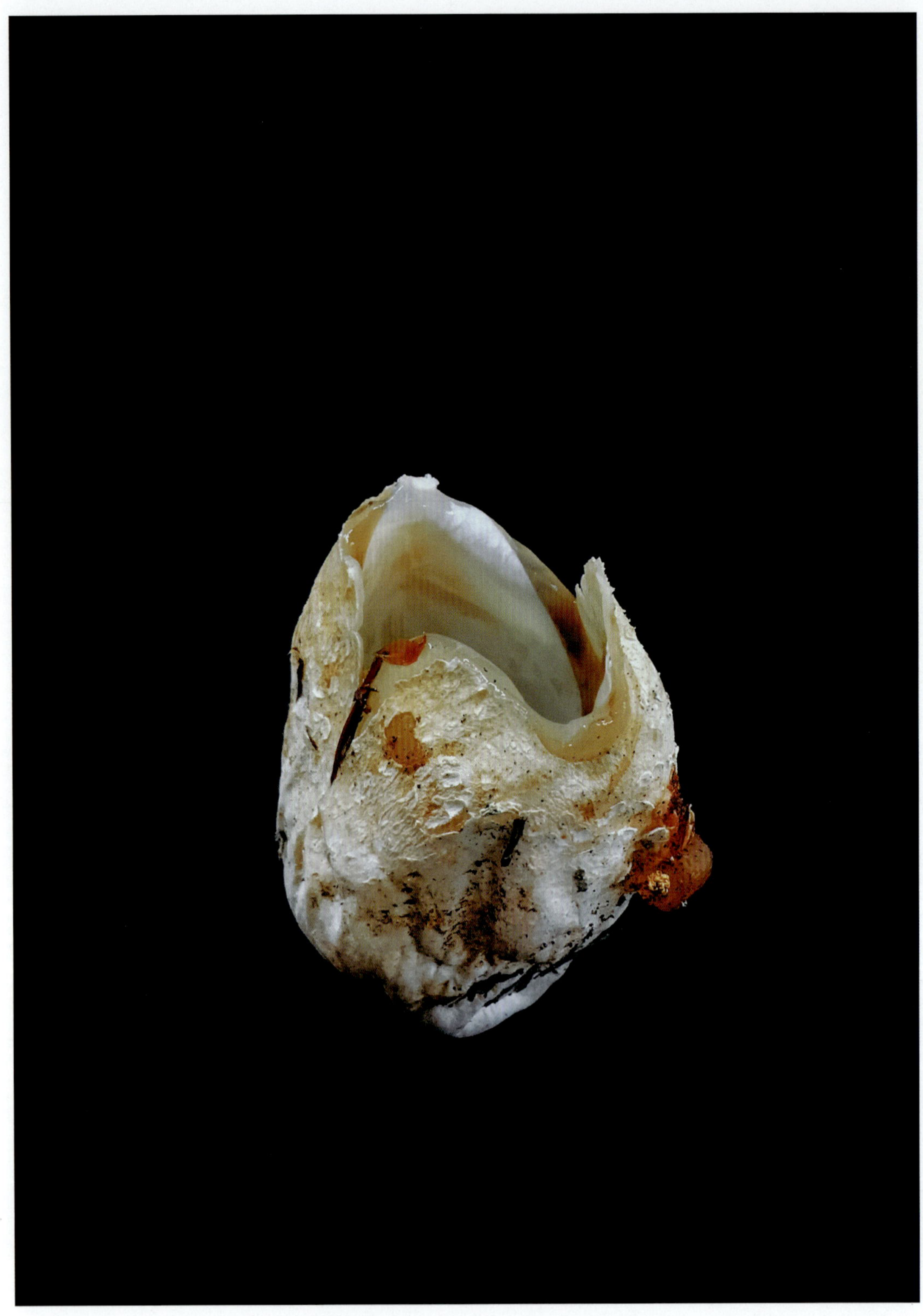

Ripe stinkhorn volva with stipe removed.

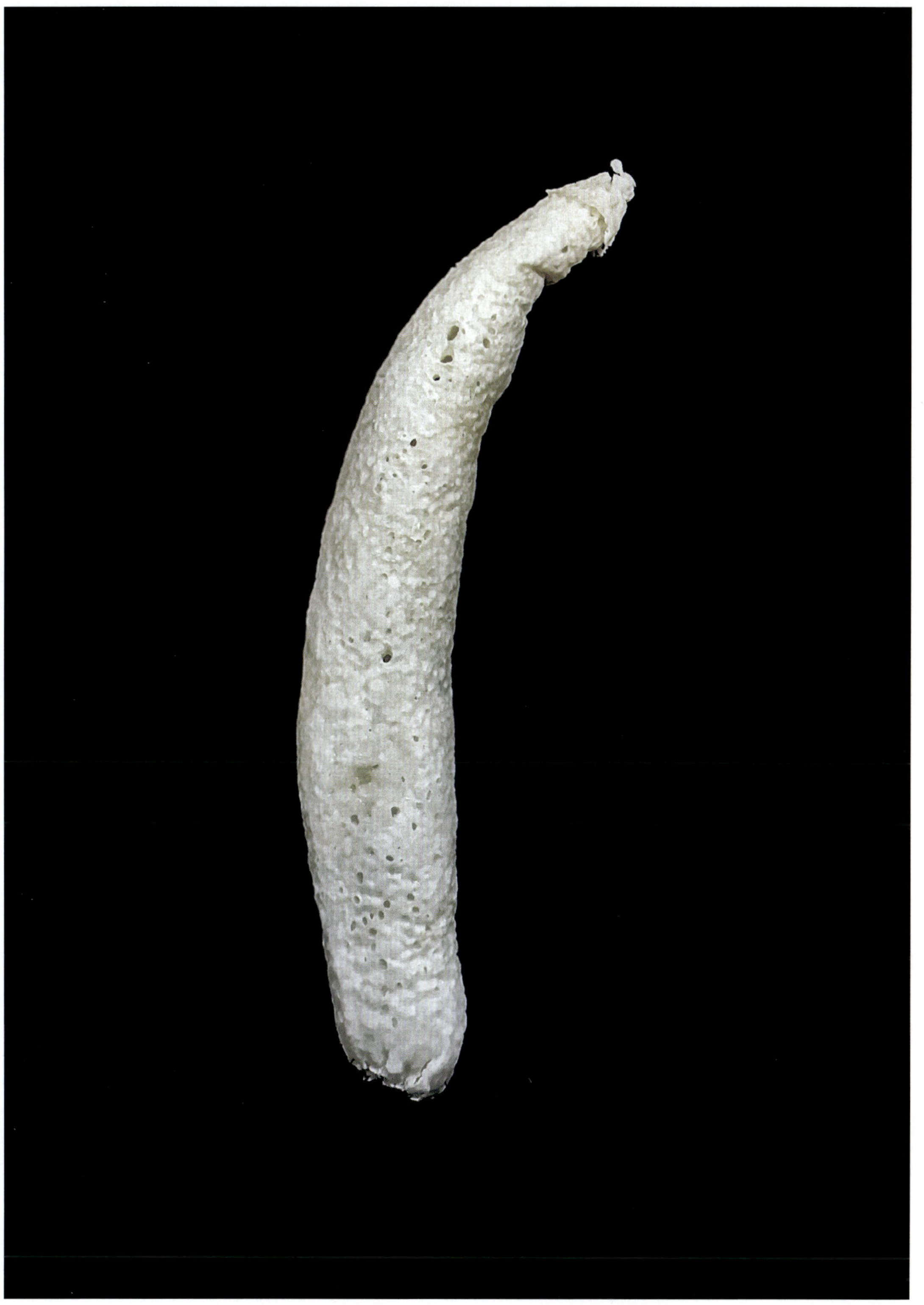

Stinkhorn stipe, or shaft, separated from its volva and cap.

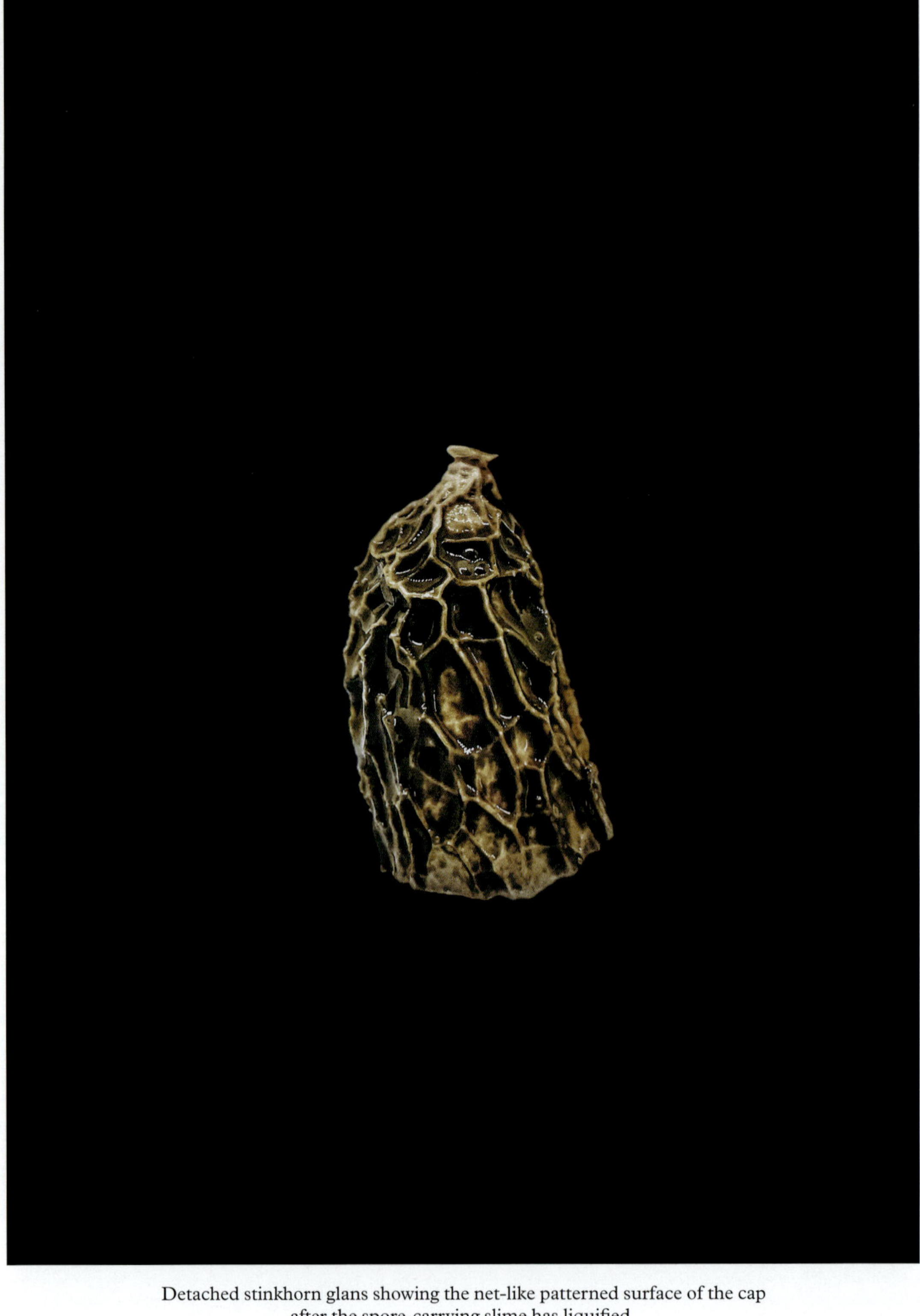

Detached stinkhorn glans showing the net-like patterned surface of the cap
after the spore-carrying slime has liquified.

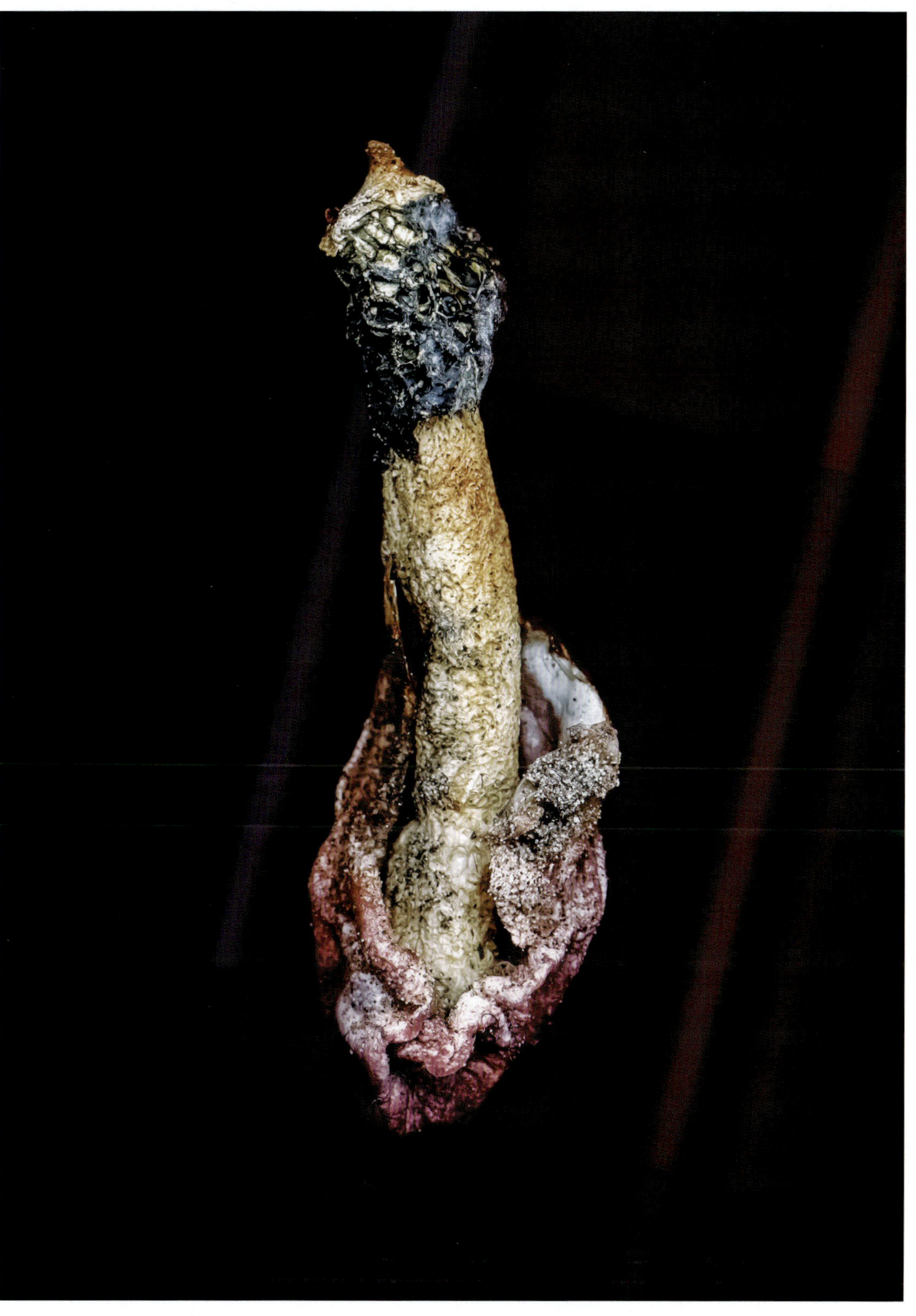

An overripe, strongly spermatic-smelling dune stinkhorn *Phallus hadriani* with loose-hanging,
violet-colored volva. A fuzzy white mold can be seen beginning to develop on its cap.
(Digital scan by Siôn Parkinson, 2022.)

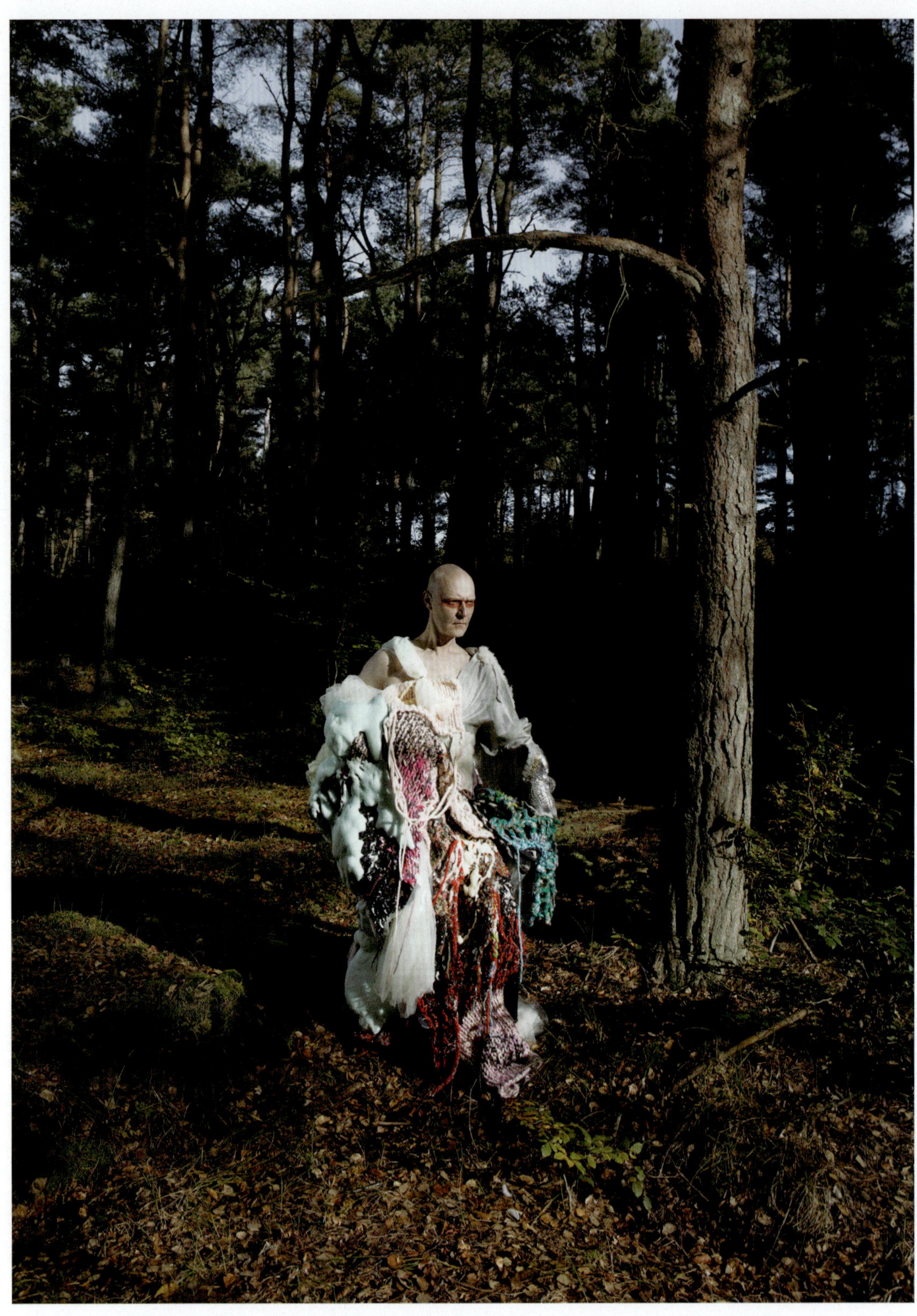

Siôn Parkinson in a stinkhorn-inspired dress, designed and constructed for him by
fashion designer Matty Bovan for a performance at Somerset House, London, 2020.
(Photograph by Donald Milne, 2020.)

our limbic system, smells that we can access only in moments of psychosis or seizure. These are not learned smells. That is, they've not been acquired though personal experience or informed through ancestral knowledge, but are completely independent from the evolution of humankind. In this way, the primitive smell memory, resurrected in the moment of phantosmia, is more like an atavism, a throwback to some point early on in the history of our existence on earth when we were simple, unicellular organisms that relied upon scent alone to navigate the world.

Shit sniffers

5.5   Freud suggests that the atrophy of human sense of smell started when our species first stood upright so that our noses were at a remove from the ground where smells are most concentrated: "The beginning of the fateful process of civilization, then, would have been marked by man's adopting of an erect posture. From then on, the chain of events proceeded, by way of the devaluation of the olfactory stimuli."[41] Freud's use of "erect" is a pun, conflating human verticalization with (male) sexual arousal and the phallus.

5.51   The withering of our olfactory sense along with our increased repulsion at the stench of others is what distinguishes us from other animals, writes Freud, who do not shun their shit but revel in it.[42] It's at this moment of erection that we ceased to be, as the French say, *renifleurs*, "sniffers."

5.511   An aside: if the renifleur is, indeed, unashamed of their love for the stench of their own piss and shit, then the civilized, upstanding human animal is, by Freud's definition, an example of some semifictional, semiflaccid mushroom-man species *Phallus pudicus*, or "shamefaced phallus." (From the Latin *pudicus* we get *pudendum*, a word for a person's external genitals, especially the vulva; literally "part to be ashamed of.")

5.512   In psychiatry, a renifleur is a person with a morbid fascination with foul smells, particularly for sexual gratification. In his notes on the Rat Man from 1909, Freud identifies his patient as such, commenting in a footnote that "in his childhood he had been subject to strong coprophilic [shit-loving] propensities."[43] Freud returns to this theory twenty years later, suggesting that in the history of hygiene, our compulsion to eradicate bad smells—specifically the smell of shit—might have had a repressive effect on the role of olfaction and sexuality in our lives.[44] He adds that "evolutionary progress notwithstanding, human beings hardly find the smell of their own excrement offensive—only that of others."[45] Our feeling of disgust is, therefore, proportionate to the degree of externality a stimulus may appear to us. It's not just the smell of any old shit we find disgusting, but the smell of someone else's shit. Someone else's shit is a stink doubly externalized, and thus twice removed from our own inner experience. Your shit will always stink more than mine. Period. According to this argument, the more outside of ourselves the source of a smell is, the more it stinks. Parents of newborn babies will know this feeling all too well, somehow finding the odors of their own children's excrement perfectly acceptable while gagging at the stench of someone else's child's shit-filled pants.

5.52   How does the condition of externality square with the phantom Stink, which, on the surface, appears to come from an entirely *internal* source, the dysfunctional mind? The answer appears to be a synthesis of multiple elements combined in the moment. They include the sheer unexpectedness of the stink, which is experienced as a violation of the background hum of the sensible world, along with the smell's novelty, intensity, and the mind's ability to distinguish it from other odors weakly perceived in the ambient environment. The latter does not mean the stink suddenly appears "in front of" this ambient environment, and therefore more proximate to our sensory experience. Quite the opposite. The interpretation of the smell as being discordant with our phenomenology means we imagine it originating from someplace entirely outwith the physical world. As such, even though the source of the smell may be very intimate indeed—the very center of the brain, the uncus—the *feeling* is of absolute externality to the point where the odor appears other-worldly. And it's this Otherness that makes it appear stinking.

5.521   The phantom stink yearns for a time when we crawled about on all fours, when we too were renifleurs. As Adorno and Horkheimer remark:

> In the ambiguous partialities of the sense of smell the old nostalgia for what is lower lives on, the longing for immediate union with surrounding nature, with earth and slime. Of all the senses the act of smelling, which is attracted without objectifying, reveals most sensuously the urge to lose oneself in identification with the Other. That is why smell, as both the perception and the perceived—which are one in the act of olfaction—is more expressive than other senses. When we see we remain who we are, when we smell we are absorbed entirely.[46]

The dysfunctional brain pierces the membrane that separates the long-forgotten primordial Stink. Though we cannot objectify or name it, we can still feel it, lose ourselves in it, for a moment shrug off our restrictive, civilizing faculties in favor of a deeper, fantastically crude knowledge of "earth and slime."

"No more aroma in matter"

5.6   Though there is no external source of the phantom stink, as I have argued, this does not mean that the feeling of the perception of the smell is necessarily "false," or that the malodor itself originates from nothing. Conversely, I've tried to illustrate how the phantom stink in fact originates *from* and *through* something. Whether that's an overload of abnormal electrical activity happening behind the ear, or the synthesized emissions of the uncus, or whether it has its roots in an ancient smell-memory—or a combination of all of these—the phantom stink (and when co-occurring with a hallucinated sound, a Stink with a capital "S") should be considered a reality in that it feels real. What's more, the phantom stink is potentially a proto-stink, a pure stink. Surpassing even nostalgia, it's a stink as yet unmediated by language and unprejudiced by autobiographical connotations or cultural associations. It's a stink because of its extreme externality, bypassing the nose and the phenomenological world to appear in the mind as something doubly strange, a *weird weird*.

5.61   Since my diagnosis of epilepsy a few years back, I feel as if I've been granted a special insight by which I'm able to spot affinities between myself and other artists and authors whose work, I can intuit, is inflected by sensory revelations as a result of their own peeks behind the curtain. "Definitely an epileptic," I'll think to myself after hearing a certain section of music or reading a passage of prose that seems to play in the space between ecstasy and dread. Most times I'm proven wrong, guilty of trying to find too much meaning in what are rather small and smeared reflections of my own morbid and excessive interest in my illness. I admit it's a silly, reductive, and potentially dangerous exercise. But sometimes I'm right. Or, if not epilepsy, then some other relatable condition or exquisite episode that could be said to have awakened the artist's mind to an "extraordinary intensification of self-awareness," as Dostoevsky called it.[47]

5.62   I had this feeling most intensely when reading Emil Cioran's collection of philosophical aphorisms, *A Short History of Decay*, first published in 1949. (Cioran did not have epilepsy, as it turns out, but famously did suffer from insomnia his whole life, a tortuous condition that permeated his writing.)[48] In a section titled "Indefinite Horror," Cioran writes about the "approach of disgust" as the moment where the human mind becomes most alert to itself and its separateness to the rest of the world.[49] In these moments, disgust is the symptom of discord: between the mind and the body, between health and unhealth. The following passage, which, like much of Cioran's writing has an odor of dead flowers about it, is the closest in tone to what I've encountered in my own experiences of phantosmia. It's necessary to quote it at length:

> It is not the outbreak of a specific evil which reminds us of our fragility: there are vaguer but more troublesome warnings to signify our imminent excommunication from the temporal. The approach of disgust, of that sensation which physiologically separates us from

the world, shows how destructible is the solidity of our instincts or the consistency of our attachments. In health, our flesh echoes the universal pulsation and our blood reproduces its cadence; in disgust, which lies in wait for us like a potential hell in order to suddenly seize upon us afterwards, we are as isolated in the whole as a monster imagined by some teratology of solitude.

The critical point of our vitality is not disease—which is struggle—but that indefinite horror which rejects everything and strips our desires of the power to procreate new mistakes. The senses lose their sap, the veins dry up, and the organs no longer perceive anything but the interval separating them from their own functions. Everything turns insipid: provender and dreams. No more aroma in matter and no more enigma in meditations; gastronomy and metaphysics both become victims of our want of appetite. We spend hours waiting for other hours, waiting for the moments which no longer flee time, the faithful moments which reinstate us in the mediocrity of health [...] and the amnesia of its dangers.[50]

5.621   Several things jump out. Disgust itself as the "monster" waiting to seize the mind (*epilepsy* literally means "to seize upon" or "take possession of").[51] There are the vague "troublesome warnings" that echo the premonitory signs of the sensory, gustatory, and psychic auras, and the "approach of disgust" like the cold breeze rising from the stomach. The "excommunication with the temporal" as the dreamy state or double consciousness of the focal-aware epileptic. "No more aroma in matter" as both the smell hallucination itself, and the olfactory distortions that follow a seizure (and read in the context of post-COVID recovery, as the nauseating effects of anosmia and our "want of appetite"). And finally, the episode of amnesia that erases the experience of one's seizure and returns us to the oblivion of so-called good health.

5.63   If there's any benefit to having epilepsy it is this: the feeling of being more attuned to a world rich in sound and scent, even if those ecstatic sensations shortly give way to disgust and dread. Through chance or meditation, I've become increasingly alert to how thin the skin is that separates one thing from another, both within the external world of objects and the internal world of the imagination. Such was the feeling I had moments before an epileptic attack while standing in a clearing in Wistman's Wood in Dartmoor, England, in the summer of 2020, the damp, musty air emanating from ancient oaks, the sound of my own breath muffled by a fist-thick mass of moss, lichen, liverworts, and fungi, and where I felt for two precious seconds what Dostoevsky—that most famous of epileptics—described as "the presence of the eternal harmony perfectly attained."[52] The sensation of Stink that fast replaced it, though equally potent and revelatory, was by comparison utterly inconsequential.

Epilogue: Stinkhorns as medicine

5.7   Since the sixteenth century, there has long been a belief among certain cultures and folk traditions of the therapeutic benefits of eating, smearing, or wearing about the body stinkhorns in order to ameliorate all manner of ailments. Carolus Clusius (1601), for example, describes how he'd been presented with several specimens of stinkhorn eggs in Amsterdam and that they were always so cold to touch that he felt a certain numbness [*torpor*] in his hands.[53] The numbing effect of what French botanist Étienne Pierre Ventenat (1798) describes as the "viscous, fetid liquor" contained within a fresh stinkhorn egg (which is in fact pretty odorless) was widely believed at the time to be an excellent topical treatment for gout and rheumatism, conditions that both cause swelling, stiffness, and pain in the joints. Other healing powers historically attributed to stinkhorns include their efficacy in treating gangrenous wounds, skin cancer, and—weirder and weirder—epilepsy.

5.71   At this, I think back to a comment made to me by psychiatrist Alain Sebille: "It's funny that you were thinking so hard about phallic-shaped mushrooms [...] around the time when you experienced your first olfactory hallucination." The synchronicity of stinkhorns in the mind—not as a cure, but as a cause for my epileptic seizures—seems to me remarkable in this context.

5.72   Although none of the claims for stinkhorns as medicine have been substantiated by recent evidence, it's easy to see how pharmacopeial superstitions regarding the specific use of stinkhorn mucus to relieve skin irritations, wounds, and swollen joints persisted in the early modern period. The clear, sticky, jelly-like substance that surrounds and protects the embryonic stinkhorn is of a similar consistency and appearance to aloe vera, the leaf pulp of aloe plants long used for its anti-inflammatory properties. When a stinkhorn egg is plucked straight from the ground and its rubbery skin sliced open, the glutinous insides that spill out onto one's fingers and hands do indeed appear strangely cool to touch, a quality Junius himself comments upon in his pamphlet. The coolness of the volva's mucilage might go some way to explaining the palliative use of immature stinkhorn eggs in treating gout or other ulcerated lesions, say. But what about their supposed use as a "cure" for epilepsy?

5.73   Pinpointing the first reference connecting stinkhorns to epilepsy is by no means straightforward. Various authors writing today about stinkhorns seem to repeat the same list of afflictions reputedly remedied by the fungus, sometimes with erectile dysfunction thrown in.[54] This same line—that stinkhorns are "reputed to cure epilepsy, gout, and rheumatism"—appears in dozens of chapters, articles, and online blog posts about the mushroom. Beyond this, any specific, historical reference to stinkhorns and their therapeutic potential for epilepsy becomes hazy.

5.731   The earliest mention of any mushroom in connection to epilepsy I can find is in Pliny's *Natural History* (completed in 77 CE), in which the author advises the use of a small amount of white agaric mushroom infused in vinegar and honey (oxymel) as a cure for epilepsy.[55] However, in his *Advice for an Epileptic Boy* (written around 190 CE), Claudius Galen warns of the dangers of inducing seizures as a result of eating foods with a "viscous or cold, thick juice," such as oysters, cartilaginous fish, bulbous roots, snails, cheese, cucumber, and eggs, before claiming mushrooms to be the worst.[56] Mushrooms should be avoided at all costs, advises Galen. He goes on to qualify that the epileptic "may have plenty of such food as contains something sharp and pungent, and which does not obviously engender bad humors nor has a smell which might affect the head."[57]

5.732   According to Galen's hypothesis, a development of Hippocrates's Theory of Humors, all matter consists of four elements: fire (hot and dry); air or vapors (hot and wet); water (cold and wet); and earth (cold and dry). These elements are reflected in four vital fluids contained within the human body: black bile, yellow bile, blood, and phlegm. Good health, per Galen's theory, depends on these humors being maintained in balanced combination, or harmony. The thickening of the humors may worsen or exacerbate certain conditions, including epilepsy. Galen described mushrooms as being potentially catastrophic in this regard, describing them thus: "Among all foods, the mushroom has the coldest humor, the most viscous, and at the same time the thickest."[58] Following his philosophy of "*contraria contrariis curantur*" (opposites are the cure of opposites) Galen would've surely taken issue with stinkhorns as a dietetic remedy for epilepsy because of the fungus's ability to affect the head with its deathly smell, along with the cold, sticky goop from which it is delivered into the world from the moist earth.

What eats, or licks, around itself

5.8   The theory that certain visual or smelly properties of plants and fungi may be a clue to their curative powers is called the Doctrine of Signatures. According to this belief, when creating diseases a benign God would surely have also peppered the natural world with signs to mark an individual plant or fungus's corresponding function. It was inevitable, therefore, that the phallic stinkhorns should be recommended as an aphrodisiac.

5.81   Writing in 1982, W.P.K. Findlay states, "Even until quite recently in Germany, [stinkhorns were] given to cattle to render them fertile; and in some tropical countries the ash from burnt stinkhorns was applied to the genitalia of infertile women."[59] No doubt stinkhorn eggs' resemblance to swollen, semen-bursting testicles was yet another clue to the mushroom's erotic, invigorating powers for humans and animals. As one German trade and industry guide (published in 1920) recommends, dried stinkhorn eggs can be used by farmers as a "jumping aid" [*Sprungmittel*] for breeding livestock.[60] I've read in a number of other sources that in German folklore the word for stinkhorn eggs is *Hirschbrunst* or *Hirschbrunft*, which loosely translates into English as "stag's lust."[61] In their *Encyclopedia of Mushrooms*, Colin Dickinson and John Lucas claim that the name *Hirschbrunft* arose from "local hunters' belief that these toadstools grew where stags had rutted."[62] The etymology of the word *Brunft*, meaning "rutting-time," combines the sense of "heat" (as in the fires of sexual desire) plus a curious sonic nuance that mimics the low, continuous grumbling noises the stag makes when crying out for a mate, and their subsequent grunting during sex. *Brunft* is connected to the Middle High German word *brummen* meaning to "hum, buzz, growl," which itself is thought to derive from the Latin verb *fremere*, "to make an inarticulate sound, murmur."[63] Implicit in the *mm* sound is the deep vibrating noise of fucking—of deer in the dark calling out to fuck or be fucked—a sound that can be heard from miles away, and marked in damp patches for days after.

5.811   The Doctrine of Signatures theory was developed and popularized in central Europe in the Middle Ages by the Swiss physician and philosopher Theophrastus von Hohenheim, better known by their Latin name Paracelsus (1493–1541). In contrast to the Galenic principle that "opposites cure opposites," the Paracelsian view of the Doctrine of Signatures proposed that "like cures like." Early modern medicine favored sympathetic qualities or characteristics rather than antipathetic ones expressed by Galen. An excellent example of this sympathetic view—that certain morphological features of an individual plant, herb, or fungus may reflect its pharmaceutical purpose—is skull moss.

5.82   Starting sometime around the 1550s and lasting for about two hundred years, there was throughout parts of Central and Northern Europe a belief among physicians and apothecaries that "moss" scraped from a deceased human skull—preferably skulls of those who had died prematurely or violently, especially strangulated criminals)—"fetched its weight in gold" as a cure for epilepsy.[64] (There is a link between stinkhorns and crime also. In parts of Europe, it was thought that if a stinkhorn were to grow upon the grave, it was a sign that the deceased had died unpunished for their crimes.) In John Gerard's *Herball* (1597), his largely plagiarized translation of Dodoens's *Cruydeboeck* (first published in Flemish in 1554), Gerard inserts a reproduction of a truly bizarre illustration by another botanist, Jacobus Theodorus, otherwise called Tabernaemontanus. Even in its original context, this image sits strangely alongside the more than two thousand plant illustrations in Tabernaemontanus's volume, *Eicones plantarum seu stirpium* (published in 1590, the same year the author died).

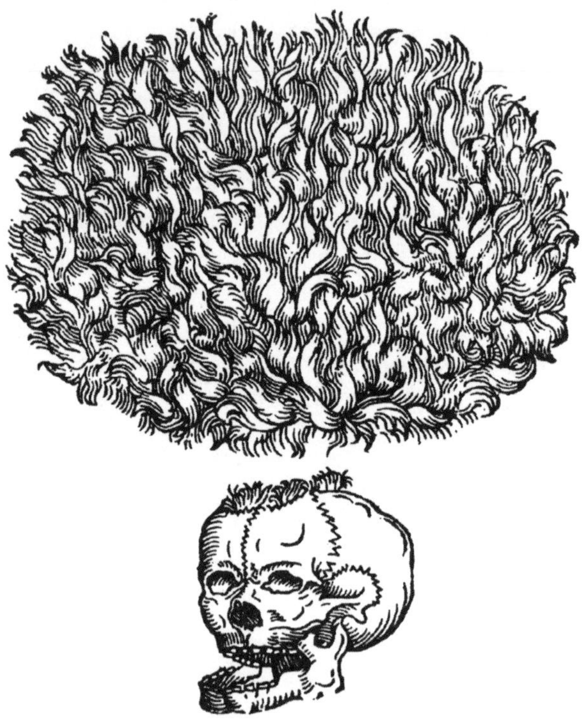

5.83   The image shows a human skull, its lower jaw drawn with extreme underbite, with what appears to be three tufts of hair growing from its crown. One of these tufts is shown in detail, floating in the air above the skull like a thought bubble, or disembodied (hairy)

brain. With its concentration of wavy lines like cartoon plumes of fire smoke, or dark, poisonous vapors—a perfume cloud separate from, and yet connected to the head itself—it's a brilliantly succinct visual representation of the quality and explosive intensity of a phantosmic epilepsy aura.

5.84   The hovering hairball in Tabernaemontanus's picture is in fact a depiction of a type of fruticose, or "bushy," lichen that typically grows on the surface of old bones. Paracelsus called it *usnea*.[65] Precisely what species of lichen portrayed in this image, or described in other pharmacopeia of the time, is not entirely clear. Speculations by present-day writers range from the shield lichen *Parmelia saxatilis* to the oakmoss *Evernia prunastri*.[66] (Oakmoss is a traditional ingredient used in perfumery dating back centuries due to its fixative powers and redolent notes of "damp forest." However, since 2017 it has been all but banned in the E.U., and its use heavily restricted worldwide since 2020, because of the risk of skin rashes it may cause.) But what's more important than identifying the exact species of lichen is the concatenation of discrete, observable elements in the moment; that is, of what, where, and how the fungus-encrusted skull must've appeared to the sixteenth-century physician and the (visual) traits they found in common with certain parts of the dysfunctional, or diseased, human body.

5.85   Paracelsus believed that after death, a body left to decay in the open air allows the vital spirit, or "Mumie," to concentrate in the skull.[67] A prolonged period of exposure to the elements sloughs off the deceased's hair and head skin to reveal a smooth, dry cranium, upon which—like the theory of the spontaneous generation of flies—magically develops a patch of crusty or leaflike growths. The liquor of the brain dries up and is transferred to the external world in wrinkled clumps of moss, indexical of damp, boggy places, that sprout out of the skull bone's milky white envelope. In this way, the site and morphology of skull lichen (*lichen*: literally "what eats, or licks, around itself") is sympathetic to the epileptic brain in the moment of seizure and its localized spurt of cortical neurons.

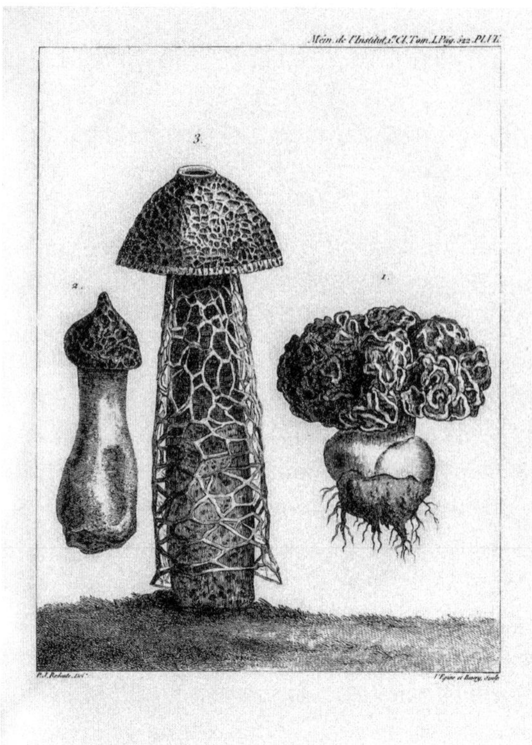

Thelma, Thelma

5.9   Despite my being unable to precisely locate in the literature the first mention of stinkhorns as a miracle cure for epilepsy, we can see from the above how folk superstitions, infused with the humoral theories of ancient and early modern medicine, could have so easily been influenced by a superficial reading of the corporeal mushroom in nature. There's the smooth, creamy-white surface of the stinkhorn peridium poking up through the earth like a bulging fetal skull. There's the cold, thick jelly that squirts out of the slit in its crown as if an excess of intracranial phlegm exiting a trepanned burr hole scraped into the fontanelle. There's the reticulated cap of the mature mushroom raised upon its bony stalk (known in German as the "corpse's finger" [*Leichenfinger*]), which, once bare of its slime, is decidedly brain-like. Then there's the invisible specter of dung and death—the "mumial spirit"—an echo of the potent smell aura that presages a generalized seizure.[68] And creeping about its base are beetles and slugs, and in the air a dense cloud of flies, insects everywhere, concentrated together only to split apart and scatter again like so many disordered thoughts.

5.91   The only remaining question I have is this. Say the stinkhorn *is* a cure for epilepsy. How should one take it? By ingesting it? Dried, powdered, and drunk (presumably with vinegar)? Or eaten fresh and whole? By smearing its green slime upon one's scalp? Or simply by inhaling its ripe gas whenever one starts to feel funny, like smelling salts?

5.92   The latter suggestion may not be as ridiculous as it sounds. In 1956, the neurologist Robert Efron reported "astonishing success" in the use of strong, unpleasant odors (an ancient theory developed in 1881 by groundbreaking English neurologist William Gowers) during the sensory aura stage of an epileptic attack in some patients—especially those who experienced phantosmia—in halting seizures spreading to other parts of the brain.[69] In his investigation, Efron presented one such patient, Mrs. T. B., a professional singer in her early forties, with vials of hydrogen sulfide (rotten eggs) which she was encouraged to sniff "just *before* the 'half-way point'" of her attack when she would typically anticipate an olfactory aura together with the hallucinated sound of a voice calling her name, "Thelma, Thelma."[70] Details within Mrs. T. B.'s story of her smell seizures are astonishingly close to my own experience of phantosmia, which she explains in precise, illuminating prose. Maybe it's because she is a singer and therefore more attuned to sound and silence that I feel a certain affinity with her account, which is worth quoting here at length:

> At the half-way point [...] I get a funny idea in my head. It is hard to put into words. It is just that I expect to smell something any moment [...]. The first time it ever happened, I was out in the country and I was feeling funny. I was in a field picking forget-me-nots. [...] For

about half an hour I kept sniffing them because I was sure they would begin to smell soon. I was somehow expecting them to smell even though I knew perfectly well at that time that forget-me-nots have no odour at all. When I'm getting this feeling of a smell coming I'm so far away from the world that I almost don't know I'm so remote, but yet a corner of my mind still knows I'm remote. I know it and I don't know it at the same time. It is so intense that I don't seem to be aware of anything but this feeling of remoteness and the feeling that the smell is coming. This feeling gets worse and worse and I seem to be floating away. Yet I know what is happening all the time. I can read and talk but I don't like it. [...]

Then, just when I seem to be as remote as I possibly could get I suddenly get a smell like an explosion or a crash. There is no buildup. It is there at once. At the same moment that the smell crashes through, I'm back in the real world—I no longer feel remote. The smell is a disgusting sweet, penetrating odour like very cheap perfume. I just stop when I smell it. Everything seems very quiet. I don't know if I can hear. I am all alone with the smell. I don't think this lasts for more than a few seconds and then the smell rapidly goes away. Then I find myself almost normal except that it still seems very quiet. This quietness lasts about five to ten seconds but I'm really not sure. Then I hear a voice off to the right calling my name, 'Thelma, Thelma.' It keeps calling. This is not like hearing a voice in a dream. It is a *real* voice.[71]

Mrs. T. B. concludes by explaining how the voice calling her name, which she describes as neither male nor female, is "irresistible," and that when her head is finally compelled to turn towards the source of the sound on the right, it is with a jerk. "That's it," she says. "I'm out. I have a convulsion after that."[72]

5.921   The mention of forget-me-nots (the genus name *Myosotis* is from Greek meaning "mouse's ear" because of the blossom's petals resembling a furry rodent ear—another nonhearing ear) is intriguing, a potential smell source that she knows is odorless, yet which over a prolonged period of repeated sniffing she almost wills into smelling, as if performing a conjuration of spirits. The sound of the hallucinated voice repeating the word "Thelma, Thelma," is itself imbued with a murmuring, muted quality: starting with the voiceless dental fricative *th*, and ending in the bilabial nasal *ma*, it is a name willed by teeth and lips. Spatially oriented to the right, but still unattached to a body or gender, the sound—like the disgusting smell that immediately precedes it—is nevertheless "*real*," as she emphasizes in italics.

5.922   Efron's experiment to halt Mrs. T. B.'s seizures by administering a foul-smelling substance at the "half-way point" was repeated several times. In the majority of occasions, the introduction of the smell effectively interrupted an attack from developing into a tonic-clonic (*grand mal*) seizure. After testing other smelly stimuli, including amyl nitrate (dirty socks), ethyl butyrate (overripe pineapple), plus a solution of skatole (a sickly-sweet aroma found in human and animal shit, as well as in flowering plants that mimic the smell of dung, such as the voodoo lily *Typhonium venosum*), Efron concluded that "it was thus apparent that any powerful, unpleasant odour would abort a seizure."[73] With this information, suddenly the supernatural idea of poking the fetid tip of a ripe stinkhorn under the nose of a person with epilepsy as an antagonist to a developing seizure seems very plausible indeed.

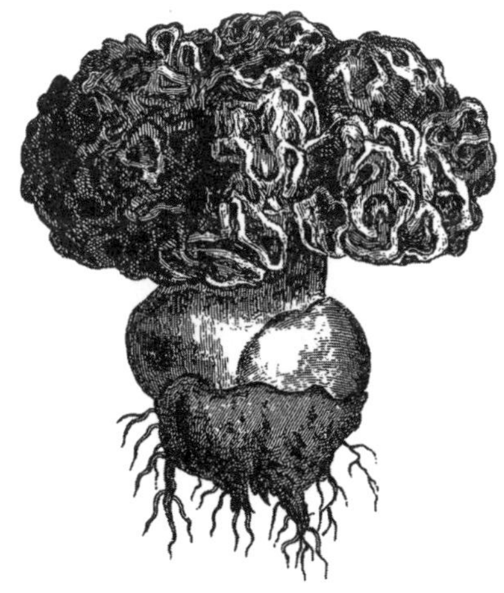

6. Conclusion

The more you know them, the less sure you feel about identifying them. Each one is itself. Each mushroom is what it is—its own center. It's useless to pretend to know mushrooms. They escape your erudition.

—John Cage, *For the Birds*

Mushrooming

6.1   At the time of writing, there's been something of a mushroom renaissance in the arts and humanities. Mushrooms as metaphors are thick on the ground. The mushroom as the horror of Otherness. The mushroom as not-knowing. The mushroom as creative impulse. The mushroom as exemplar of connectivity and collaborative spirit, and so on. Whether its professional jealousy, artistic territorialism, or the curse of a short attention span, I must admit, I worry that I'm beginning to tire of all these mushroom metaphors going around with overblown promises of saving our species. However, I'm still surprised and heartened by how often a new book, artwork, film, or other imaginative approach to mycological thinking will rise above the others to carry me off once again into the forest or sand hills in search of a new idea of my own. This book is the result of one such adventure.

6.11   "To mushroom" means to go out in search of fungi. It describes an intrepid and passionate project, one that, if you're lucky, ends in a prize. But the word has another less favorable meaning. When we talk about something "mushrooming," we mean the rapid increase or spread of a usually disastrous series of events. The term is used metaphorically to invoke the shape of a typical cap-and-stalk mushroom, narrow at its base and widening dramatically at the top, to describe a concern that starts small and spreads fast to the point of catastrophe. The proto-metaphor of mushrooming in this sense has to be the ten-mile-high mushroom cloud that emerged from the blasts of Little Boy and Fat Man, the two atomic bombs that devastated the Japanese cities of Hiroshima and Nagasaki in August 1945.

6.12   Mushrooming can be global, such as the effects of the climate crisis. It can also be local, both literal and nonliteral, such as the spread of COVID-19-associated mucormycosis, or CAM, reported in patients in India in early 2021, a rare, noncontagious fungal infection mistakenly called "black fungus." But the metaphor implies more than a comparison to the typical mushroom shape. More subtly, the fear of an event mushrooming carries with it an idea of an unseen and unstoppable force, a degenerative process happening just below the level of sense perception. This interpretation is played out literally in David Foster Wallace's novel *Infinite Jest*, when the young Hal returns from a basement, running to his mother in the backyard, and baring in his hand a partially chewed patch of mold, which Foster describes as "horrific: darkly green, glossy, vaguely hirsute, speckled with parasitic fungal points of yellow, orange, red."[1] "I ate this," he cries to his mother, who, seeing bits of the fungus smeared around her son's mouth, becomes hysterical. "Help! My son ate this!" she shrieks, running around yelling over and over, "God! Help! My son ate this! Help!"

6.121   Hal's and his mother's fear is of an unknown and unnamable *this*. The conditions of dampness and darkness that make it possible for a pathogenic fungus to thrive and fill a space with its spores are all elements that combine to create a single atmosphere, one that Hal breathes in, eats, and absorbs into his body. The impact this atmosphere has on the collective imagination of both Hal and his mother is one of horror, a shared but unspoken horror, a horror of the potential effects mysterious molds might have on the mind and body. In Wallace's suburban America, much the same as in many other largely mycophobic nations, such as where I'm now writing in the UK, the image of an unknown fungus is an image of death, for it carries with it the very real possibility of poison, disease, and dying.

6.13   We've read plenty in recent literature about how fungi are more closely related to animals than plants. (As Nicholas P. Money points out, we shouldn't get too excited by this fact: it also means that every other animal is also more connected to fungi than plants. We humans need to stop thinking we're so damn special.)[2] One of the main distinctions between plants and fungi is that fungi move towards their food, whereas plants produce their own food through photosynthesis. Fungi are ravening lifeforms. Our fear and disgust of mushrooms is therefore a disgust with ourselves. As Vilém Flusser notes, "the farther an animal is from man, the more disgust it causes."[3] But instinctively the reverse is true: our fear of fungi stems from our subconscious, a feeling in our gut, a fear of our bodies being devoured by an insatiable zombie. Such is our experience with the aura of death that signals in us a compulsion to flee. This is our experience as we sense the rotting animal carcass in the woods, or as we sniff out a frightening malodor emanating from somewhere behind the walls, or rising up from under the floorboards come the heat of summertime. We can't help ourselves. We move in closer to discover its source before finally it fills our noses, realization hits us, and we violently pull back. This book implores us to do the opposite, to act in a way that seems counterintuitive and stay with the stink.

Why Stink matters

6.2   Since I started this book, the COVID-19 pandemic has seen the death of over 6.5 million people worldwide. With infection marked by a symptom of loss of taste or smell, the advent of the coronavirus disease in December 2019 could be considered the beginning of the most anosmic plagues in human history. Since then, the world has seen three of the warmest years on record—a fact that will likely be out of date soon after this book is published.[4] The accelerated release into the Earth's atmosphere of potentially catastrophic levels of methane (caused by farting livestock and burning fossil fuels), sulfur dioxide (the smell of the Devil himself), and other malodorous gases, are indicative of a distempered planet out of tune with its human inhabitants—or vice versa.[5] Ongoing genocides in several countries, illegal land grabs, the global rise of populism, and the increasingly vocal divisions within and between nations, cultures, and communities similarly speak of a widespread discordance that is only getting noisier. Contagion. Climate change. Conflict. In a short time, the world has become an increasingly stinky place to live. And this stink, as this book has shown, is audible as well as smellable.

6.21   Stink conveys an ontic note of the humming world's sonic-osmic becoming. Stink is borne out of disharmony, symptomatic that something is dreadfully wrong. Or, perhaps more hopefully, that the world is, at last, righting itself, though not before expelling us like some feculent flatus. Stink is not always something to be repelled by, therefore, for it may divulge a quality that, for the sake of our species' continued existence, we must urgently move towards rather than shy away from. And if this sounds hyperbolic, raise your nose and sniff the air.

6.22   This investigation started with the figure of the artist at the mouth of the forest striking out in search of the source of a *smelling sound*, a paradoxical element I've named Stink. Like the poet Dante "impelled by a spirit of exploration and experiment," I have shown how, by following one's nose and slowly inching forward, an advance can be achieved.[6] As I begin to exit my own dark wood, looking back, the path reveals itself. Standing at its lip, I find myself changed—neurologically no less than intellectually.

6.221   Here at the end, emerging into the light, I am reminded of Cage's famous account of his time in an anechoic chamber at Harvard University in 1951. In an anecdote repeated many times throughout his life, Cage reported how the silence he anticipated within the chamber was unexpectedly obscured by the presence of two persistent sounds: one pitched high, one low. These twin noises, Harvard engineer Peter Gena explained to him, were likely the buzzing of Cage's nervous system together with the humming of his blood flowing through his veins.[7] In an address he gave at the Music Teachers National Association convention several years later, Cage remarked that the silence he was denied in that moment was, for him, cause for comfort rather than concern. Cage: "Until I die there will be sounds. And they will continue following my death. One need not fear about the future of music."[8] Emerging from the anechoic chamber, a humming in his ears, Cage found his faith in the future of music reaffirmed. Whereas I, emerging from the forest, a humming in my ears *and* my nose, have found the conditions of all listening transformed.

6.23   It might be claimed that the work of the artist, like the poet, is to demonstrate the extent of their discoveries. Yet for this knowledge to matter means it must *pervade* the artist's subjective experience to the world beyond.[9] Stink matters because it challenges the seemingly unshakeable conviction of sound as sound, as something that "passes through" the external world of objects into the ear alone. This book has potentially significant benefits, therefore, to the work of other composers and artists working with sound, and to musicologists writing about music, by affording them a creative and critical tool for listening beyond the ear to include the nose and the nasal imaginary. In other words, by daring to insert smell into the practices of listening, making, and writing about sound—musical or otherwise—a theory of Stink may allow us to rediscover a path that we have lost. However, the diverse and divergent examples included in this inquiry reveal that this path is by no means straightforward. What's at stake for others who choose to follow after is that things are likely to become, at least for a while, confused and a bit weird. But a path exists nonetheless.

6.24   As discussed in my introduction, my theory of sound as Stink attempts to highlight the ongoing discord within sound studies organized along historical-philosophical lines. It appears that the conclusions I arrived at in chapters four and five in particular have led me to come down strongly on the side of philosophy. This can be seen as a direct consequence of the nose-led approach I have chosen to take; specifically, the fact that I've made my discoveries openly and intuitively by following a foul smell to its source. Whether that source is empiric, cosmic, etymologic, or neurologic, each demonstrates in different yet overlapping ways how sound, in *smelling*, can be experienced beyond the dumb appendages of the ears and nose to something felt as a reality within the awakening mind of the artist or poet.

6.25   Finally, it's worth remarking on some of the pitfalls that this inquiry reveals. For example, it's clear how Stink, through the process of writing, quickly becomes prolix. Stink is thus airborne, inarticulate, ambivalent. Stink is pervasive, primordial, discordant, disgusting, dreadful. Stink is musical, mycological, malodorous. Stink is a humming swarm, an incessant sound, an incensing scent. Stink is a seizure, a specter, a symptom of a disordered mind and a distempered world. In other words, Stink is *linguistic*, that is to say, "language-producing." However, in attempting to name Stink by way of yet more language, of yet more epithets and morphological mutations, the exercise reveals the limits of the thing we are trying to describe, something Barthes warns us about when attempting to write about music. The more one pursues this path, therefore, the more it becomes apparent how Stink, like Cage's mushroom, "escapes erudition."[10]

6.251   I admit to this contradiction. I also admit to how, throughout this book, I have attempted to have it both ways by proclaiming Stink as an inarticulate phenomenon before working hard to articulate it all the same. And so, as I begin to run out of words and mushroom metaphors of my own, let me conclude by saying this. Although the practices of thinking Stink, writing Stink, and making Stink are all imbricated in this study, I believe only the latter—the making of art and music; the artist attempting to articulate the inarticulable—can help sidestep the foul pitfalls language exposes in itself. Above all else, it is by this work that music makes Stink listenable.

NOTES

0. Introduction

1. David Toop, "It Is Nothing," in *On Listening*, ed. Angus Carlyle and Cathy Lane (Padstow: Uniformbooks, 2015), 38.

2. Ivor Cutler, "The Path," *Jammy Smears* (Virgin, 1976).

3. Seth Kim-Cohen, *In the Blink of an Ear: Towards a Non-cochlear Sonic Art* (London: Bloomsbury, 2009), xviii.

4. David Toop, *Sinister Resonance: The Mediumship of the Listener* (London: Continuum, 2010), xi.

5. The image of a cartoon character floating as a result of the odorous allure of food has been a common trope in TV and film since the early years of animation. In the animated short *The Little Whirlwind* (directed by Riley Thomson, Walt Disney Production: RKO Radio Pictures, 1941), Mickey Mouse is shown levitating, lured by the smell of a freshly baked pie drifting in from offscreen.

6. See a transcript of Eno's talk, "Perfume," which he gave in Barcelona in 1992 at https://www.moredarkthanshark.org/feature_opal_info_22-1992.html.

7. Ibid.

8. Brian Eno, liner notes to *Neroli* (All Saints Records, 1993).

9. "Neroli," *Wikipedia*, last updated February 20, 2024, https://en.wikipedia.org/wiki/Neroli.

10. Eno, "Perfume."

11. Ibid.

12. In 1920 in his laboratory in Cannes, perfumer Ernest Beaux presented Coco Chanel with ten samples of a new fragrance in a series of small glass vials numbered—incongruously, it seems—one to five, and twenty to twenty-four. Chanel selected the fifth, hence the name Chanel No. 5. In her book *The Secret of Chanel No. 5: The Biography of a Scent*, author Tilar J. Mazzeo accounts for this gap in the sequence as a result of several vials having been spoiled by a careless lab assistant, who accidentally added a much-too-high percentage of what was then a new fragrance material known as aldehydes. As a result of this overdose, it appears vials six to nineteen were either too crude or too cloying for Chanel to even contemplate. There's also something "off" about the potion in Leiber and Stoller's song "Love Potion No. 9" (first released by The Clovers in 1960), a song I sang many times during my early twenties. A couple of lines in the third verse come back to haunt me: "It smelled like turpentine, it looked like Indian ink / I held my nose, I closed my eyes, I took a drink." The idea is that no matter how magical the medicine might be, the stuff still stinks. And with each variation, or "take," as Mazzeo puts it, the concoction does not improve. See Tilar J. Mazzeo, *The Secret of Chanel No. 5* (New York: HarperCollins, 2010), 60.

13. Lana Vasung et al., "Exploring Early Human Brain Development with Structural and Physiological Neuroimaging," *NeuroImage*, 187 (2019): 226–54 (233).

14. Ibid.

15. Toop, *Sinister Resonance*, ix.

16. Didier Anzieu, *The Skin Ego*, trans. Chris Turner (New Haven, CT: Yale University Press, 1989), 47.

17. Julia Simner, *Synaesthesia: A Very Short Introduction* (Oxford: Oxford University Press, 2019), 4.

18. Thomas E. Jackson and Soupramanien Sandramouli, "Auditory-Olfactory Synaesthesia Coexisting with Auditory-Visual Synaesthesia," *Journal of Neuro-Ophthalmology* 32, no. 3 (2012): 221–23.

19. William James, *The Principles of Psychology* (1890; London: Dover, 1950), 251.

20. Roland Barthes, "The Grain of the Voice," *Image, Music, Text*, trans. Stephen Heath (London: Fontana Press, 1982), 179.

21. Ibid.

22. Ibid.

23. Ibid., 180.

24. Roland Barthes, *The Pleasure of the Text*, trans. Roland Miller (New York: Hill and Wang, 1975), 61.

25. Roland Barthes, *Camera Lucida: Reflections on Photography*, trans. Richard Howard (London: Vintage, 2000), 26–27.

26. Ibid, 27.

27. John Cage, "Music Lover's Field Companion," *A Mycological Foray* (Italy: Atelier Éditions, 2020), 9.

28. Michel Foucault, *The Order of Things* (London: Routledge, 2005), 10.

29. Emphasis in the original. Jean-Luc Nancy, *Listening*, trans. Charlotte Mandell (New York: Fordham University Press, 2007), 3.

30. A 2020 study conducted by a team of neuroscientists in Saarland, Germany, shows that it so happens that humans are capable of pricking up their ears to listen more intently to novel sounds, though in much more subtle ways than their canine, feline, or simian cousins. See Daniel J. Strauss et al., "Vestigial Auriculomotor Activity Indicated the Direction of Auditory Attention in Humans," *eLife*, 9 (2020): e54536.

31. "Visualism," as termed by Don Ihde in *Listening and Voice*, is used to describe the privileging of sight over other senses in the history of Western philosophy. Don Ihde, *Listening and Voice: Phenomenologies of Sound* (New York: SUNY Press, 2007), 6–10.

32. Robert Pasnau, "What is Sound?" *The Philosophical Quarterly* 49, no. 196 (1999): 309–24 (313).

33. Andreas Keller, *Philosophy of Olfactory Perception* (New York: Palgrave Macmillan, 2016), 64–71.

34. David Howes, "Intersensoriality: Music to the Eyes," *The Routledge Companion to Sounding Art*, ed. Marcel Cobussen et al. (London: Routledge, 2017), 165.

35. Katelynn Robinson, *The Sense of Smell in the Middle Ages* (London: Routledge, 2020), 6.

36. Robert Muchembled, *Smells*, trans. Susan Pickford (Cambridge: Polity Press, 2020), 96.

37. Ibid., 65.

38. See Rodolphe el-Khoury's introduction to Dominique Laporte's *History of Shit*, trans. Nadia Benabid and Rodolphe el-Khoury (Cambridge, MA: MIT Press, 2000), viii.

39. This quote from Stravinsky is from one of six lectures he delivered between 1939 and 1940, just as he was entering his seventh decade. In it, Stravinsky challenges the pejorative implication of the word dissonance, of something that must always be resolved, made "fragrant." Instead, he implores us to liberate the term from its suggestion of harmonic disorder. See Igor Stravinsky, *Poetics of Music in the Form of Six Lessons* (New York: Vintage, 1947), 36–37.

40. Jonathan Sterne, "Sonic Imaginations," *The Sound Studies Reader*, ed. Jonathan Sterne (London: Routledge, 2012), 1–18 (2).

1. On Stink

1. The name is shared by a species of fungus, *Coprinus sterquilinus*, the midden inkcap, that typically grows in horse shit, rabbit dung, and rotting vegetation. Like other inkcaps, *C. sterquilinus* autodigests as it matures, turning itself into its own shit, so to speak.

2. Constance Classen, David Howes, and Anthony Synnott, *Aroma: The Cultural History of Smell* (London: Routledge, 2002), 97.

3. See Ivonne Wallrabenstein et al., "Smelling of Hedione Results in Sex Differentiated Human Brain Activity," *NeuroImage*, 113 (2015): 365–73.

4. Nadine S. Fischer and Martin Steinhaus, "Identification of an Important Odorant Precursor in Durian: First Evidence of Ethionine in Plants," *Journal of Agricultural and Food Chemistry* 68, no. 38 (2019); 10397–402 (10401).

5. Muchembled, *Smells*, 160.

6. Alain Corbin, *The Foul and the Fragrant: Odour and the Social Imagination* (London: Papermac, 1996), 200.

7. Erica Hellerstein and Ken Fine, "A Million Tons of Feces and an Unbearable Stench: Life near Industrial Pig Farms," *Guardian*, September 20, 2017, https://www.theguardian.com/us-news/2017/sep/20/north-carolina-hog-industry-pig-farms.

8. Muchembled, *Smells*, 160.

9. Dante Alighieri, *Inferno: The Divine Comedy I*, trans. and ed. by Robin Kirkpatrick (London: Penguin, 2010), 92 (Canto 11, line 12).

10. *Labyrinth*, dir. Jim Henson (Columbia TriStar, 1986).

11. Megan Garber, "What Space Smells Like," *Atlantic*, July 19, 2012, https://www.theatlantic.com/technology/archive/2012/07/what-space-smells-like/259903/.

12. Ibid.

13. David Whitehouse, "Black Hole Hums in B flat," *BBC News*, September 10, 2003, http://news.bbc.co.uk/1/hi/sci/tech/3096776.stm.

14. "Chandra 'Hears' a Black Hole for the First Time," Chandra X-Ray Observatory, NASA (September 9, 2003), https://chandra.harvard.edu/press/03_releases/press_090903.html.

15. Peter Szendy, *Listen: A History of Our Ears*, trans. Charlotte Mandell (New York: Fordham University Press, 2008), 141.

16. As Szendy points out in *Listen* (p. 140), Duchamp went on to reiterate the same sentiment over thirty years later, though updating and transposing his terminology to distinguish between seeing and looking, hearing and listening. Duchamp: "One can

see looking. Can one hear listening, smell smelling, etc.?" Szendy, Nancy, and others have remarked that Duchamp's subtle shifts in language are philosophically useful for thinking about how we might differentiate between verbs that describe a passive, or unintentional sense (i.e. hearing) versus an active, or intentional one (i.e. listening). But, as we can sense in the trailing off of Duchamp's question in the second version of his thought, the same transposition cannot be so easily achieved for *smell* and *smelling*. As a verbal noun, *smell* behaves differently.

17. The alternative title for this section is taken from a chapter in Dostoevsky's *The Brothers Karamazov* (1880), titled "A Putrid Smell" (as translator David McDuff notes, probably named after a poem by Fyodor Tyutchev, 1836). The chapter tells the story of the half-day-old corpse of Elder Zosima, a senior monk believed by his brethren to be free from sin and therefore, in death, beyond the reach of "God and His deliberate finger" (a line that brings to mind the figa-like "fuck you" gesture drawn by Albrecht Dürer in his *Study of Three Hands*, c.1490). Yet, less than twelve hours after his death, Zosima's body has started to decompose at such an astonishing rate that its odor has filled the small cell in which he lies and is drifting out to fill the porch of the monastery. The unusually fast putrefaction of the holy body is considered a "defamation, a disgrace." However, to the townsfolk who have gathered in the porch, the effect of this unholy stench is so irreconcilable with the idea of the Elder's inviolability that it causes their faith to waver. The stench quickly intensifies, becoming so unspeakably evil that even those who have taken a vow of silence at once break their pledge and "open their lips," sighing and murmuring. The scene ends with the sounds of a bell summoning the monks to service mixed with the "frenzied shrieking" of zealots. Stink is a blasphemer, an oath-breaker. To others, it is a trial of faith. Fyodor Dostoevsky, *The Brothers Karamazov*, trans. David McDuff (London: Penguin, 2003), 423–37.

18. See Thomas Miller's translation of Bede's *Ecclesiastical History of the English People* (Cambridge: In Parentheses, 1999), book 3, vi, 80–81.

19. Robert Holt, ed., *The Ormulum* (Oxford: Clarendon Press, 1878), book 2, 8,191–98,196.

20. Roland Barthes, *Sade, Foruier, Loyola*, trans. Richard Miller (Berkeley, CA: University of California Press, 1989), 137.

21. Corbin, *Foul and the Fragrant*, 214.

22. Plato, *Cratylus*, trans. Benjamin Jowett, Project Gutenberg, https://www.gutenberg.org/files/1616/1616-h/1616-h.htm.

23. Classen, *Aroma*, 119. Steven Connor also picks up on this association, quoting the Dogon in a passage about "nasality and negativity." See Connor, *Beyond Words* (London: Reaktion Books, 2014), 89–90.

24. Samuel Taylor Coleridge, "Ancyent Marinere," part v, in William Wordsworth and Samuel Taylor Coleridge, *Lyrical Ballads*, vol. 1 (Bristol: T. N. Longman, 1798), 30.

25. Paul Hegarty, *Noise/Music* (London: Bloomsbury, 2018), 3.

26. John Jamieson, "noisome," *Supplement to the Etymological Dictionary of the Scottish Language*, vol. 2. (Edinburgh: University of Edinburgh Press, 1825), 160.

27. Connor, *Beyond Words*, 104.

28. Ibid.

2. Sight

1. Vilém Flusser, *Vampyroteuthis infernalis*, trans. Rodrigo Maltez Novaes (New York: Atropos Press, 2011), 27.

2. Judith Butler, *Bodies That Matter: On the Discursive Limits of Sex* (London: Routledge, 2011), 31.

3. Donna J. Haraway, "Receiving Three Mochilas in Colombia: Carrier Bags for Staying with the Trouble," introduction to Ursula Le Guin, *The Carrier Bag Theory of Fiction* (London: Terra Ignota, 2019), 11.

4. Nicholas P. Money, *Mushrooms: A Natural and Cultural History* (London: Reaktion Books, 2017), 63.

5. Le Guin, *Carrier Bag Theory*, 29, 37.

6. Money, *Mushrooms*, 63.

7. Judith Butler, "Reply from Judith Butler," *Philosophy and Phenomenological Research* 96, no. 1 (2018): 243–49 (246).

8. David Arora, *Mushrooms Demystified* (Berkeley, CA: Ten Speed Press, 1986), 766–67.

9. Charles David Badham, *A Treatise on the Esculent Funguses of England: Containing an Account of Their Classical History, Uses, Characters, Development, Structure, Nutritious Properties, Modes of Cooking and Preserving, Etc.*, 2nd ed. (London: Lovell Reeve & Co., 1863), 13.

10. Miomir Nikšić, Ivan Hadzic, and Milan Glišić, "Is *Phallus impudicus* a Mycological Giant?" *Mycologist* 18, no. 1 (2004): 21–22.

11. Hadrianus Junius, *The Description of the Phallus*, translated for this book by Caroline Spearing (65–80).

12. Carolus Clusius, *Rariorum plantarum historia* (Antwerp: Officina Plantiniana, Ioannem Moretum, 1601), 295, my translation.

13. Junius, *Phallus*.

14. See D. P. Sleeman, P. Jones, and J. N. Cronin, "Investigations of an Association between the Stinkhorn Fungus and Badger Setts," *Journal of Natural History* 31, no. 6 (1997): 983–92: https://doi.org/10.1080/00222939700770481.

15. Ibid., 986.

16. Gwen Raverat, *Period Piece* (New York: W. W. Norton & Company, 1953), 121.

17. Ibid., 135–36, emphasis in the original.

18. Elio Schaechter, *In The Company of Mushrooms: A Biologist's Tale* (Cambridge, MA: Harvard University Press, 1989), 169.

19. Pliny, *The Natural History*, book XXII, 360–61.

20. *Hortus sanitatis. De Herbis et Plantis, de Animalibus et Reptilibus, de Avibus et Volatilibus, de Piscibus et Natatilibus, de Lapidibus et in terre venis nascentibus, de Urinis et earum speciebus* (Mainz: Jacob Meydenbach, 1491), book 1, plate CCCIII.

21. This literal definition of autopsy was used by American experimental filmmaker Stan Brakhage as the title for his 1971 silent film *The Act of Seeing With One's Own Eyes* (Canyon, 1971). The film documents in graphic detail (though dispassionately) the various postmortem methods of forensic pathologists in a morgue in Pittsburgh over a period of days.

22. Junius, *Phallus*.

23. Dirk van Miert, *Hadrianus Junius (1511–1575): Een humanist uit Hoorn* (Hoorn: Bas Baltus, 2011), 70–71, my translation.

24. Ibid.

25. Ibid.

26. See *OED*, "empiric," sense A.2.

27. Junius, *Phallus*.

28. Ibid.

29. Alexander Stuart Macmillan, *Popular Names of Flowers, Fruits, Etc., As Used in the County of Somerset and the Adjacent Parts of Devon, Dorset and Wilts* (Yeovil: Western Gazette, 1922), 209.

30. *Geldersche volksalmanak*, vols. 21–22 (Arnhem: Nijhoff en Zoon, 1855), 11, my translation.

31. Ibid., 10.

32. Van Miert, *Hadrianus Junius*, 157.

33. Junius, *Phallus*.

34. Ibid.

35. Ibid.

36. Ibid.

37. Van Miert, *Hadrianus Junius*, 69.

38. Junius, *Phallus*.

39. Étienne Pierre Ventenat, "Dissertation sur la genre phallus," *Mémoires de l'Institut des Sciences et Arts Sciences de Mathématique et de Physique*, vol. 1 (Paris: Institut de France, 1798): 503–23 (509).

40. Gerard, *Herball*, 1583.

41. John Parkinson, *Theatrum Botanicum, or, An Universal and Compleat Herball* (London: Thomas Cotes, 1640), 1322.

42. Other species of stinkhorns have similarly lewd names. For example, *Mutinus caninus*, or the dog stinkhorn as it is more commonly known due its resemblance to a dog's penis, stems from the name for the phallic deity Mutinus Mutunus, known to the Greeks as Priapus. (Note, Mutinus, alternatively spelled "Mutunus," is in fact the name of another phallic god often conflated with Priapus.)

43. E. C. Large, "Pursuits of Mycology: Presidential Address to the British Mycological Society, March 1961," *Transactions of the British Mycological Society*, 44 (March 1961): 1–23 (12).

44. Anna Pavord, *The Naming of the Names: The Search for Order in the World of Plants* (New York: Bloomsbury, 2005), 260.

45. Ibid.

46. Schaechter also reproduces Gerard's misprint —a version of an inversion of a version—in his (also out of print) book *In the Company of Mushrooms*, 171.

47. W.P.K. Findlay, *Fungi: Folklore, Fiction, & Fact* (Richmond, UK: The Richmond Publishing Company, 1982), 4.

48. Robert Boyle, "Experiment 27," in Boyle, *New Experiments Physico-Mechanicall, Touching the Spring of the Air, and its Effects* (Oxford: H. Hall, 1660), 205–14.

49. Pliny: "If the hole of a serpent has been near the mushroom, or should a serpent have breathed on it as it first opened, its kinship to poisons makes it capable of absorbing the venom." Pliny the Elder, *Natural History*, vol. 6, book 22, trans. Horace Rackham (Cambridge, MA: Harvard University Press, 1938).

50. Petro Andreae Matthiolus, *Commentarii secundo aucti, in libros sex* (Venice: Vincenzo Valgrisi, 1558), 545.

51. John Gerard, *The Herball, or, Generall Historie of Plantes*, ed. Thomas Johnson (London: Adam Islip, Joice Norton, and Richard Whitakers, 1633), 1582–583 (1583).

52. Albrecht Dürer, *Vier bücher von menschlider Proportion* (Nuremberg, 1528), n.p.n.

53. Franciscus van Sterbeeck, *Theatrum fungorum oft het tooneel der campernoelien* (Antwerp: Josef Jakobs, 1675), 276–85.

54. These three "rods" are also copies from Clusius. From Sterbeeck's descriptions, they are likely variations of the common, dune, and dog stinkhorn ("*Veretrum canini*" [dog's privates], or in vernacular Flemish "*Honts roede*" [dog's dick]). Another name Sterbeeck ascribes to these that I'm particularly fond of is "*Moerbesi fungi*" on account of the stinkhorn's blackened, indented cap bearing a passing resemblance to a mulberry. Ibid., 280.

55. Possibly an alternative spelling of Christianus Kislingh, or Hisling; both are mentioned by Sterbeeck in his book. Ibid., 281–82.

56. Ibid., 282, my translation.

57. Ibid.

58. Ibid.

59. Ibid. 284.

60. *Society*, directed by Brian Yuzna (Wild Street Pictures, 1989).

61. "*Fungus anthropomorphas* [sic]," plate 29, Sterbeeck, *Theatrum fungorum*.

62. Georgius Seger, "Observatio LV., *Fungus anthropomorphos* [sic]," in *Miscellanea Curiosa Medico-Physica Academiae Naturae Curiosorum*, vol. 2 (Leipzig: Samuel Krebs, 1671), 112–13.

63. *Society*, 1:12:12–1:12:25.

3. Smell

1. Roger Phillips, *Mushrooms* (London: Macmillan: 2006).

2. Ibid., 123, 262, 231, 236–41.

3. M. C. Cooke, *Fungi: Their Nature, Influence, and Uses* (London: Henry S. King & Co., 1875), 116.

4. Ibid.

5. Phillips, in an interview with me at his home in London, March 15, 2019.

6. Richard Mabey, *The Perfumier and the Stinkhorn* (London: Profile Books, 2011), 59–60.

7. James Sowerby, *Coloured Figures of English Fungi or Mushrooms*, vol. 3 (London: R. Wilks, Chancery-Lane, 1803), notes to plate 291.

8. Pliny's assertion concerning the edibility of the larvae *Cossus cossus* is taken up by Friedrich S. Bodenheimer in his book *Insects as Human Food*. Bodenheimer concludes, however, that it's more likely the larvae of *Cerambyx heros*, a type of long-horned beetle, that was favored by the Romans. See Bodenheimer, *Insects as Human Food* (The Hague: Dr W. Junk, 1951), 43.

9. Pliny the Elder, *Natural History*, vol. 3, trans. Horace Rackham (Cambridge, MA: Harvard University Press, 1938), eBook, 1588.

10. See Ken Murata et al., "Identification of an Olfactory Signal Molecule that Activates the Central Regulator of Reproduction in Goats," *Current Biology* 24, no. 6 (2014): 681–86.

11. Eristanna Palazzolo et al., "Volatile Organic Compounds in Wild Fungi from Mediterranean Forest Ecosystems," *Journal of Essential Oil Research* 29, no. 5 (2017): 385–90 (388).

12. Ibid.

13. See Donald I. Williamson, *Larvae and Evolution: Toward a New Zoology* (New York: Chapman and Hall, 1992).

14. Bernd Heinrich, *Life Everlasting: The Animal Way of Death* (Boston: Houghton Mifflin Harcourt, 2012), 183.

15. R. T. Rolfe and F. W. Rolfe, *The Romance of the Fungus World* (London: Chapman & Hall, 1925), 25–26, 263.

16. W.P.K. Findlay, *Fungi, Fiction, & Fact* (Richmond, UK: The Richmond Publishing Company, 1982), 52.

17. Phillips, *Mushrooms*, 338.

18. "Damp earth" and "spent incense" are from David Arora, *Mushrooms Demystified* (Berkeley, CA: Ten Speed Press, 1986), 561. "Spermatic" is generally reserved for describing the smell of several members of *Inocybe*, including *Inocybe lacera* and *Inocybe rimosa*, although Camille Montagne also observed this scent in the bright-orange-colored stinkhorn *Phallus aurantiacus* (see Montagne, *Annales des Sciences Naturelles*, 16 [1841], 277). "Rotten Limburger cheese" is from William Herbst's description of the "very repugnant odor" of the netted stinkhorn *Phallus duplicatus* in his book *Fungal Flora of the Lehigh Valley*, Pennsylvania (Allentown: Berkemeyer, Keck & Co., 1899), 159: https://doi .org/10.5962/bhl.title.3600. "Scorched linen" is used by Daniel McAlpine to describe the yellow dog stinkhorn *Mutinus borneensis*, a rare species found in Australia, Borneo, and China. See Daniel McAlpine, "Janisa Truncata," in Curtis Gates Lloyd, *Mycological Notes*, no. 36 (1910): 477–92 (485): https://www .biodiversitylibrary.org/partpdf/329350. Descriptions of the common stinkhorn smelling like "burning bricks," "bones," and "hartshorn manufactories" are from Sowerby, *English Fungi*, n.p.n.

19. Charles David Badham, *A Treatise on the Esculent Funguses of England* (London: Lovell Reeve & Co., 1863), 13.

20. Sowerby, *English Fungi*, vol. 3, notes to plate 291.

21. Carelton Rea, *British Basidiomycetae: A Handbook to the Larger British Fungi* (Cambridge: Cambridge University Press, 1922), 24.

22. John Curtis, *British Entomology; being illustrations and descriptions of the genera of insects found in Great Britain and Ireland* (London: E. Ellis and Co., 1823–1840), vol. 10, plate 469.

23. M. J. Berkeley, "Egg Fungi," *The Intellectual Observer* 9 (July 1866): 402.

24. See Guy Fourré, *Pièges et curiosités des Champignons* (Maulévrier, France: self-pub., 1985.

25. Ibid.

26. C. G. Lloyd, *Mycological Writings of C. G. Lloyd*, vol. 2 (Cincinnati: self-pub., 1898–1925), 328.

27. Interview with Roger Phillips.

28. See Steven D. Johnson and Florian P. Schiestl, "Convergent Evolution of Carrion and Faecal Scent," *South African Journal of Botany*, 76 (2010): 796–807.

29. Nazni Wasi Ahmad et al., "Determination of the Flight Range and Dispersal of the House Fly, *Musca domestica* (L.) Using Mark Release Recapture Technique," *Tropical Biomedicine* 22, no. 1 (2005): 53–54.

30. For a brief but fascinating review of the arum lily *Rafflesia*, see Elaine Ayers, "Noble Rot: On Joseph Arnold and the Discovery of the Corpse Flower," *Cabinet Magazine*, no. 64 (March 2017): 71–76.

31. D. P. Sleeman, P. Jones, and J. N. Cronin, "Investigations of an Association between the Stinkhorn Fungus and Badger Setts," *Journal of Natural History* 31, no. 6 (1996): 983–92.

32. Junius, *Description of the Phallus*, trans. Caroline Spearing in this book. Charles Badham (1863) pretty much repeats the same anecdote three hundred years later: "A botanist had by mistaken one of the former into his bedroom; he was soon awakened by an intolerable fœtor, and was glad to open up his window and get rid of it, as he hoped, and the Phallus together. Here he was disappointed; '*sublatâ causâ non tollitur effectus*,' [removing the cause does not remove the effect] the fœtor remaining nearly the same for some hours afterwards."

33. Findlay, *Fungi*, 52.

34. Sleeman et al., "Stinkhorn Fungus and Badger Setts," 983.

35. Pudil, "Volatile Compounds in Stinkhorns," 167–68.

36. Ibid.

37. "Dimethyl trisulfide," The Good Scents Company (website), http://www.thegoodscents company.com/data/rw1008101.html.

38. Mark C. Taylor, *Erring: A Postmodern A/theology* (London: University of Chicago Press, 1984), 107.

39. Toop, *Sinister Resonance*, vii–viii.

40. Jacques Derrida, "The Hinge [*La Brisure*]," *Of Grammatology*, trans. Gayatri Chakravorty Spivak (Baltimore: John Hopkins University Press, 1997), 65–73 (65).

41. Ibid., 66.

42. Pascal Quignard, *Abysses*, trans. Chris Turner (London: Seagull Books, 2015), 154.

43. Cooke, *Fungi*, 116.

44. Ibid.

4. Sound

1. In Australian and British English, "honking," like "humming," also doubles up to mean both a harsh or irritating sound and an unpleasant smell.

2. To read a more in-depth analysis of the phenomenon of multiple pitches being perceivable in a single bell, see Gareth Loy, *Musimathics: The Mathematical Foundations of Music*, vol. 1 (Cambridge, MA: MIT Press, 2006), 156–57.

3. Sallie Tisdale, "The Sutra of Maggots and Blowflies," *Conjunctions*, no. 51 (2008): 10.

4. Alexander B. Klots and Elsie B. Klots, *1001 Questions Answered about Insects* (New York: Dover, 1977), 48.

5. April Daley, "Do All Houseflies Hum in Key?" *Mental Floss*, October 14, 2015, https://www.mentalfloss.com/article/69639/do-all-houseflies-hum-key.

6. "Buzz off," *New Scientist*, no. 24 (2012), 65.

7. Tisdale, "Sutra of Maggots," 12.

8. Scott Walker (credited as Noel Scott Engel), "It's Raining Today," *Scott 3* (Philips/Fontana, 1969).

9. Radiohead, "How to Disappear Completely," *Kid A* (Parlophone/Capitol, 2000); Mica Levi, "Drift," *Under the Skin: Original Motion Picture Soundtrack* (Rough Trade, 2014).

10. Rob Haskins, *John Cage* (London: Reaktion Books, 2012), 75–76.

11. Steven Connor, *Fly* (London: Reaktion Books, 2006), 172.

12. Steven Connor, *Beyond Words*, (London: Reaktion Books, 2014), 72.

13. William Shakespeare, *The Tempest*, act 3, scene 2, lines 50–51.

14. Connor, *Beyond Words*, 90.

15. Walter Skeat, *An Etymological Dictionary of the English Language* (Oxford: Clarendon Press, 1910), 392.

16. Connor cites Ambrose Bierce's entry on "fly speck" as the "proto-type of punctuation" from Bierce's satirical work, *The Devil's Dictionary* (1911). See Connor, *Fly*, 178–79.

17. For more on flies and the belief of spontaneous generation, see Robert Muchembled, *A History of the Devil: From the Middle Ages to the Present*, trans. Jean Birrel (London: Polity Press, 2003), 84, 102, 178.

18. Anna Lowenhaupt Tsing, *The Mushroom at the End of the World: On the Possibility of Life in Capitalist Ruins* (Princeton, NJ: Princeton University Press, 2015), 47.

19. Pascal Quignard, *Abysses*, trans. Chris Turner (London: Seagull Books, 2015), 164.

20. Connor, *Fly*, 90.

21. Christine Hume, *Saturation Project* (New York: Solid Objects, 2021), 81–82.

22. Ibid.

23. Lawrence Kramer, *The Hum of the World* (Oakland, CA: University of California Press, 2018), 4.

24. Ibid., 5–6.

25. Pascal Quignard, *Petits traités*, vol. 4 (Paris: Maeght, 1990), 22. The phrase "sonorous scent" first appeared in English in Jean-François Lyotard's essay "Music, Mutic," *Postmodern Fables*, trans. Georges van Den Abbeele (Minneapolis, MN: University of Minnesota Press, 1997), 208.

26. See John G. Cramer, "The Sound of the Big Bang," University of Washington, March 30, 2013, https://faculty.washington.edu/jcramer/BBSound.html.

27. Suk-Jun Kim, *Humming* (New York: Bloomsbury, 2019), 77. Emphasis in the original.

28. Ibid., 79.

29. C.H.E Brookfield, *Random reminiscences* (1902), "hum," quoted at *OED*.

30. Kramer, *Hum of the World*, 5.

31. Cathy Lynn Cripps, *Fungi in Forest Ecosystems: Systematics, Diversity and Ecology* (New York: New York Botanical Press, 2004), 17.

5. Phantom Stink

1. In David Foster Wallace's novel *Infinite Jest*, the character Poor Tony "P. T." Krause also has a seizure on a train, though his was down to alcohol Withdrawal (with a capital "W," as Wallace writes it). P. T.'s collapse on the carriage is similarly preceded by a phantom smell, a "sudden and incongruous smell of Old Spice Stick Deodorant, Classic Original Scent—unbidden and unexplainable, his late obstetric Poppa's brand, not smelled for years." David Foster Wallace, *Infinite Jest* (New York: Little Brown and Company, 1996), 268.

NOTES

2. See Owsei Temkin, *The Falling Sickness: A History of Epilepsy from the Greeks to the Beginnings of Modern Neurology* (Baltimore, MD: Johns Hopkins University Press, 1994), 92–96.

3. *Not I* by Samuel Beckett, first aired on BBC2, April 17, 1977 as part of an episode titled *Shades: Three Plays by Samuel Beckett*, dir. Donald McWhinnie and Anthony Page.

4. In medicine *aura* implies a premonition, a sense that something more momentous is on its way. In epilepsy, sensory auras are considered a type of seizure in their own right, albeit a "mild" one. Auras can lead to other types of seizure, including bilateral *grand mal* seizures causing loss of consciousness and bodily convulsions.

5. Alain Sebille, email to the author, August 31, 2020.

6. Timothy Morton, *Dark Ecology: For a Logic of Future Coexistence* (New York: Colombia University Press, 2016), 5.

7. *Lemon*, dir. Hollis Frampton (1969).

8. Akif İşlek and Mustafa Koray Balcı, "Phantosmia with COVID-19 Related Olfactory Dysfunction: Report of Nine Cases," *Indian Journal of Otolaryngology and Head and Neck Surgery*, 74 (2022): 2893.

9. This list of words used to described the qualities of hallucinated smells is gathered from multiple sources, including: Sara Sjölund et al., "Phantom Smells: Prevalence and Correlates in a Population-Based Sample of Older Adults," *Chemical Senses* 42, no. 4 (2017): 309–18 (315); Donald Leopold, "Distortion of Olfactory Perception: Diagnosis and Treatment," *Chemical Senses* 27, no. 7 (2002): 611–15 (611, 612); Colin Grant, *The Smell of Burning: A Memoir of Epilepsy* (London: Vintage, 2017), 34; William Gowers, "A Clinical Lecture On Minor Epilepsy," *The British Medical Journal* 1, no. 2036 (1900): 1–5 (3); also Emmanouil Magiorkinis, Kalliopi Sidiropoulou, and Aristidis Diamantis, "Hallmarks in the History of Epilepsy: From Antiquity Till the Twentieth Century," *Novel Aspects on Epilepsy*, ed. Humberto Foyaca-Sibat (Rijeka: IntechOpen, 2011), 134.

10. See Louis Carp, "George Gershwin—Illustrious American Composer: His Fatal Glioblastoma," *The American Journal of Surgical Pathology* 3, no. 5 (1979): 473–77 (474).

11. Elena Gasenzer and Edmund A. M. Neugebauer, "George Gershwin: A Case of New Ways in Neurosurgery as Well as in the History of Western Music," *Acta Neurochirurgica*, 156 (2014): 1251–258 (1254).

12. Ibid., 1256.

13. Sjölund, *Phantom Smells*, 315.

14. Ibid.

15. Ibid.

16. See Hughlings Jackson, "Remarks on Dissolution of the Nervous System as Exemplified by Certain Post-epileptic Conditions," *The Selected Writings of John Hughlings Jackson*, vol. 2, ed. James Taylor (London: Staples Press, 1958), 3–28.

17. Leopold, "Olfactory Perception," 612.

18. Sjölund, *Phantom Smells*, 315.

19. Quoted in Temkin, *The Falling Sickness*, 37.

20. Ibid.

21. Ibid.

22. Aretaeus, "On the Paroxysm of Epileptics," *De causis et signis acutorum morborum*, book 1, chapter 5, available at http://www.perseus.tufts.edu.

23. Critchley cites such an instance whereby a thirty-year-old man experiences seizures even when imagining a certain song. See Macdonald Critchley, "Musicogenic Epilepsy," *Brain* 60, no. 1 (1937): 13–27 (20).

24. Ibid., 14, 16, 17, 18, 20.

25. Ibid.

26. There's still some discussion about whether these types of hallucinated noises, heard during an auditory aura, are induced by an equivalent sound heard in the real world at the onset of a seizure, or whether subsequent musicogenic epileptic seizures are the result of an associative response to a memory of the feeling of fear of that sound. See Critchley, "Musicogenic Epilepsy," 26.

27. See Hegarty's introduction to *Noise/Music*, Paul Hegarty (London: Bloomsbury, 2018), 3–19.

28. Timothy Morton riffs on Kant's distinction of the real and reality in a passage on the philosophical concept of "object-oriented ontology," in an extract of one of his lectures published as *All Art is Ecological* (London: Penguin, 2021), 10–15.

29. Ibid., 12.

30. Martin Heidegger, "The Origin of the Work of Art," in *Off the Beaten Track*, ed. and trans. Julian Young and Kenneth Haynes (Cambridge: Cambridge University Press, 2002), 1, 8.

31. Andreas Keller, *Philosophy of Olfactory Perception* (New York: Palgrave Macmillan, 2016), 83.

32. Ibid., 74.

33. Ibid.

34. "Hallucination," *OED*.

35. *A Matter of Life and Death*, dir. Michael Powell and Emeric Pressburger (Criterion Collection, 2018).

36. Keller, *Olfactory Perception*, 82–83.

37. This is a paraphrase of Keller's expression "some sort of smelliness." Ibid., 85.

38. Oliver Sacks, *Hallucinations* (London: Picador, 2012), 277.

39. Ibid., 52.

40. Ibid.

41. Sigmund Freud, *Civilization and its Discontents*, trans. David McLintock (London: Penguin, 2002), 42.

42. In a footnote to his translation of Freud's "Notes Upon a Case of Obsessional Neurosis (1909)," James Strachey points out how Freud returned to this question of human-versus-animal olfactory repression, first in 1897 in two letters to Fliess, then in 1909 in his notes on the "Rat Man," and finally twenty years later in *Civilisation* (1929), as quoted from above. See Freud, *The Standard Edition of The Complete Psychological Works of Sigmund Freud: Volume X: Two Cases: 'Little Hans' & The 'Rat Man,'* trans. James Strachey (London: Hogarth Press, 1981), 248.

43. Freud reports that the Rat Man had an extraordinarily heightened awareness of smell, comparing his ability to distinguish family members by their smell alone as being "like a dog." Freud, *Complete Psychological Works*, 247.

44. Freud, *Civilization*, 41–44

45. Ibid., 42.

46. Max Horkheimer and Theodor W. Adorno, *Dialectic of Enlightenment*, trans. Edmund Jephcott (Stanford, CA: Stanford University Press, 2002), 151.

47. Fyodor Dostoevsky, *The Idiot*, trans. David McDuff (London: Penguin Books, 2004), 264.

48. On the influence of insomnia on Cioran's writing, see Willis G. Regier's essay, "Cioran's Insomnia," *MLN: Comparative Literature Issue* 119, no. 5 (December 2004): 994–1012.

49. E. M. Cioran, *A Short History of Decay*, trans. Richard Howard (London: Penguin Books, 2018), 60.

50. Ibid., 60–61.

51. There's an interesting discussion to be had about the change in preference for the word "epilepsy" over "the falling sickness," its origins in botany, and, significantly for our discussion, some curious pharmacopeial links to some strong-smelling plants, herbs, and spices. Writing about the same time as Junius, fellow physician and botanist Rembert Doedens published his *Cruydeboeck* in 1554. In it, he mentions several plant-based remedies for epilepsy, then almost exclusively known as "the falling sickness." Some of the plants Doedens recommends as remedies for epilepsy (almost always taken with vinegar) include: anthyllis, conyza, betony, galbanum, gentian, hyacinth, laserpitium (possibly silphion or laserwort, a fennel-like plant commonly used in classical antiquity as a perfume and medicine), pennyroyal, sagapenum, seseli, thyme, and white hellebore. The recommendation of white hellebore is a frightening addition, for all parts of the plant are known to be poisonous, even its aroma. English botanist Henry Lyte's translation of Doedens's herbal in 1578, *A New Herbal, or Historie of Plants*, has been cited as the starting point for this shift in favor towards the word "epilepsy" and its consideration as a medical disease rather than some sacred affliction metered out by a malevolent God. See Dodoens, *A New Herbal, or Historie of Plants*, trans. Henry Lyte (London: Gerard Dewes, 1578), 14, 35, 41, 206, 230, 232, 283, 291, 305, 307, 335, 347; see also Howard Marcel, "Science Diction: The Origin of the Word 'Epilepsy,'" *NPR*, September 30, 2011, https://www.npr.org/2011/09/30/140954025/science-diction-the-origin-of-the-word-epilepsy.

52. Fyodor Dostoevsky, *The Possessed* (*The Devils*), trans. Constance Garnett, available at https://www.gutenberg.org/cache/epub/8117/pg8117-images.html.

53. Carolus Clusius, *Rariorum plantarum historia* (Antwerp: Officina Plantiniana, Ioannem Moretum, 1601), 672.

54. Among those who've notably reported these claims (and who are most often cited by others) include: David Arora, *Mushrooms Demystified* (Berkeley, CA: Ten Speed Press, 1986), 766; Colin Dickinson and John Lucas, eds., *The Encyclopedia of Mushrooms* (London: Orbis, 1979), 29; Elio Schaechter, *In the Company of Mushrooms: A Biologist's Tale* (Cambridge, MA: Harvard University Press, 1997), 170; and M. Nikšić, I. Hadzic, and M. Glišić, "Is *Phallus impudicus* a Mycological Giant?" *Mycologist*, no. 18 (2004): 21–22 (21).

55. Pliny the Elder, *Natural History*, trans. W. H. S. Jones (Cambridge, MA: Harvard University Press, 1980), 349.

56. Galen, "Advice for an Epileptic Boy," trans. Owsei Temkin, *Bulletin of the Institute of the History of Medicine* 2, no. 3 (May 1934): 179–89 (185, 188).

57. Ibid., 185.

58. My translation from Karl Gottlob Kühn's Latin translation of Galen's "*De probis pravisque alimentorum succis*," *Galeni opera omnia*, ed. K. G. Kühn (Leipzig: Car. Cnoblochii, 1823), vol. 6, 770–71.

59. Finlay, *Fungi*, 52.

60. Adolf Beythien and Ernst Dressler, eds., *Klemens Merck's Warenlexikon*, seventh edition (Leipzig: Gloeckner, 1920). Note, the mention of "stinkhorn" is missing from previous editions of the *Warenlexikon*. (For example, see the third edition, published in 1884, page 203.) It appears that over time there's been some confusion about the German folk name *Hirschbrunst* (and latterly *Hirschtrüffel*) being synonymous with the embryonic common stinkhorn *Phallus impudicus* in the UK. This is understandable given the ways both stinkhorn eggs and false truffles *Elaphomyces granulatus* develop beneath the ground, and the similarities in their outward appearance. However, whereas the outer skin of the stinkhorn egg is smooth, rubbery, and creamy-colored, the false truffle is brown, covered in tiny warts, and is dusty-looking, as if sprinkled all over with cinnamon.

61. *Hirschbrunft* has now been replaced with the word *Hirschtrüffel*, literally "deer truffle," though this typically refers to the species *Elaphomyces granulatus* (*elaph-* meaning "deer," and -*myces* meaning "fungus"), also known as false truffles.

62. Dickinson, *Encyclopedia of Mushrooms*, 29.

63. "Brummen," "Brunft," Friedrich Kluge, *Etymological Dictionary of the German Language* (London: Bell, 1891), 45.

64. Christopher J. Duffin, "'The Periwig of a Dead cranium': Medicinal Skull Moss," *Pharmaceutical Historian* 52, no. 3 (September 2022): 75–85 (77–78).

65. *Usnea*, from the Arabic *ušna*, literally "moss," is now used to describe a genus of beard lichens.

66. Elena González-Burgos, Carlos Fernández-Moriano, M. Pilar Gómez-Serranillos, "Current Knowledge on Parmelia Genus: Ecological Interest, Phytochemistry, Biological Activities and Therpeautic Potential," *Phytochemistry*, 165 (September 2019): 112051, https://doi.org/10.1016/j.phytochem.2019.112051; Paolo Modenesi "Skull Lichens: A Curious Chapter in the History of Phytotherapy," *Fitoterapia* 80, no. 3 (January 2009): 145–48 (147), https://doi.org/10.1016/j.fitote.2008.12.005.

67. Andrea Tentzelius, *Medicina diastatica, or Sympatheticall Mumie: Containing Many Mysterious and Hidden Secrets in Philosophy and Physick* (London: T. Newcomb for T. Heath, 1653), 30–31.

68. Tentzelius, *Medicina diastatica*, 34.

69. Robert Efron, "The Effect of Olfactory Stimuli in Arresting Uncinate Fits," *Brain* 79, no. 2 (June 1956): 267–81 (274), https://doi.org/10.1093/brain/79.2.267.

70. Ibid., 273.

71. Ibid., 271.

72. Ibid.

73. Ibid., 275. In *The Pharmacopoeia Londinensis* (first published in 1618 and translated into English by Nicholas Culperer in 1649), castoreum, a perfume ingredient derived from the anal glands of beavers and which smells strongly of leather, is similarly ascribed such healing properties: "The smell of it allays the fits of the Mother. Inwardly given, it helps tremblings, Falling sickness [epilepsy], and other such ill effects of the Brain and Nerves." Nicholas Culpeper, John Allen, *Pharmacopoeia Londinensis* (London: Royal College of Physicians of London, 1720), 46.

6. Conclusion

1. David Foster Wallace, *Infinite Jest* (New York: Little Brown and Company, 1996), 20.

2. Nicholas P. Money, *Mr. Bloomfield's Orchard: The Mysterious World of Mushrooms, Molds, and Mycologists* (Oxford: Oxford University Press, 2002), 10.

3. Vilém Flusser, *Vampyroteuthis infernalis*, trans. Rodrigo Maltez Novaes (New York: Atropos, 2011), 32.

4. According to the World Meteorological Organization, 2019, 2020, and 2023 were three of the warmest years since records began, with 2023 smashing the record "by a huge margin."

5. On the sulfurous smell of the Devil, as well as an account of the stink of sin and sickness in early modern Europe and the olfactory remedies

often prescribed to survive them, see Robert
Muchembled's excellent chapter "Towards
a History of the Senses: The Demonizing of Smell,"
in *A History of the Devil: From the Middle Ages
to the Present*, trans. Jean Birrel (London: Polity
Press, 2003), 99–107.

6. Robin Kirkpatrick, "Commentary to Canto 1,"
in Dante Alighieri, *Inferno*, trans. and ed. Robin
Kirkpatrick (London: Penguin Classics, 2010), 316.

7. Some have challenged the notion that the high-
pitched noise Cage reportedly heard was, as Gena
attributed it to, the sound of his nervous system,
suggesting it was more likely the effects of tinnitus.
See David Revill, *The Roaring Silence: John Cage—
A Life* (London: Bloomsbury, 1992), 162; and Craig
Dworkin, *No Medium* (London: MIT Press, 2015),
190, n.12. On tinnitus as a sometimes precedent
or accompaniment to auditory hallucinations,
see Oliver Sacks, *Musicophilia: Tales of Music and
the Brain* (London: Picador, 2011), 69.

8. John Cage, *Silence: Lectures and Writings by
John Cage* (Middletown, CT: Wesleyan University
Press, 1973), 8.

9. In a lecture delivered in 1997, Russian philosopher
Vladimir Bibikhin explored how humans have
"exhausted" both living and ancient (fossilized)
forests by "burning" the elements they have yielded.
Discussing forests as a potential site for renewing
our philosophical energy, Bibikhin dwells on the
curious history of the word matter [Greek: ὑλη, *hyle*]
and its origins in ancient Greek philosophy meaning
"wood," "forest." See Vladimir Bibikhin, "Lecture
1," *The Woods (Hyle)*, ed. Artemy Magun, trans.
Arch Tait (Cambridge: Polity Press, 2021), 6–16 (8).

10. John Cage, *For the Birds: John Cage in
Conversation with Daniel Charles* (London: Marion
Boyars, 2000), 188.

ILLUSTRATIONS

0. Introduction

p. 10: Paul Gustave Doré's illustration to Dante's *Inferno*, Canto 1. (Copperplate etching. In *Divine Comedy: Hell, Purgatory, Paradise*, plate 1. By Dante Alighieri. Translation by Henry W. Longfellow. London: Arcturus Books, 2007.)

p. 13: Examples of "stink lines" used to illustrate unseen smells emanating from a malodorous object offscreen. (Video still. From "Son of Stimpy" a.k.a. "Stimpy's First Fart." *The Ren & Stimpy Show*. Directed by Kelly Armstrong, Bob Camp, and John K. Spumco: 1993.)

p. 15: Slide from performance lecture by Siôn Parkinson titled *On Sound and Smell* (2019) showing a limestone votive ear (Cypriot, 4th–3rd century BCE) and nose from terracotta mask (Greek, Laconian, 6th century BCE). (Color photographs. The Metropolitan Museum of Art, New York. Public domain.)

p. 19: The anatomy of the ear showing the gap between the nasal cavity and inner ear connected by the eustachian tube. (Drawing. By John Cunningham Saunders. 1806. Wellcome Collection. Public domain.)

p. 20: An abstract illustration purportedly showing the conflicting emotions of "Selfish Affection," a synesthetic "cloud-like ovoid, or aura." (Color illustration. In *Thought-Forms*, plate 9. By Annie Besant and Charles Leadbeater. Bradford: Percy Lund, Humphries & Co., 1901.)

1. On Stink

p. 30: "'Solar protuberances' observed on May 5, 1873 at 9:40am." Print showing massive eruptions of hydrogen gas from the surface of the sun. (Lithographic color print. By Étienne Léopold Trouvelot. 1881–1882. Rare Book Division, The New York Public Library Digital Collections. Public domain.)

p. 32: "A durian (*Durio zibethinus*); an entire and sectioned fruit." Note, the epithet *zibethinus* derives from the name of the large Indian civet *Viverra zibetha*. (Monochrome photograph. By Scowen & Co. Date unknown. Wellcome Collection. Public domain.)

p. 36: The body of Saint Thérèse de Lisieux in the choir, Notre Dame du Mont Carmel, Lisieux, photographed by her sister on October 3, 1897, three days after her death. (Photograph. By Céline Martin. Les Archives du Carmel de Lisieux. Public domain.)

p. 40: Neo-Assyrian bell, (Transcaucasia or Iran), bronze, iron c.8th–7th century BCE. (Monochrome photograph. The Metropolitan Museum of Art, New York. Public domain.)

p. 42: A Limoges porcelain box in the shape of a cornucopia, or "Horn of Plenty." (Slide from performance lecture *On Sound and Smell*. By Siôn Parkinson. 2019.)

2. Sight

p. 44: An early woodblock, shown here the right way up, of the dune stinkhorn *Phallus hadriani* made for the famous Plantin Press, first used to illustrate Clusius's *Rariorum plantarum historia* (1601). The block was subsequently loaned to other publishers across Europe, including Norton, the London printers of Gerard's *Herball* (1633). The original woodblock housed in the Plantin-Moretus Museum, Antwerp, shows a piece of paper affixed to the reverse. Written in ink, the following can be made out: "Plant. Phallus [text unclear], Dod'. Herbal. 1618, 3.15,25 [presumably the woodcut's catalog number], p. 785." It's not known when this piece of paper was pasted to the back of the block, obscuring another earlier inscription written directly onto the wood. What *is* clear is that this was the block that was used by Francis van Ravelinghen in Plantin's Leiden shop to illustrate Rembert Dodoens's second edition of his successful *Cruydt-Boeck* (1618). (Photograph. Museum Plantin-Moretus, Antwerp. Public domain.)

p. 50: A whole fly in segments showing the side of the chest and stomach. (Hand-colored copperplate engraving by Wolfgang Winterschmidt. In *Mikroskopische Gemüths- und Augen-Ergötzung* [Microscopic Delights of the Mind and Eyes], vol. 3, plate 42. By Martin Frobenius Ledermüller. Nuremberg: Christian de Launoy, 1768.)

p. 53: The earliest example of a printed fungus in a published book. (Woodcut. In *Hortus sanitatis. De Herbis et Plantis, de Animalibus et Reptilibus, de Avibus et Volatilibus, de Piscibus et Natatilibus, de Lapidibus et in terre venis nascentibus, de Urinis et earum speciebus*, book 1, plate 302. Author unknown. Mainz: Jacob Meydenbach, 1491.)

p. 56: "Stinking Morell or Stink Horn, *Phallus impudicus*." (Watercolor drawing. In *Icons fungorum circa Halifax sponte Nascentium* [An History of Fungesses Growing about Halifax], vol. 1, plate 31. By James Bolton. Printed by him in 1784.)

p. 62: The misprinted stinkhorn, described as "Fungus virilis penis effigie, or Pricke Mushroom," on p. 1583 of Gerard's *Herball*. (Woodcut. In *The Herball, or, Generall Historie of Plantes*. By John Gerard. London: John Norton, 1633 and 1636.)

p. 64: "The Circle of the Falsifiers: Dante and Virgil Covering Their Noses Because of the Stench." From Dante's *Inferno*, Canto 29. (Unfinished line engraving. In *Illustrations to Dante's Divine Comedy*. By William Blake. c.1826–1827. Buffalo AKG Art Museum. Public domain.)

p. 81: A sixteenth-century woodcut showing mushrooms, described as "agarics," growing amid snakes, snails, and rotting a tree stump. (Woodcut. In *Commentarii secundo aucti, in libros sex*. By Petro Andreae Matthiolus. Venice: Vincenzo Valgrisi, 1558.)

p. 82: Detail of serpent from *Commentarii*. (Matthiolus. 1558.)

p. 83: "Description of all the genera of the Phallus." (Copperplate engraving. In *Theatrum fungorum*, Plate 30. By Franciscus van Sterbeeck. Antwerp: Josef Jakobs, 1675.)

p. 85: Detail of figures K, L, and M from "Description of all the genera of the Phallus." (Sterbeeck. 1675.)

p. 86: A scene from the motion picture *Society* showing "The Shunt" in full flow. Special effects by Screaming Mad George. (Video still. From *Society*. Directed by Brian Yuzna. Wild Street Pictures: 1989.)

p. 87: George Seger's imaginative depiction of the earthstar "*Fungus anthropomorhpus*," first published in 1671, reproduced by Sterbeeck a few years later in his major fungi book, *Theatrum fungorum*. (Copperplate engraving. In *Theatrum fungorum*, plate 29. By Franciscus van Sterbeeck. Antwerp: Josef Jakobs, 1675.)

3. Smell

p. 88: Dune stinkhorn slime smeared on torn endpaper. (Photograph. By Siôn Parkinson. 2022.)

p. 91: Goat moth wax cap *Hygrophorus cossus*. (Monochrome photograph. By Siôn Parkinson. 2022.)

p. 91: Goat moth caterpillar *Cossus cossus*. (Photograph. By D. Dreise Bothe. 2011. Via Wikimedia Commons: CC BY-SA 3.0.)

p. 92: A feral billy goat with long horns. (Wood engraving [Dutch]. Artist and date unknown. Wellcome Collection. Public domain.)

p. 93: Goat moth caterpillar and adult moth *Cossus ligniperda*, now *Cossus cossus*. (Lithograph. Colored by Joseph Standish. In *British Entomology*, vol. 5, plate 60. By John Curtis. London: E. Ellis and Co., 1823–1840.)

p. 98: John Curtis's illustration of a large fly drawn towards the tip of a supposedly violet-smelling dune stinkhorn *Phallus hadriani*, shown here without any of its reeking slime. (Colored lithograph. In *British Entomology*, vol. 10, plate 469. By John Curtis. London: printed for the author by E. Ellis and Co., 1823–1840).

p. 100: The corpse flower *Rafflesia arnoldii*. (Colored copperplate engraving by Franz Bauer. In *An Account of a New Genus of Plants, Named Rafflesia*, plate 15. By Robert Brown. London: Richard and Arthur Taylor, 1821.)

p. 100: Underside view of a giant bud of the corpse flower *Rafflesia arnoldii*, showing the bracket root where the plant parasitizes a vine (looking here like a severed finger shushing an open, necrotic wound). (Copperplate engraving [rotated] by Franz Bauer. In *Rafflesia*, plate 17. By Robert Brown. London: Richard and Arthur Taylor, 1821.)

p. 101: Dead horse arum lily *Dracunculus crinitus* (now *Helicodiceros muscivorus*) with blowflies. (Hand-colored lithograph. In *Flore des Serres et des Jardins del Europe*, vol. 5. By Louis van Houtte. Ghent, Belgium: A. Gand, 1849.)

p. 108: A mature dune stinkhorn *Phallus hadrianus* growing in a clump of marram grass, St Cyrus, Scotland, September 2022. (Monochrome photograph. By Siôn Parkinson. 2022.)

p. 111: M. C. Cooke's drawing of the red cage stinkhorn, a mushroom described by him as smelling "intensely fetid" and "unbearable." (Colored lithograph. In *Fungi: Their Nature, Influence, and Uses*, plate 20. By Mordecai Cubitt Cooke. London: Henry S. King & Co., 1875.)

4. Sound

p. 112: Common houseflies and cheese skippers *Piophilia casei*. Cheese skipper flies are one of the longest-known domestic pests. Their larvae—which have been reported to leap, or "skip," up to twelve centimeters—are known to infest cheese, cured meats, and fish. Cheese skipper larvae are introduced to *pecorino* to form *casu martzu* (literally "rotten cheese"), a traditional Sardinian sheep milk cheese served with live maggots. The metaphor of maggots springing from a lump of cheese as angels, or humans, emerging from chaotic matter inspired the title of Carlo Ginzburg's famous treatise on sixteenth-century cosmologies, *Il formaggio e i vermi* (The cheese and the worms), published in 1976. (Scanned page from book. In "The cheese skipper as a pest in cured meats," *U.S. Department of Agriculture Bulletin*, no. 1453. By Perez Simmons. 1927. Via Wikimedia Commons. Public domain.)

p. 115: "The larva and mature form of a female housefly (*Musca domestica*) magnified twenty-four times its actual size." (Pen and ink drawing with watercolor. By A.J.E. Terzi. Date unknown. Wellcome Collection. Public domain.)

p. 117: Fragment from a marble head of a man, preserving the nose and mouth, mid-second century CE. (Photograph. The Metropolitan Museum of Art, New York. Public domain.)

p. 118: The plural anatomies of the housefly *Musca domestica*, showing (clockwise) eggs, larvae, pupae, and mature flies. (Photograph. Photographer and date unknown. Clemson University, South Carolina, USA. Via Wikimedia Commons: CC BY-SA 3.0.)

p. 122: The gleba of a ripe stinkhorn *Phallus impudicus* being devoured by a frenzy of flies. (Photograph. By Hildesvini. 2011. Via Wikimedia Commons: CC BY 4.0.)

p. 125: Wood ear fungus *Auricularia auricula-judae* growing on dead branch. (Color photograph. By Dominicus Johannes Bergsma. 2017. Via Wikimedia Commons: CC BY 4.0.)

p. 126: Postcard collected by John Cage c. 1980. (Photo collage. By Gerry Miller. Reproduced with kind permission by the Library and Archives of the University of California Santa Cruz, home to the John Cage Mycology Collection.)

5. Phantom Stink

p. 128: MRI visualization (sagittal view) of the author's brain showing at its center the dark, hook-shaped uncus, the part of the brain where olfactory and auditory hallucinations are thought to originate as part of epileptic sensory auras. (MRI digital image. Courtesy of Ninewells Hospital, NHS Dundee. 2021.)

p. 132: Rotated still of artist Hollis Frampton's experimental short film *Lemon* showing the nose-like blossom end of the fruit. (Video still. From *Lemon*. Directed by Hollis Frampton. 1969.)

p. 133: MRI visualization (axial view) of the author's brain showing the external sensory organs: eyes, ears, and nose. (MRI digital image. Courtesy of Ninewells Hospital, NHS Dundee. 2021.)

p. 137: A woman referred to only as "M …" in the grips of an epileptic seizure with sensory hallucination "seeming to show a strong repugnance," possibly phantosmia. The photograph by physician and medical photographer Paul-Marie-Léon Regnard was taken at La Salpêtrière hospice, Paris. Salpêtrière was originally a gunpowder factory, hence its name. Since the mid-1600s, the hospice was dedicated to the care for women "of bad behavior," or those with learning disabilities, mental illness, and epilepsy. This image is one of over a hundred photographs depicting young women in various phases of epileptic "attacks," including several hallucinations, published in a book commissioned by the pioneering French neurologist Jean-Martin Charcot. (Albumen photographic print with letterpress caption. In *Iconographie photographique de la Salpêtrière*, plate 35. By Jean-Martin Charcot with text by Désiré-Magloire Bourneville. Paris: Les Bureaux du progrès medical, 1875.)

p. 140: A volva cross section of the stinkhorn *Diectyophora duplicata*, now *Phallus duplicatus*, the netted stinkhorn or wood witch. (Photograph. In "Wild Mushrooms as Food." By William Alphonso Murrill. *The American Museum Journal*, no. 17, May 1917, p. 323.)

p. 162: *Skull lichen Muscus ex Craneo Humano*, first printed as part of a volume of 2,255 plant illustrations by German botanist Jacobus Theodorus. (Woodcut. In *Eicones plantarum seu stirpium*, 805. By Tabernaemontanus. Frankfurt am Main: Nicolaus Bassaeus, 1590.)

p. 164: Illustration of three phallic fungi: right (no. 1), *Phallus tremelloides*, now *Morchella esculenta*, the common morel; left (no. 2), *Phallus crassipes*, now *Morchella semilibera*, the half-free morel;

and middle (no. 3), *Phallus indusiatus*, the bridal veil stinkhorn or bamboo fungus. Note, only the latter is a true phalloid. (Copperplate engraving. From "Dissertation sur le genre phallus," *Mémoires de l'Institut des Sciences et Arts*, vol. 1, 503. By Étienne Pierre Ventenat. Paris: printed by Baudouin on behalf of Institut de France, 1798.)

p. 167: Detail of the brain-like common morel (no. 1) from Ventenat's illustration in his "Dissertation sur le genre phallus," 1798.

Photographs on pages 145–51 by Siôn Parkinson, 2021–22.

BIBLIOGRAPHY

A Matter of Life and Death. Directed by Michael Powell and Emeric Pressburger. Criterion Collection, 2018.

The Act of Seeing with One's Own Eyes. Directed by Stan Brakhage. Canyon, 1971.

Ackerman, Diane. *A Natural History of the Senses*. London: Vintage, 1990.

Adorno, Theodor W. "Music, Language, and Composition." *The Musical Quarterly* 77, no. 3 (1993): 401–14.
———. *Current of Music*. Edited by Robert Hullot-Kentor. Cambridge: Polity Press, 2009.
———. *Essays on Music*. Edited by Richard Leppert. Berkeley, CA: University of California Press, 2002.
———. *Philosophy of New Music*. Translated by Robert Hullot-Kentor. Minneapolis, MN: University of Minnesota Press, 2006.

Alighieri, Dante. *Divine Comedy*. Translated by Henry Wadsworth Longfellow. eBook: Digiread, 1997.
———. *Inferno*. Translated and edited by Robin Kirkpatrick. London: Penguin Classics, 2010.

Allegro, John M. *The Sacred Mushroom and the Cross*. London: Gnostic Media, 2009.

Annand, Sam. *Four Celestial Bodies*. Unreleased EP, 2019.

Anzieu, Didier. *The Skin Ego*. Translated by Chris Turner. New Haven, CT: Yale University Press, 1989.

Aretaeus. "On the Paroxysm of Epileptics." *De causis et signis acutorum Morborum*. eBook: Perseus Digital Library.

Artuad, Antonin. "All Writing Is Pigshit." *Antonin Anthology*. Edited by Jack Hirschman. San Francisco: City Lights Books, 2008.

Ashton, Rosemary. *One Hot Summer: Dickens, Darwin, Disraeli, and the Great Stink of 1858*. London: Yale University Press, 2017.

Ashworth, J. M., and Jennifer Dee. *The Biology of Slime Moulds*. London: Edward Arnold, 1975.

Atali, Jacques. *Noise: The Political Economy of Music*. Translated by Brian Massumi. Minneapolis, MN: University of Minnesota Press, 2017.

Author unknown. "Ammonia (NH3) Emissions." European Environment Agency. January 29, 2014. https://www.eea.europa.eu/data-and-maps/indicators/eea-32-ammonia-nh3-emissions-1/assessment-4.

Author unknown. "Buzz off." *New Scientist* 214, no. 2865 (2012): 65. https://doi.org/10.1016/S0262-4079(12)61310-4.

Author unknown. "Chandra 'Hears' a Black Hole For the First Time." Chandra X-Ray Observatory, NASA. September 9, 2003. https://chandra.harvard.edu/press/03_releases/press_090903.html.

Author unknown. *Geldersche Volksalmanak*. Arnhem: Nijhoff en Zoon, 1855: 10–11.

Author unknown. *The Priapeia: Sportive Epigrams of divers Poets on Priapus*. Translated by Leonard C. Smithers and Richard Burton. Charlston: Biblio Bazaar Reproduction, 2008.

Axel, Richard. "Lecture: Scents and Sensibility: A Molecular Logic of Olfactory Perception." Nobel Prize. December 8, 2004. https://www.nobelprize.org/prizes/medicine/2004/axel/lecture/.

Ayers, Elaine. "Noble Rot." *Cabinet Magazine*, no. 64 (March 2017): 71–75.

B., David. *Epileptic*. London: Jonathan Cape, 2005.

Baba, Masashi, Fumio Ogawaa, Shinsaku Hiuraa, and Naoki Asada. "Height Estimation of Hiroshima A-bomb Mushroom Cloud from Photos." *Revisit The Hiroshima A-bomb with a Database: Latest Scientific View on Local Fallout and Black Rain*. Edited by Michio Aoyama and Yutaka Oochi. Hiroshima: Hiroshima City, 2013.

Badham, Charles David. *A Treatise on the Esculent Funguses of England*. London: Lovell Reeve & Co., 1863.

Bailey, Derek. *Improvisation: Its Nature and Practice in Music*. London: The British Library National Sound Archive, 1992.

Bakkar, Sally, Sherif Abdel-Aal, and Amany Nafee. "Erectile dysfunction among patients with chronic brucellosis." *International Journal of Impotence Research*, no. 30 (2018): 230–36. https://doi.org/10.1038/s41443-018-0068-9.

Barbour, J. Murray. *Tuning and Temperament: A Historical Survey*. New York: Da Capo Press, 1972.

Barkham, Patrick. "UK Scientists Confirm Arrival of Brown Marmorated Stink Bugs." *Guardian*. March 1, 2021. https://www.theguardian

.com/environment/2021/mar/01/uk-scientists-confirm-arrival-of-brown-marmorated-stink-bugs.

Barthes, Roland. *Camera Lucida*. Translated by Richard Howard. London: Vintage, 2000.
———. *Image, Music, Text*. Translated by Stephen Heath. London: Fontana Press, 1982.
———. *Sade, Foruier, Loyola*. Translated by Richard Miller. Berkeley, CA: University of California Press, 1989.
———. *The Pleasure of the Text*. Translated by Richard Miller. New York: Hill and Wang, 1975.

Barwich, A. S. *Smellosophy: What the Nose Tells the Mind*. Cambridge, MA: Harvard University Press, 2020.

Bataille, Georges. "'The Big Toe' and 'The Jesuve: The Pineal Eye.'" *Georges Bataille: Visions of Excess: Selected Writings, 1927–1939*. Edited by Allan Stoekl, 20–23, 73–90. Minneapolis, MN: University of Minnesota Press, 1985.

Batty, Clare. "Smelling Lessons." *Philosophical Studies: An International Journal for Philosophy in the Analytic Tradition* 153, no. 1 (2011): 161–74. https://www.jstor.org/stable/41487622.

Baumeister, Roy. *The Cultural Animal: Human Nature, Meaning, and Social Life*. Oxford: Oxford University Press, 2005.

Beament, James. *How We Hear Music: The Relationship Between Music and the Hearing Mechanism*. Woodbridge: Boydell Press, 2005.

Bede. *The Ecclesiastical History of the English People*. Translated by Thomas Miller. Cambridge, ON: In Parentheses Publications, 1999.

Berkeley, M. J. "Egg Fungi." *The Intellectual Observer* 9:7 (July, 1866), 401–406 (402).

Bibikhin, Vladimir. *The Woods (Hyle)*. Edited by Artemy Magun. Translated by Arch Tait. Cambridge: Polity Press, 2021.

Bierce, Ambrose. *The Devil's Dictionary*. New York: Dover Publications, 1993.

Blanco, María del Pilar, and Esther Peeren, eds. *The Spectralities Reader: Ghosts and Haunting in Contemporary Cultural Theory*. London: Bloomsbury, 2013.

Blodgett, Bonnie. *Remembering Smell: A Memoir of Losing—and Discovering—The Primal Sense*. New York: Houghton Mifflin Harcourt, 2010.

Bodenheimer, Friedrich S. *Insects as Human Food*. The Hague: Dr W. Junk, 1951.

Boisver, Donald L. "The Temple of Priapus: Contemporary Phallus Worshippers in Montreal." *The Mystical Geography of Quebec: Catholic Schisms and New Religious Movements*. Edited by Susan J. Palmer, Martin Geoffroy, and Paul L. Gareau, 151–65. Cham: Palgrave Macmillan, 2020.

Bové, Frank James. *The Story of Ergot*. Basel: S. Karger, 1970.

Breton, André. *Poems of André Breton: A Bilingual Anthology*. Translated by Jean-Pierre Cauvin and Mary Caws. Boston: Black Widow, 2006.

Briggs, Kate. *This Little Art*. London: Fitzcarraldo Editions, 2017.

Brown, Mark, and Robert Booth. "Death of two-year-old from mould in flat a 'defining moment', says coroner." *The Guardian*. November 15, 2022. https://www.theguardian.com/uk-news/2022/nov/15/death-of-two-year-old-awaab-ishak-chronic-mould-in-flat-a-defining-moment-says-coroner.

Buxton, Julian. "National life tables—life expectancy in the UK: 2018 to 2020." Office for National Statistics. September 23, 2011. https://www.ons.gov.uk/peoplepopulationandcommunity/birthsdeathsandmarriages/lifeexpectancies/bulletins/nationallifetablesunitedkingdom/2018to2020.

Butler, Judith. "Reply from Judith Butler." *Philosophy and Phenomenological Research* 96, no. 1 (2018): 243–49. https://doi.org/10.1111/phpr.12481.
———. *Bodies That Matter: On the Discursive Limits of Sex*. London: Routledge, 2011.

Cage, John. *A Mycological Foray*. Los Angeles: Atelier Éditions, 2020.
———. *For the Birds: John Cage in Conservation with Daniel Charles*. London: Marion Boyars, 2000.
———. *Notations*. New York: Something Else Press, 1969.
———. *Silence: Lectures and Writings by John Cage*. Middletown, CT: Wesleyan University Press, 1973.
———. *Works for Prepared Piano*. Col Legno, 1998.

Cardew, Cornelius. *Treatise*. Buffalo, NY: The Gallery Upstairs Press, 1967.

Carlyle, Angus, and Cathy Lane, eds. *On Listening*. Padstow: Uniformbooks, 2015.

Carp, Louis. "George Gershwin, Illustrious American composer: His fatal Glioblastoma." *The American Journal of Surgical Pathology* 3, no. 5 (1979): 473–77.

Carroll, Noel. *The Philosophy of Horror.* New York: Routledge, 1990.

Chion, Michel. *Sound: An Ecological Treatise.* Translated by James A. Steintrager. Durham, NC: Duke University Press, 2016.

Cioran, E. M. *A Short History of Decay.* Translated by Richard Howard. London: Penguin Books, 2018.
———. *The Trouble with Being Born.* Translated by Richard Howard. London: Penguin Books, 2020.

Classen, Constance, David Howers, and Anthony Synott. *Aroma: The Cultural History of Smell.* London: Routledge, 2002.

Cobb, Matthew. *Smell: A Very Short Introduction.* Oxford: Oxford University Press, 2020.

Cobussen, Marcel, Vincent Meelberg, and Barry Turax, eds. *The Routledge Companion to Sounding Art.* London: Routledge, 2017.

Collins, Percy. "Insects That Are Eaten." *Scientific American* 98, no. 4 (1908): 63–64. https://www.jstor.org/stable/26006884.

Connor, Steven. *Beyond Words.* London: Reaktion Books, 2014.
———. *Fly.* London: Reaktion Books, 2009.
———. *The Book of Skin.* London: Reaction Books, 2004.
———. *The Matter of Air: Science and Art of the Ethereal.* London: Reaction Books, 2010.

Cooke, M. C. *Fungi: Their Nature, Influence, and Uses.* London: Henry S. King & Co., 1875.

Corbin, Alain. *The Foul & The Fragrant: Odor and the Social Imagination.* London: Papermac, 1996.
———. *Village Bells: Sound and Meaning in the 19th Century French Countryside.* Translated by Martin Thom. Cambridge: Papermac, 1999.

Corngold, Stanley. "Nietzsche's Moods." *Studies in Romanticism: Nietzsche and Romanticism* 29, no. 1 (1990): 67–90. http://www.jstor.org/stable/25600822.

Cossé, Allard A., and Thomas C. Baker. "House Flies and Pig Manure Volatiles: Wind Tunnel Behavioral Studies and Electrophysiological Evaluations." *Journal of Agricultural Entomology* 13, no. 4 (1996): 301–17.

Coulter, Charles Russel, and Patricia Turner, eds. *Encyclopaedia of Ancient Deities.* London: Fitzroy Dearborn, 2000.

Cox, Christopher, and Daniel Warner, eds. *Audio Culture: Readings in Modern Music.* London: Continuum, 2017.

Cramer, John G. "The Sound of the Big Bang." University of Washington. March 30, 2013. https://faculty.washington.edu/jcramer/BBSound.html.

Cripps, Cathy Lynn. *Fungi in Forest Ecosystems: Systematics, Diversity and Ecology.* New York: The New York Botanical Press, 2004.

Critchley, Macdonald. "Musicogenic Epilepsy." *Brain* 60, no. 1 (1937): 13–27. https://doi.org/10.1093/brain/60.1.13.

Curtis, Abi. "Mushrooming: Resistance and Creativity in Sigmund Freud and Emily Dickinson." *Angelaki* 18, no. 2 (2013): 29–44. https://doi.org/10.1080/0969725X.2013.804989.

Curtis, John. *British Entomology; being illustrations and descriptions of the genera of insects found in Great Britain and Ireland.* London: E. Ellis and Co., 1823–1840.

Cutler, Ivor. "The Path." *Jammy Smears.* Virgin, 1976.

Daley, April. "Do All Houseflies Hum in Key?" *Mental Floss.* October 14, 2015. https://www.mentalfloss.com/article/69639/do-all-houseflies-hum-key.

Daniel, Chris. "What causes the fresh smell before a storm?" *New Scientist.* June 26, 2019. https://www.newscientist.com/lastword/mg24232361-300-what-causes-the-fresh-smell-beforeastorm.

Darrieussecq, Marie. *Pig Tales: A Novel of Lust and Transformation.* Translated by Linda Coverdale. New York: The New Press, 1997.

Darwin, Erasmus. *The Botanic Garden: A Poem in Two Parts.* eBook: Project Gutenberg, 2006. https://books.apple.com/us/book/the-botanic-garden/id506180580.

Davachi, Sara. "Perfumes I–II." *Pale Bloom.* W. 25th, 2019.

Davey, Melissa. "What is the deadly 'black fungus' seen in Covid patients in India?" *The Guardian.* May 11, 2021. https://www.theguardian.com/global/2021/may/11/what-is-the-dangerous-black-fungus-being-seen-in-covid-patients-in-india-mucormycosis.

Davis, Miles. "Blue in Green." *Kind of Blue.* Columbia Records, 2008.

Del Amo, Jean-Baptise. *Animalia.* Translated by Frank Wynne. London: Fitzcarraldo Editions, 2019.

Derrida, Jacques. *Of Grammatology*. Translated by Gayatri Chakravorty Spivak. London: John Hopkins University Press, 1997.
———. *Resistances of Psychoanalysis*. Translated by Peggy Kamuf, Pascale-Anne Brault and Michael Naas. Stanford, CA: Stanford University Press, 1998.

Dickinson, Emily. "The Mushroom is the Elf of Plants – (1350)." *Poetry Foundation*. https://www.poetryfoundation.org/poems/56458/the-mushroom-is-the-elf-of-plants-1350.

Dillon, Brian. *Objects in This Mirror: Essays*. Berlin: Sternberg, 2014.

Dodoens, Rembert. *A Nievve Herball, or Historie of Plantes*. Translated by Henry Lyte. London: Gerard Dewes, 1578.

Dolar, Mladen. *The Voice and Nothing More*. Cambridge, MA: MIT Press, 2006.

Dongen, Pieter W. J. van, and Akosua N. J. A. de Groot. "History of ergot alkaloids from ergotism to ergometrine." *European Journal of Obstetrics & Gynaecology and Reproductive Biology* 60, no. 2 (1995): 109–16. https://doi.org/10.1016/0028-2243(95)02104-Z.

Dostoevsky, Fyodor. *The Brothers Karamazov*. Translated by David McDuff. London: Penguin Books, 2003.
———. *The Idiot*. Translated by David McDuff. London: Penguin Books, 2004.
———. *The Possessed or The Devils*. Translated by Constance Garnett. eBook: Project Gutenberg, 2010.

The Duke of Burgundy. Directed by Peter Strickland. Film4, 2014.

Drobnick, Jim, ed. *The Smell Culture Reader*. Oxford: Berg, 2006.

Drury, Susan. "Funeral Plants and Flowers in England: Some Examples." *Folklore*, 105 (1994): 101–103.

Duffin, Christopher J. "'The periwig of a dead cranium': medicinal skull moss." *Pharmaceutical Historian* 52, no. 3: (September 2022), 75–85 (77–78).

Dugan, Holly. *The Ephemeral History of Perfume: Scent and Sense in Early Modern England*. Baltimore, MD: John Hopkins University Press, 2011.

Dworkin, Craig. "Mycopedagogy." *College English* 66, no. 6 (2004): 603–11. https://www.jstor.org/stable/4140742.
———. *No Medium*. London: MIT Press, 2015.

Efron, Robert. "The Effect of Olfactory Stimuli in Arresting Uncinate Fits." *Brain* 79, no. 2 (June 1956): 267–81. https://doi.org/10.1093/brain/79.2.267.

Eno, Brian. "The Future Will Be Like Perfume." *More Dark Than Shark*. https://www.moredarkthanshark.org/feature_opal_info_22-1992.html.
———. *Neroli*. All Saints Records, 1993.

Euripides. *Suppliant Women. Electra. Heracles.* Translated and Edited by David Kovacs. Cambridge, MA: Harvard University Press, 1998.

Fantastic Fungi. Directed by Louis Schwartzberg. Moving Art, 2019.

Findlay, W.P.K. *Fungi: Folklore, Fiction, & Fact*. Richmond, UK: The Richmond Publishing Company, 1982.

Fischer, Nadine S., and Martin Steinhaus. "Identification of an Important Odorant Precursor in Durian: First Evidence of Ethionine in Plants." *Journal of Agricultural and Food Chemistry* 68, no. 38 (2019): 10397–402. https://doi.org/10.1021/acs.jafc.9b07065.

Flusser, Vilém. *Vampyroteuthis infernalis*. Translated by Rodrigo Maltez Novaes. Milton Keynes: Atropos Press, 2011.

Foucault, Michel. *The Order of Things*. London: Routledge, 2005.

Fourré, Guy "Potirinus." *Pièges et curiosités des Champignons*. Maulévrier, France: self-published, printed by André-Hubert Hérault, 1985.

Foyaca-Sibat, Humberto. *Novel Aspects on Epilepsy*. Rijeka: Intech, 2011.

Freud, Sigmund. *Civilization and Its Discontents*. Translated by David McLintock. London: Penguin, 2004.
———. *The Interpretation of Dreams*. Translated and edited by James Strachey. London: Hogarth, 1990.
———. *The Standard Edition of The Complete Psychological Works of Sigmund Freud: Volume X: Two Cases: 'Little Hans' & 'The Rat Man.'* Translated by James Strachey. London: Hogarth Press, 1981.

Galen, Aelius. "Advice for an Epileptic Boy." Translated by Owen Temkin. *Bulletin of the Institute of the History of Medicine* 2, no. 3 (1934): 179–89. https://www.jstor.org/stable/44437787.

Gasenzer, Elena, and Edmund A. M. Neugebauer. "George Gershwin: A case of new ways in neurosurgery as well as in the history of western music." *Acta Neurochirurgica*, 156 (2014): 1251–258. https://doi.org/10.1007/s00701-014-2045-5.

Garber, Megan. "What Space Smells Like." *The Atlantic*. July 19, 2012. https://www.theatlantic.com/technology/archive/2012/07what-space-smells-like/259903/.

Gavin, Francesca, ed. *Mushrooms: The Art, Design and Future of Fungi*. London: Somerset House, 2020. Exhibition catalogue.

Gellen, Kate. "Stimmung, Sound, and Space in Robert Musil's 'Die Versuchung der stillen Veronika.'" *Seminar: A Journal of Germanic Studies* 54, no. 3, (2018): 328–49. https://doi.org/10.3138/seminar.54.3.003.

Gerard, John. *The Herball, or, Generall Historie of Plantes*. London: John Norton, 1597.

Ginzburg, Carlo. *Ecstasies: Deciphering the Witches' Sabbath*. Translated by Raymond Rosenthal. Chicago: University of Chicago Press, 1991.

Gisbertz, Anna-Katharina, ed. *Stimmung: Zur Wiederkehr einer ästhetischen Kategorie*. Munich: Wilhelm Fink Verlag, 2011.

Glindemann, Dietmar, Andrea Dietrich, Hans-Joachim Staerk, and Peter Kuschk. "The Two Odors of Iron when Touched or Pickled: (Skin) Carbonyl Compounds and Organophosphines." *Angewandte Chemie* 45, no. 42 (2006): 7,006–7,009. https://doi.org/10.1002/anie.200602100.

Glinsky, Albert. *Theremin: Ether Music and Espionage*. Champaign, IL: University of Illinois Press, 2005.

Goddard, Michael, Benjamin Halligan, and Paul Hegarty, eds. *Reverberations: The Philosophy, Aesthetics and Politics of Noise*. London: Continuum, 2012.

González-Burgos Elena, Carlos Fernández-Moriano, and M. Pilar Gómez-Serranillos. "Current knowledge on Parmelia genus: Ecological interest, phytochemistry, biological activities and therapeutic potential." *Phytochemistry* 165 (September 2019): 112,051. https://doi.org/10.1016/j.phytochem.2019.112051.

Goodman, Steve. *Sonic Warfare: Sound, Affect, and the Ecology of Fear*. Cambridge, MA: MIT Press, 2012.

Gowers, William. "A Clinical Lecture on Minor Epilepsy." *The British Medical Journal* 1, no. 2036 (1900): 1–5. https://www.jstor.org/stable/20263008.

Grant, Colin. *The Smell of Burning: A Memoir of Epilepsy*. London: Vintage, 2017.

Graves, Robert. *The Shout & Other Stories*. Middlesex: Penguin Books, 1978.

Greshoff, Maurits. "Een Natuurhistorisch Ducument Der 16de Eeuw." *De Levende Natuur* 11, no. 8 (1906): 141–44. https://www.dbnl.org/arch/_lev013190601_01/pag/_lev013190601_01.pdf.

Grieg, Edvard. "Peer Gynt Suite Nr. 1, Op. 46: 2. The Death of Aase." *Grieg: Peer Gynt*. Haenssler Classic, 2007.

Grimay, Aracelis. *Kingdom Animalia*. Rochester, NY: BOA Editions, 2011.

Grimm, Jacob, and Wilhem Grimm. "Mutterkorn." *Deutsches Wörterbuch*. Trier: Universität Trier, 2004.

Guerney, Edmund, Frederic W. H. Myers, and Frank Podmore. *Phantasms of the Living*, vol. I. eBook: Rooms of the Society for Psychical Research; Trübner and Co, 1886.

Gulland, Anne. "Revealed: why meat processing plants are the ideal incubator of the coronavirus." *The Telegraph*. June 19, 2020. https://www.telegraph.co.uk/global-health/science-and-disease/revealed-meat-processing-plants-ideal-incubator-coronavirus/.

Gumbrecht, Hans Ulrich. *Atmosphere, Mood, Stimmung: On a Hidden Potential of Literature*. Translated by Erik Butler. Stanford, CA: Stanford University Press, 2012.

Haarmann, Thomas, Yvonne Rolle, Sabine Giesbert, and Paul Tudzynski. "Ergot: from witchcraft to biotechnology." *Molecular Plant Pathology* 10, no. 4 (2009): 563–77. https://doi.org/10.1111/j.1364-3703.2009.00548.x.

Hainge, Greg. *Noise Matters: Towards an Ontology of Noise*. London: Bloomsbury, 2013.

Hamilton, John. "Philology and Music in the Work of Pascal Quignard." *Studies in 20th & 21st Century Literature* 33, no. 1 (2009): 141–65. https://doi:10.4148/2334-4415.1696.

Han, Byung-Chul. *The Scent of Time: A Philosophical Essay on the Art of Lingering*. Translated by Daniel Steuer. Cambridge: Polity Press, 2018.

Haraway, Donna J. *Staying with the Trouble: Making Kin in the Cthulucene*. Durham, NC: Duke University Press, 2016.

Haskins, Rob. *John Cage*. London: Reaktion Books, 2012.

Hegarty, Paul. *Noise/Music*. London: Bloomsbury, 2018.

Heidegger, Martin. "The Origin of the Work of Art." *Off the Beaten Track*. Edited by Julian Young and Kenneth Haynes. Cambridge: Cambridge University Press, 2002.

———. *Being and Time*. Translated by John Macquarrie and Edward Robinson. London: Martino Fine Books, 2019.

Heinrich, Bernd. *Life Everlasting: The Animal Way of Death*. New York: Houghton Mifflin Harcourt, 2012.

Hellerstein, Erica, and Ken Fine. "A million tons of feces and an unbearable stench: life near industrial pig farms." *The Guardian*. September 20, 2017. https://www.theguardian.com/us-news /2017/sep/20/north-carolina-hog-industry-pig -farms.
———. "Hogwashed, Part 2." *Indyweek*. July 12, 2017. https://indyweek.com/news/longform /hogwashed-part-2-environmental- advocates-say -hog-facilities-antiquated-waste-disposal-systems -threatening-state-s-waterways/.

Holt, Robert, ed. *The Ormulum*. Oxford: Clarendon Press, 1878.

Hope Hodgson, William. *The Voice in The Night*. Amazon: Profundis Publishing, 2020.

Horkheimer, Max, and Theodor W. Adorno. *Dialectic of Enlightenment*. Translated by Edmund Jephcott. Stanford, CA: Stanford University Press, 2002.

Hughes, Geoffrey. *Swearing: A Social History of Foul Language, Oaths and Profanity in English*. Oxford: Blackwell, 1991.

Hullot-Kentor, Robert. "Second Salvage: Prolegomenon to a Reconstruction of 'Current of Music.'" *Cultural Critique*, 60 (2005): 134–69.

Hume, Christine. *Musca Domestica*. Boston, MA: Beacon Press, 2000.
———. *Saturation Project*. New York: Solid Objects, 2021.

Ihde, Don. *Listening and Voice: Phenomenologies of Sound*. Albany: University of New York Press, 2007.
———. *Postphenomenology: Essays in the Postmodern Context*. Evanston, IL: Northwestern University Press, 1995.

İşlek, Akif, and Mustafa Koray Balcı. "Phantosmia with COVID-19 Related Olfactory Dysfunction: Report of Nine Case." *Indian journal of otolaryngology and head and neck surgery: official publication of the Association of Otolaryngologists of India*, 74 (2022): 2891–93. https://doi.org/10.1007/s12070-021 -02505-z.

Jackson, David, and Gary Marx. "Spills of pig waste kill hundreds of thousands of fish in Illinois." *Chicago Tribune*. August 5, 2016. https://www .chicagotribune.com/2016/08/05/spills-of-pig-waste -kill-hundreds-of-thousands-of-fish-in-illinois/.

Jackson, Thomas E., and Soupramanien Sandramouli. "Auditory-Olfactory Synaesthesia Coexisting With Auditory-Visual Synaesthesia." *Journal of Neuro-Ophthalmology* 32, no. 3 (2012): 221–23. https://doi.org/10.1097/WNO .0b013e31825d3c44.

Jacobi, Carol. *Out of the Cage: The Art of Isabel Rawsthorne* (Studies in Art). London: Thames & Hudson, 2021.

Jacobson, Rowan. *Truffle Hound: On the Trail of the World's Most Seductive Scent, with Dreamers, Schemers, and Some Extraordinary Dogs*. London: Bloomsbury, 2021.

James, William. *The Principles of Psychology*. eBook: Public Library, 2000. http://www.public -library.uk/ebooks/50/61.pdf.

Jamieson, John. *Supplement to the Etymological Dictionary of the Scottish Language*, vol. 2. Edinburgh: University of Edinburgh Press for W. & C. Tait, 1825).

Jion, Yasmin I., Brian M. Grosberg, and Randolph W. Evans. "Phantosmia and Migraine With and Without Headache." *Headache: The Journal of Head and Face Pain* 56, no. 9 (2016): 1494–502. https://doi.org/10.1111/head.12890.

Johnson, Steven D., and Florian P. Schiestl. "Convergent evolution of carrion and faecal scent mimicry in fly-pollinated angiosperm flowers and a stinkhorn fungus." *South African Journal of Botany*, 76 (2010): 796–807.

Junius, Hadrianus, *Phalli, ex fungorum genere in Hollandiae sabuletis passim crescentis descriptio, & ad viuum expressa pictura*. Delft: Schinckelius, 1564.

Kafka, Franz. *Metamorphosis and Other Stories*. Translated by Michael Hofmann. London: Penguin Books, 2007.

Kahn, Douglas. *Noise, Water, Meat: A History of Sound in the Arts*. London: MIT Press, 2001.

Karesh, William B., Andy Dobson, James O. Lloyd-Smith, Juan Lubroth, Matthew A. Dixon, Malcolm Bennett, Stephen Aldrich, Todd Harrington, Pierre Formenty, Elizabeth H. Loh, Catherine C. Machalaba, Mathew Jason Thomas, and David L. Heymann. "Ecology of Zoonoses: Natural and Unnatural Histories." *The Lancet* 389, no. 9857 (2012): 1936–945. https://doi.org /10.1016/S0140-6736(12)61678-X.

Keller, Andreas. *Philosophy of Olfactory Perception.* New York: Palgrave Macmillan, 2016.

Kelly, Caleb, ed. *Sound.* London: Whitechapel Gallery, 2011.

Kettler, Andrew. *The Smell of Slavery: Olfactory Racism and the Atlantic World.* Cambridge: Cambridge University Press, 2020.

Kim-Cohen, Seth. *In the Blink of an Ear: Towards a Non-Cochlear Sonic Art.* London: Bloomsbury, 2009.

Kim, Suk-Jun. *Humming.* New York: Bloomsbury, 2019.

Kindy, Kimberly. "Consumers are buying contaminated meat, doctors' group says in lawsuit." *The Washington Post.* April 17, 2019. https://www.washingtonpost.com/national/consumers-are-buying-contaminated-meat-doctors-group-says/2019/04/16/978eed32-6073-11e9-9412-daf3d2e67c6d_story.html.

Kirk, Paul M., Paul F. Cannon, and J. A. Stalpers. *Dictionary of the Fungi.* Wallingford: CABI, 2008.

Klots, Alexander B., and Elsie B. Klots. *1001 Questions Answered about Insects.* New York: Dover Publications, 1977.

Kohn, Eduardo. *How Forests Think: Toward an Anthropology Beyond the Human.* Berkeley, CA: University of California Press, 2013.

Kramer, Lawrence. *The Hum of the World.* Oakland, CA: University of California Press, 2018.

Kristeva, Julia. *Powers of Horror: An Essay on Abjection.* Translated by Leon D. Roudiez. New York: Columbia University Press, 1982.
———. *Revolution in Poetic Language.* Translated by Margaret Waller. New York: Columbia University Press, 1984.

LaBelle, Brandon. *Lexicon of the Mouth: Poetics and Politics of Voice and the Oral Imaginary.* London: Bloomsbury, 2014.
———. *Sonic Agency: Sound and Emergent Forms of Resistance.* London: Goldsmiths Press, 2018.

Labyrinth. Directed by Jim Henson. Columbia TriStar, 1986.

Lacan, Jacques. "The Signification of the Phallus." *Écrits.* Translated by Bruce Fink. New York: Norton & Company, 2006.

Laporte, Dominique. *History of Shit.* Translated by Nadia Benabid and Rodolphe el-Khoury. Cambridge, MA: MIT Press, 2000.

Large, E. C. "Pursuits of Mycology: Presidential Address to the British Mycological Society, March 1961." *Transactions of the British Mycological Society,* 44 (1961): 1–23.
———. *The Advance of the Fungi.* New York: Dover Books, 1962.

Le Guin, Ursula K. *The Carrier Bag Theory of Fiction.* London: Terra Ignota, 2019.

Lee, Martin R. "The history of ergot of rye (Claviceps purpurea) I: From antiquity to 1900." *The Journal of the Royal College of Physicians of Edinburgh* 39, no. 2 (2009): 179–84.

Leiber, Jerry, and Mike Stoller. "Love Potion No. 9." Capitol, 1959.

Leipert, Trent. "Destination Unknown: Jean-François Lyotard and Orienting Musical Affect." *Contemporary Music Review,* 31 (2012): 425–38.

Lemon. Directed by Hollis Frampton (1969). YouTube. Last updated December 16, 2022. https://www.youtube.com/watch?v=6gnz1pIy6l4.

Leopold, Donald. "Distortion of Olfactory Perception: Diagnosis and Treatment." *Chemical Senses* 27, no. 7 (2002): 611–15. https://doi.org/10.1093/chemse/27.7.611.

Letcher, Andy. *Shroom: A Cultural History of the Magic Mushroom.* London: Faber and Faber, 2006.

Levi, Mica. "Drift." *Under the Skin* (Original Motion Picture Soundtrack). Rough Trade, 2013.

Leys, Ruth, ed. *The Ascent of Affect: Genealogy and Critique.* Chicago: University of Chicago Press, 2017.

Ligeti, György. "Atmosphères." *Ligeti Project, Vol. 2 —Lontano, Atmosphères, Apparitions,* San Francisco Polyphony & Concert Românesc. Warner Music, 2002.
———. "Continuum." *Ligeti Project, Vol. 6— Keyboard Works.* Sony Classical, 1997.

Lindermann, Charles B. "A Wonderous Tale of a Sperm Tail." *Oakland Journal,* 19 (2010): 51–56.

Lister, Arthur. *A Monograph of the Mycetozoa.* London: British Museum, 1911.

Little Joe. Directed by Jessica Hausner. BFI, 2020.

The Little Whirlwind. Directed by Riley Thomson. Walt Disney / RKO Radio Pictures, 1941.

Littré, Émile. *Dictionnaire de la Langue Française.* Paris: Hachette, 1883.

Lloyd, C. G. *Mycological writings of C. G. Lloyd*, vol. 2. Cincinnati: self-published, 1898–1925.

Lo, Yin-Cheung M., Jacek A. Koziel, Lingshuang Cai, Steven J. Hoff, William S. Jenks, and Hongwei Xin. "Simultaneous Chemical and Sensory Characterization of Volatile Organic Compounds and Semi-Volatile Organic Compounds Emitted from Swine Manure Using Solid Phase Microextraction and Multidimensional Gas Chromatography–Mass Spectrometry–Olfactometry." *Journal of Environmental Quality* 37, no. 2 (2008): 521–34. https://doi.org/10.2134/jeq2006.0382.

Lockwood, Patricia. "The Communal Mind: Patricia Lockwood travels through the Internet." *London Review of Books*, 41 (February 21, 2019).

Loy, Gareth. *Musimathics: The Mathematical Foundations of Music*, vol. 1. Cambridge, MA: MIT Press, 2006.

Lucie-Smith, Edward. *Sexuality in Western Art*. London: Thames and Hudson, 1991.

Lyotard, Jean-François. *Postmodern Fables*. Translated by Georges van Den Abbeele. Minneapolis, MN: University of Minnesota Press, 1997.

Mabey, Richard. *The Perfumier and the Stinkhorn*. London: Profile Books, 2011.

Macpherson, Fiona, and Dimitris Platchias, eds. *Hallucination: Philosophy and Psychology*. Cambridge, MA: MIT Press, 2013.

Mahon, Lee. "New NASA Black Hole Sonifications with a Remix." NASA. May 4, 2022. https://www.nasa.gov/universe/new-nasa-black-hole-sonifications-with-a-remix/.

Marcel, Howard. "Science Diction: The Origin of the Word 'Epilepsy.'" NPR. September 30, 2011. https://www.npr.org/2011/09/30/140954025/science-diction-the-origin-of-the-word-epilepsy.

Maruo, Viviane Mayumi, Ana Paula Bracarense, Jean-Paul Metayer, Maria Vilarino, Isabelle P. Oswald, and Philippe Pinton. "Ergot Alkaloids at Doses Close to EU Regulatory Limits Induce Alterations of the Liver and Intestine." *Toxins* 10, no. 5 (2018): 1–13. https://doi.org/10.3390/toxins10050183.

Matango: Attack of the Mushroom People. Directed by Ishirô Honda. Toho Co., 1963.

Maxmen, Amy. "'Penis worm' pokes holes in evolutionary dogma." *Nature*. October 26, 2012. https://doi.org/10.1038/nature.2012.11667.

Mazzeo, Tilar J. *The Secret of Chanel No. 5: The Biography of a Scent*. New York: HarperCollins, 2010.

McCartney, William. *Olfaction and Odors: An Osphrésiological Essay*. Berlin: Springer-Verlag, 1968.

Merrie Melodies: Bugs Bunny and the Three Bears. Directed by Chuck Jones. Warner Brothers, 1944.

Metzger, Nadine. "Battling demons with medical authority: werewolves, physicians and rationalization." *History of Psychiatry* 24, no. 3 (2013): 341–55. https://doi.org/10.1177/0957154X13482835.

Miller, William Ian. *The Anatomy of Disgust*. Cambridge, MA: Harvard University Press, 1997.

Miert, Dirk van. *Hardianus Junius (15–11–1575) Een humanist uit Hoorn*. Hoorn: Bas Baltus, 2011.
———, ed. *The Kaleidoscopic Scholarship of Hardianus Junius*. Leiden: Koninklijke Brill, 2011.

Mizrahi, Vivian. "Sniff, smell, and stuff." *Philosophical Studies: An International Journal for Philosophy in the Analytic Tradition* 171, no. 2 (2014): 233–50. https://www.jstor.org/stable/24704128.

Modenesi, Paolo. "Skull lichens: A curious chapter in the history of phytotherapy." *Fitoterapia* 80, no. 3 (January 2009): 145–48 (147). https://doi.org/10.1016/j.fitote.2008.12.005.

Money, Nicholas P. "Against the naming of fungi." *Fungal Biology* 117, nos. 7–8 (2013): 463–65. https://doi.org/10.1016/j.funbio.2013.05.007.
———. *Fungi: A Very Short Introduction*. Oxford: Oxford University Press, 2016.
———. *Mushrooms: A Natural and Cultural History*. London: Reaction Books, 2017.

Montaigne, Michel de. "On the Power of the Imagination." *The Complete Essays of Montaigne*. Translated by Donald M. Frame. Stanford: Stanford University Press, 1966), 68–76.

Morton, Timothy. *All Art Is Ecological*. London: Penguin, 2021.
———. *Dark Ecology: For a Logic of Future Coexistence*. New York: Colombia University Press, 2016.

Mowitt, John. *Radio: Essays in Bad Reception*. Berkeley, CA: University of California Press, 2011.
———. *Sounds: The Ambient Humanities*. Oakland, CA: University of California Press, 2015.

Muchembled, Robert. *A History of the Devil: From the Middle Ages to the Present*. Translated by Jean Birrel. London: Polity Press, 2003.
———. *Smells*. Translated by Susan Pickford. Cambridge: Polity Press, 2020.

Murata, K., S. Tamogami, M. Itou, Y. Ohkubo, Y. Wakabayashi, H. Watanabe, H. Okamura, Y. Takeuchi, and Y. Mori. "Identification of an Olfactory Signal Molecule that Activates the Central Regulator of Reproduction in Goats." *Current Biology* 24, no. 6 (2014): 681–86. https://doi.org/10.1016/j.cub.2014.01.073.

Nancy, Jean-Luc. *Corpus.* Translated by Richard A. Rand. New York: Fordham University Press, 2008.
———. *Listening.* Translated by Charlotte Mandell. New York: Fordham University Press, 2007.

Nazni, W. A., H. Luke, W. M. Wan Rozita, A. G. Abdullah, I. Sa'diyah, A. H. Azahari, I. Zamree, S. B. Tan, H. L. Lee, and M. A. Sofian. "Determination of the flight range and dispersal of the house fly, Musca domestica (L.) using mark release recapture technique." *Tropical Biomedicine* 22, no. 1 (2005): 53–61.

Newhauser, Richard G., ed. *A Cultural History of the Senses in the Middle Ages.* London: Bloomsbury, 2019.

Nicastro, Nicolas, and Fabienne Picard. "Joan of Arc: Sanctity, witchcraft or epilepsy?" *Epilepsy Behavior,* 57 (2016): 247–50. https://doi.org/10.1016/j.yebeh.2015.12.043.

Nietzsche, Friedrich. *Human, All Too Human: A Book for Free Spirits.* Translated by Alexander Hardy. Chicago: Charles H. Kerr and Company, 1908.

Nikši , M., I. Hadzic, and M. Glisic. "Is *Phallus impudicus* a mycological giant?" *Mycologist* 18, no. 1 (2004): 21–22. https://doi.org/10.1017/S0269915X04001041.

Nyman, Michael. "1–100." *Decay Music.* EMI/Virgin, 2004.

Oam, Sarah Lloyd. *Where the Slime Mould Creeps.* Tasmania: Tympanocryptis Press, 2014.

Olds, Sharon. *Odes.* Padstow: Jonathan Cape, 2016.

Oram, Daphne. *An Individual Note: of Music, Sound and Electronics.* London: Galliard, 1972.

Otte, Willem M., Eric van Diessen, Gail S. Bell, and Josemir W. Sander. "Web-search trends shed light on the nature of lunacy: Relationship between moon phases and epilepsy information-seeking behavior." *Epilepsy & Behaviour* 29, no. 3 (2013): 571–73. https://doi.org/10.1016/j.yebeh.2013.10.013.

Pagel, Caryl. "Driving at Night: A Chorus." *Agni,* no. 74 (2011): 157–72. https://www.jstor.org/stable/23316055.

Palazzolo, Eristanna, Filippo Saiano, Vito Armando Laudicina, Maria Letizia Gargano, and Giuseppe Venturella. "Volatile organic compounds in wild fungi from Mediterranean forest ecosystems." *Journal of Essential Oil Research,* no. 29 (2017): 385–90. https://doi.org/10.1080/10412905.2017.1302896.

Parbery, D. G. "Trophism and the ecology of fungi associated with plants." *Biological Reviews* 71, no. 3 (1996): 473–27. https://doi.org/10.1111/j.1469-185X.1996.tb01282.x.

Parkinson, John. *Theatrum Botanicum, or, An Universall and Compleat Herbal.* London: Thomas Cotes, 1640.

Parkinson, Siôn. "The Stink of the Stinkhorn." *The Mushroom* 1, no. 3 (2021): 45–51.

Pasnau, Robert. "What is Sound?" *The Philosophical Quarterly* 49, no. 196 (1999): 309–24. http://www.jstor.org/stable/2660396.

Passarello, Elena. *Animals Strike Curious Poses.* Louisville: Sarabande, 2017.
———. *Let Me Clear My Throat: Essays.* Louisville, KT: Sarabande Books, 2012.

Payne Knight, Richard, and Thomas Wright. *Two Essays on the Worship of Priapus.* Leeds: Celephaïs Press, 2003.

Pearson, Keith Ansell, and Duncan Large, eds. *The Nietzsche Reader.* Oxford: Blackwell, 2006.

Pegler, D. N., T. Læssøe, and B. M. Spooner. *British Puffballs, Earthstars and Stinkhorns: An Account of the British Gasteroid Fungi.* London: Royal Botanic Gardens, Kew, 1995.

Peintner, Ursula, and Thomas Pümpel. "The Iceman's fungi." *Mycological Research* 102, no. 10 (1998): 1153–162. https://doi.org/10.1017/S0953756298006546.

Penman, Ian. *It Gets Me Home, This Curving Track.* London: Fitzcarraldo Editions, 2019.

Phillips, Roger. *Mushrooms.* London: Macmillan: 2006.

Plato. *Cratylus.* Translated by Benjamin Jowett. eBook: Project Gutenberg. https://www.gutenberg.org/files/1616/1616-h/1616-h.htm.

Pliny the Elder. *The Natural History.* eBook: Loeb Classics. https://doi.org/10.4159/DLCL.pliny_elder-natural_history.1938.

Pocci, Stefano. "John Cage a Lascia o raddoppia? (Milano 1959)." *John Cage in Italia.* http://www.johncage.it/1959-lascia-o-raddoppia.html.

Pudil, František, Roamn Uvíra, and Václav Janda. "Volatile Compounds in Stinkhorn (Phallus impudicus L. ex Pers.) at Different Stages of Growth." *European Scientific Journal* 10, no. 9 (2014): 163–71.

Quignard, Pascal. *Abysses*. Translated by Chris Turner. London: Seagull Books, 2015.
———. *Petits traités*. vol. IV. Paris: Maeght, 1990.
———. *Sex and Terror*. Translated by Chris Turner. Chicago: University of Chicago Press, 2012.
———. *The Hatred of Music*. Translated by Matthew Amos and Fredrik Rönnbäck. New Haven, CT: Yale University Press, 2016.

Radigue, Éliane. *Adnos I–III*. Table Of The Elements, 2002.
———. *Geelriandre—Arthesis*. Fringes Recordings, 2003.
———. *Jetsun Mila*. Lovely Music, Ltd, 1987.
———. *L'Île Re-Sonante*. Shiiin, 2005.
———. *Trilogie de la Mort*. Experimental Intermedia Foundation, 1998.
———. *Triptych*. Important Records, 2009.
———. Ψ 847. Oral, 2013.

Radiohead. "How to Disappear Completely." *Kid A*. Parlophone/Capitol, 2000.

Rainsford, Sarah. "'Scent of terror' created in protest against Moscow perfume Store." *BBC News*. February 27, 2020. https://www.bbc.co.uk/news/av/world-europe-51647596.

Rayner, M. C. *Trees and Toadstools*. London: Faber and Faber, 1945.

Rea, Carelton. *British Basidiomycetae: A Handbook to the Larger British Fungi*. Cambridge: Cambridge University Press, 1922.

Redlich, Susanne. *Slime: A Natural History*. Translated by Ayça Türkoğlu. London: Granta, 2021.

Regier, Willis G. "Cioran's Insomnia." *MLN* 119, no. 5 (December 2004): 994–1012.

Reiners, Jonathan. *Past Scents: Historical Perspectives on Smell*. Chicago: University of Illinois Press, 2014.

Revill, David. *The Roaring Silence: John Cage: A Life*. London: Bloomsbury, 1992.

Richards, Sam. *John Cage as…*. Oxford: Amber Lane Press, 1996.

Riedel, Friedlind, and Juha Torvinen, eds. *Music as Atmosphere: Collective Feelings and Affective Sounds*. London: Routledge, 2019.

Roach, Mary. *Stiff: The Curious Lives of Human Cadavers*. New York: Norton, 2003.

Robbins, Tom. *Jitterbug Perfume*. Harpenden: No Exit Press, 2001.

Robinson, Katelynn. *The Sense of Smell in the Middle Ages: A Source of Certainty*. London: Routledge, 2020.

Rolfe, R. T., and F. W. Rolfe. *The Romance of the Fungus World*. London: Chapman and Hall, 1925.

Rose-Innes, Henrietta. *Animalia Paradoxa*. Norwich: Boiler House Press, 2019.

Rosolato, Guy. "The Voice: Between Body and Language." *Psychoanalytic Quarterly*, 46 (1977): 75–94.

Rothstien, Edward. "Sounds and Mushrooms." *The New York Times*. November 22, 1981. https://www.nytimes.com/1981/11/22/books/sounds-and-mushrooms.html.

Ruck, Carl, Mark Alwin Hoffman, and Jose Alfredo González Celdrán. *Mushrooms, Myth and Mithras: The Drug Cult that Civilized Europe*. San Francisco: City Light Books, 2011.

Russolo, Luigi. *The Art of Noises*. Translated by Barclay Brown. New York: Pendragon Press, 1986.

Sacks, Oliver. *Hallucinations*. London: Picador, 2012.
———. *Musicophilia: Tales of Music and the Brain*. London: Picador, 2011.

Sandner, Andreas. "Visible Odors? On the Issue of Visuocentrism in 'Olfactory Austerity.'" *British Society for the Phenomenology Annual Conference* 2019. July 11, 2020. https://www.podbean.com/ew/pb-b78vm-e20469.

Sarafoleanu, C., C. Mella, M. Georgescu, and C. Perederco. "The importance of the olfactory sense in the human behavior and evolution." *Journal of Medicine and Life* 2, no. 2 (2009): 196–98.

Schaecter, Elio. *In the Company of Mushrooms: A Biologist's Tale*. Cambridge, MA: Harvard University Press, 1998.

Schafer, R. Murray. *Soundscapes: Our Sonic Environment and the Tuning of the World*. Rochester, VT: Destiny, 1977.

Schlögel, Karl. *The Scent of Empire: Chanel No. 5 and Red Moscow*. Translated by Jessica Spengler. Cambridge: Polity Press, 2021.

Schoenberg, Arnold. *Theory of Harmony*. Translated by Roy E. Carter. Berkeley, CA: University of California Press, 2009.

Scott Walker: *30th Century Man*. Directed by Stephen Kijak. Oscilloscope, 2006.

Seger, Georgius. "Observatio LV., Fungus anthropomorphos [sic]." *Miscellanea Curiosa Medico-Physica Academiae Naturae Curiosorum*, vol. 2. Leipzig: printed by Samuel Krebs, 1671.

Sheldrake, Merlin. *Entangled Life: How Fungi Make Our Worlds, Change Our Minds and Shape Our Futures*. London: Random House, 2020.

Shifman, Arie. "'A Scent' of the Spirit: Exegesis of an Enigmatic Verse (Isaiah 11:3)." *Journal of Biblical Literature* 131, no. 2 (2012): 241–49. https://www.jstor.org/stable/23488223.

Sidky, Homayun. *Witchcraft, Lycanthropy, Drugs and Disease: An Anthropological Study of the European Witch-Hunts*. Eugene, OR: Wipf and Stock, 2010.

Simner, Julia. *Synaesthesia: A Very Short Introduction*. Oxford: Oxford University Press, 2019.

Sjölund, Sara, Maria Larsson, Jona K. Olofsson, Janina Seubert, and Erika J. Laukka. "Phantom Smells: Prevalence and Correlates in a Population-Based Sample of Older Adults." *Chemical Senses* 42, no. 4 (2017): 309–18. https://doi.org/10.1093/chemse/bjx006.

Skeat, Walter. *An Etymological Dictionary of the English Language*. Oxford: Clarendon Press, 1910.

Sleeman, D. P., P. Jones, and J. N. Cronin. "Investigations of an association between the stinkhorn fungus and badger setts." *Journal of Natural History* 31, no. 6 (1997): 983–92. https://doi.org/10.1080/00222939700770481.

Smith, Alexander. *Puffballs and their Allies in Michigan*. Ann Arbor, MI: University of Michigan Press, 1951.

"Son of Stimpy" a.k.a. "Stimpy's First Fart." *The Ren & Stimpy Show*. Directed by Kelly Armstrong, Bob Camp, and John K. Spumco, 1993.

Sowerby, James. *Coloured Figures of English Fungi or Mushrooms*. London: J. Davis, 1797.

Spitzer, Leo. *Classical and Christian Ideas of World Harmony: Prolegomena to an Interpretation of the Word 'Stimmung.'* Edited by Anna Graville Hatcher. Baltimore, MD: Johns Hopkins University Press, 1963.

Spooner, Brian, and Peter Roberts. *Fungi*. London: Collins, 2005.

Sprott, Boyd. *Inaugural Essay on the Structure of the Mucous Membrane of the Stomach*. PhD thesis: University of Edinburgh, 1836.

Stamets, Paul. *Mycelium Running: How Mushrooms Can Help Save the World*. Berkley, CA: Ten Speed Press, 2005.

Stearn, William T. "The Gender of the Generic Name Onosma (Boraginaceae)." *Taxon* 42, no. 3 (1993): 679–81. https://doi.org/10.2307/1222551.

Steinitz, Richard. *György Ligeti: Music of the Imagination*. London: Faber and Faber, 2003.

Sterbeeck, Franciscus van. *Theatrum fungorum oft het tooneel der campernoelien*. Antwerp: Josef Jakobs, 1675.

Sterne, Jonathan, ed. *The Sound Studies Reader*. New York: Routledge, 2012.

Sterne, Jonathan. *The Audible Past: Cultural Origins of Sound Reproduction*. Durham, NC: Duke University Press, 2003.

Stijnman, A., and E. Savage, eds. *Printing Colour 1400–1700: History, Techniques, Functions and Receptions*. Leiden: Koninklijke Brill, 2015.

Stockhausen, Karlheinz. *Stimmung, Paul Hillier and Theatre of Voices*. Harmonia Mundi, 2007.

Stoddart, David Michael. *The Scented Ape: The Biology and Culture of Human Odor*. Cambridge: Cambridge University Press, 1990.

Stommel, Jesse. "The Loveliness of Decay." *Journal of the Fantastic in the Arts*, 25 (2014): 332–46.

Strauss, Daniel J., Farah I. Corona-Strauss, Andreas Schroeer, Philipp Flotho, Ronny Hannemann, and Steven A. Hackley. "Vestigial auriculomotor activity indicates the direction of auditory attention in humans." *eLife*, 9 (2020): e54536. https://doi.org/10.7554/eLife.54536.

Stravinsky, Igor. *Poetics of Music in the Form of Six Lessons*. New York: Vintage, 1947.

Sullivan, Walter. "Truffles: Why pigs can sniff them out." *The New York Times*. March 24, 1982. https://www.nytimes.com/1982/03/24/garden/truffles-why-pigs-can-sniff-them-out.html.

Süskind, Patrick. *Perfume: The Story of a Murderer*. Translated by John E. Woods. London: Penguin Books, 2010.

Swanton, E. W. *Fungi and How to Know Them: An Introduction to Field Mycology*. London: Methuen, 1909.

Szendy, Peter. *Listen: A History of Our Ears.* Translated by Charlotte Mandell. New York: Fordham, 2008.

Talou, T., A. Gaset, M. Delmas, M. Kulifaj, and C. Montant. "Dimethyl sulphide: the Secret for black truffle hunting by animals?" *Mycological Research* 94, no. 2 (1990): 277–78. https://doi.org/10.1016/S0953-7562(09)80630-8.

Taylor, James, ed. *The Selected Writings of John Hughlings Jackson.* London: Staples Press, 1958.

Taylor, Jane. *William Kentridge: Being Led by the Nose.* London: University of Chicago Press, 2017.

Taylor, Mark C. *Erring: A Postmodern A/theology.* Chicago: University of Chicago Press, 1984.

Temkin, Oswei. *The Falling Sickness: From the Greeks to the Beginnings of Modern Neurology.* Baltimore, MD: Johns Hopkins University Press, 1994.

Thompson, Marie, ed. *Beyond Unwanted Sound: Noise, Affect & Aesthetic Moralism.* London: Bloomsbury, 2017.

Thompson, Marie, and Ian Biddle, eds. *Sound, Music, Affect: Theorizing Sonic Experience.* London: Bloomsbury, 2013.

Tisdale, Sallie. "The Sutra of Maggots and Blowflies." *Conjunctions,* no. 51 (2008): 8–29. https://www.jstor.org/stable/24517519.

Toller, Steve Van, and George H. Dodd, eds. *Perfumery: The Psychology and Biology of Fragrance.* London: Chapman and Hall, 1998.

Toop, David. *Into the Maelstrom: Music, Improvisation and the Dream of Freedom.* London: Bloomsbury, 2016.
———. *Ocean of Sound: Ambient Sound and Radical Listening in the Age of Communication.* London: Serpent's Tail, 2018.
———. *Sinister Resonance: The Mediumship of the Listener.* London: Continuum, 2010.

Toop, Richard. *György Ligeti.* London: Phaidon Press, 1999.

Tsing, Anna Lowenhaupt. "Arts of Inclusion, or How to Love a Mushroom." *Wild Hearts: Literature, Ecology, and Inclusion* 22, no. 2 (2010): 191–203. https://www.jstor.org/stable/41479491.
———. *The Mushroom at the End of the World: On the Possibility of Life in Capitalist Ruins.* Princeton, NJ: Princeton University Press, 2015.

Under the Skin. Directed by Jonathan Glazer. StudioCanal, 2013.

Vadén, Tere, and Juha Torvinen. "Musical Meaning in Between: Ineffability, Atmosphere and Asubjectivity in Musical Experience." *Journal of Aesthetics and Phenomenology* 1, no. 2 (2014): 209–30. https://doi.org/10.2752/205393214X14083775795032.

Vasung, Lana, Esra Abaci Turk, Silvina L. Ferradal, Jason Sutin, Jeffrey N. Stout, Banu Ahtam, Pei-Yi Lin, and P. Ellen Grant. "Exploring early human brain development with structural and physiological neuroimaging." *NeuroImage,* 187 (2019): 226–54. https://doi.org/10.1016/j.neuroimage.2018.07.041.

Ventenat, Étienne Pierre. "Dissertation sur la genre phallus." *Mémoires de l'Institut des Sciences et Arts Sciences de mathématique et de physique,* vol. 1. Paris: printed by Baudouin on behalf of the Institut de France, 1798.

Vuong, Léa. *Pascal Quignard: Towards the Vanishing Point.* London: Legenda, 2016.

Walker, Scott. "It's Raining Today." *Scott 3.* Philips/Fontana, 1969.

Wallace, David Foster. *Infinite Jest.* New York: Little Brown and Company, 1996.

Wallrabenstein, I., J. Gerber, S. Rasche, I. Croy, S. Kurtenbach, T. Hummel, and H. Hatt. "The smelling of Hedione results in sex-differentiated human brain activity." *NeuroImage,* 113 (2015): 365–73. https://doi.org/10.1016/j.neuroimage.2015.03.029.

Wallrup, Erik. *Being Musically Attuned: The Act of Listening to Music.* London: Routledge, 2019.

Walls, Alissa A. "Cy Twombly and the Art of Hunting Mushrooms." *American Art* 28, no. 2 (2014): 50–69. https://doi.org/10.1086/677965.

Wasson, R. Gordon. *Soma: Divine Mushroom of Immortality.* New York: Harcourt Brace Jovanovich, 1973.

Wasson, R. Gordon, Albert Hofmann, and Carla P. Ruck. *The Road to Eleusis: Unveiling the Secret of the Mysteries.* Edited by Robert Forte. Berkeley, CA: North Atlantic Books, 2008.

Watkinson, Mike, and Pete Anderson, eds. *Scott Walker: A Deep Shade of Blue.* London: Virgin Books, 1995.

Wehling, Eike, Josef J. Bless, Marco Hirnstein, Bodil Kråkvik, Einar Vedul- Kjelsås, Kenneth Hugdahl, Anne Martha Kalhovde, and Frank Larøi. "Olfactory hallucinations in a population-based sample." *Psychiatry Research,* 304 (2021): 114117. https://doi.org/10.1016/j.psychres.2021.114117.

Wellbery, David. "Stimmung." Translated by Rebecca Pohl. *new formations: a journal of culture /theory/politics*, 93 (2018): 6-45. https://muse .jhu.edu/article/699196.

Whitehouse, David. "Black hole hums in B flat." *BBC News*. September 10, 2003. http://news.bbc. co.uk/1/hi/sci/tech/3096776.stm.

Williamson, Donald I. *Larvae and Evolution: Toward a New Zoology*. New York: Chapman and Hall, 1992.

Wittgenstein, Ludwig. *Tractatus Logico-Philosophicus*. Translated by D. F. Pears and B. F. McGuiness. London: Routledge, 2006.

Woodward, Ashley. "Lyotard on Postmodern Music." *Eventual Aesthetics* 5, no. 1(2016): 118–43.

Woodward, Ben. *Slime Dynamics: Generation, Mutation, and the Creep of Life*. Winchester: Zero Books, 2012.

Wordsworth, William, and Samuel Taylor Coleridge. *Lyrical Ballads*, vol. 1. Bristol: printed by Biggs and Cottle, for T. N. Longman, Paternoster-Row London, 1798.

World Meteorological Organization (WMO). "State of the Global Climate 2023." WMO. March 19, 2024. https://library.wmo.int/idurl/4/68835.

Young, Neil. *Waging Heavy Peace*. London: Penguin Books, 2012.

INDEX

ACKNOWLEDGEMENTS

I would like to express my gratitude to John Mowitt, Sam Belinfante, and Eric Prenowitz at the University of Leeds, whose support and guidance helped me find my way through the dark wood. I am indebted to the family of Miss Amanda Burton for their award of a doctoral scholarship without which I would've in no way been able to undertake this project. Thank you.

To Caroline Spearing for her fastidious Latin-English translation of the text by Hadrianus Junius, and her kind permission to print it in full here. To Stuart Bertolotti-Bailey for his careful typesetting of Caroline's translation, which so closely echoes the sixteenth-century original; for his keen eye looking over the manuscript many times and in multiple iterations; for introducing me to the writing of E. C. Large; and for his infectious, collaborative spirit, which resulted in the beautiful design of this book. To Caroline Schneider and the staff at Sternberg for their enthusiasm for my and Stuart's reeking subject, and for taking a punt on a book that doesn't seem to fit neatly into any genre. And to the visual arts team at Creative Scotland for their financial support, which allowed valuable time and resources to make this book, and their continued faith in artists who dare to stray from the path.

Thanks also to my dear friend Richard Whitby for his collaboration on our animated short we created together for the BBC, and for his many kind comments and suggestions that have helped shape this project. To Sam Annand, whose own music has infused and affected my mind in more ways than one. To Alain Sebille for his time and generous insights into the workings of my (perhaps) phallus-fixated mind. To fashion designer Matty Bovan for designing and constructing the extraordinary stinkhorn-inspired outfit featured in this book, and to Donald Milne for his photography.

Thank you to author Roger Phillips for his hospitality, and whose passion for mushrooms and mushroom identification by smell was in part the impetus for this investigation. Likewise, to my mentor Phyllida Barlow, who in 2010—the year we both exited the Sculpture Department at The Slade School of Art, London—encouraged me to sing seriously and with abandon. Roger and Phyllida, both, rest in peace.

To my colleagues at the Royal Botanic Garden Edinburgh, especially Emma Nicolson and Lorna Mitchell, who have given me courage to pursue this mushroom-smell thought experiment a little further. To Esther van Gelder and Paulien Rings at the KB, The National Library of The Netherlands, The Hague, for letting me sniff their first edition copy of Junius's *Description of the Phallus* for myself, and to the Art Fund for granting me a Jonathan Ruffer Travel Award, which allowed me to make the journey.

To *The Mushroom Magazine* and *Odeuropa*, who published much shorter versions of chapters two and three in 2021 and 2023 respectively. To the Museum Plantin-Moretus, Antwerp, for their consent to reproduce the photograph of the original woodblock of the dune stinkhorn featured at the start of chapter two. And to the staff at the John Cage Mycological Collection, University of California Santa Cruz, and the John Cage Trust for their kind permission to use the image of the stinkhorn postcard at the end of chapter four.

Finally, to the Parkinson family, my mother, Janet Wyn, in particular. *Diolch yn fawr iawn.* To Clare, Natalia, and my Godson, conceived across borders with our help in the middle of this project, and whose arrival post-Brexit has given all or families such joy. And to my wife Hannah and our three children for their company and patience during our many excursions into Scotland's forests together, and for their shared love of the natural world more generally. Sorry (not sorry) for stinking up our home for so long.

Siôn Parkinson
Stinkhorn

Design: Stuart Bertolotti-Bailey
Copyediting: Aaron Juneau
Proofreading: Raphael Wolf
Printing: Tallinn Book Printers, Estonia

ISBN 978-1-915609-27-4

© 2024 the author, Sternberg Press

Distributed by The MIT Press, Art Data,
Les presses du réel, and Idea Books

Published by
Sternberg Press
71–75 Shelton Street
London WC2H 9JQ
UK

www.sternberg-press.com

Supported by Creative Scotland